Dedicated to my children and grandchildren
Who must somehow survive the mess we have created

WHEREVER businessmen gather the talk turns to the present prosperity in America; how long will it last, and what will follow it. Periods of prosperity like the present always have one accompaniment. Always it happens that a considerable number of people think this particular prosperity will not end, that there will never be another panic or another depression. They are always wrong. They will be wrong this time.

—New York Herald, November 27, 1925
[as quoted in *Drummer in the Dar* by T. Davis Bunn]

AUTHOR'S NOTE:

The numbers and statistics contained in this book were accurate at the time of writing – but statistics are a moving target subject to constant change. If they have changed by the time you read this, it won't affect the points I'm making, as they will almost certainly have changed for the worse.

Contents

PART
ONE

WHERE WE ARE

Preface

"And ye shall know the truth,
and the truth shall make you free."
– John 8:32

It was my privilege and good fortune to accompany President George Bush when he visited Gdansk, Poland, home of the birthplace of the freedom movement that spread like wildfire and ultimately toppled the imprisoning Communist Soviet Union's stranglehold on the peoples and nations of Eastern Europe. At the time Poland remained a Communist country, yet the stirrings and yearnings for freedom were no longer held dormant but were now aflame. As our slow-moving motorcade entered the decaying industrial city on the Baltic Sea he was greeted by hundreds of thousands of enthusiastically cheering Poles, men and women of every walk of life who hungered for the life and liberty that America represented. This was a day and a poignant expression that I was never to forget.

To my surprise, thousands of them were waving American flags—which was especially meaningful and touching as Poland was still a Communist country, where the display of American flags was against the law. Many of these flags had the wrong numbers of stars, less than fifty stars, even some less than forty-eight stars. These were American flags that freedom-seeking Poles had hidden away under mattresses and in attics for thirty or forty or fifty years as a reminder of the example for their dreams of a better way of life, a life of peace and prosperity. There were also American flags of the wrong color blues, the wrong color reds, the wrong number of stars and bars. These were flags that freedom-seeking Poles had hidden away for thirty or forty or fifty years, or had handmade for the occasion, brought out to honor this visit by America's President. And there were handmade American flags, brought out to honor the American president and as an expression of that for which they were willing to give their lives. America, to them, stood for political freedom, economic independence, and integrity in government—things for which they were willing, if need be, to sacrifice their lives.

And some of the Gdansk Poles had, when years earlier the Communist Polish government, at the behest of the Soviet Union, descended on the Gdansk shipyard with soldiers and tanks in an attempt to crush the Solidarity movement—the epicenter of the Polish struggle for freedom.

A year later I visited Gdansk again, this time as part of a freedom delegation helping Solidarity continue in its battle for democracy. Standing at the iron gates of the massive Lenin Shipyard, now the Gdansk Shipyard, I noticed the uniformed gate guard, a stooped and aging man in a weathered Navy pea coat, furtively looking up and down the street. He approached me and, through the interpreter, asked if he'd seen me there before. I assured him he had. He looked once more to make certain the dreaded secret police were nowhere near. Then, with weathered and gnarled hands, he reached into that worn coat and pulled out a rolled-up piece of cloth. When he unfurled it I recognized the red-and-white banner of the now prohibited Solidarity workers movement, a symbol of the Polish freedom fighters, hard working men and women unlike the liberal intellectuals within the Soviet political elite. I asked about the stains; with quiet tenderness he explained that he had been on duty on the day the workers rebelled against tyranny and lined up at the shipyard gates demanding freedom. The Communist government had responded with typical force, and the army tanks lined up facing the weaponless workers. These courageous lovers of freedom stood their ground and held firm to their hopes, long before Mikhail Gorbachev's perestroika (the political and economic restructuring in the former Soviet Union that created some private property ownership) and glasnost (committing the Soviet Union to greater accountability and openness) only to be crushed by the powerful tanks.

The stains on that banner were the bloodstains of those who sacrificed their all for freedom—as the gate guard said to me, "freedom like you Americans have." That day they died to have what you and I have long taken for granted, but the movement, the hopes, the dreams of freedom did not die.

Poland is now a free land, its thirty-eight million citizens still seeking for the dream of America. But it is a different America they seek, for the America of their dreams I fear may soon be no more.

Things feel of late like the planet is on a downhill runaway train and picking up speed, growing ever closer to the mountain cliff. The inevitable crash is around the next bend, or the next. There are frightening clouds of instability on the close horizon and they are easily seen by those who look. In many respects we are a nation sinking under its own weight. My restless and nagging fear is that the avalanche may suddenly come crashing down before we can get our own houses in order.

Today the breadth and complexity of factors influencing the world economy makes it difficult if not impossible to get a clear perspective of what lies ahead. Yet to survive tomorrow we need just such a perspective to make intelligent decisions now and in the future. Gone are the days of American independence from global events. Today, distant small economic movements can trigger major worldwide financial swings. It's essential today to have an educated and timely understanding of what's happening in the world and where it may indeed lead us in the days ahead. How do we get this understanding?

This is not a book saying "all is well in America". Equally it is not a book predicting dire events of apocalyptic proportions, neither is it a book of solutions but a book of warnings. I have written it to realistically assess the risks, and the dangers emanating from our pursuit of these policies.

It's not that the government and monetary officials are untruthful, though sometimes they are, but rather it is that those in charge at the highest levels are politically expedient and thus selective about which part of the truth they reveal. The rest of the truth, and probably the most important and unsettling parts, are kept from public view. Unfortunately too many in public positions forget there is a difference between telling the truth and managing the truth. This is the proverbial "what they don't know won't hurt them" approach that has been practiced by captains, kings, and presidents for centuries. If Federal Reserve Chairmen Allen Greenspan and Ben Bernanke spoke the truth plainly and fully it is entirely possible that the result would be instant economic chaos. Yet these are the facts you need to make safe financial and investment decisions.

To some extent this is a book of numbers—mostly negative numbers that tell the alarming story of our culture of foolish entitlement and wild spending that is destroying America. I have spoken plainly, like one of my heroes President Harry Truman, and I've let the chips fall where they may. This is a book born of "link analysis", sort of like predicting the future and something that's usually found only at social gatherings because there are simply too many variables to accurately predict the future. But predicting the coming dangers is rather uncomplicated because they are now pretty much unavoidable. In the following chapters, as a Washington insider of four decades I attempt to connect the dots outlining ten threatening dangers, some more dangerous than others. Honestly, I hope that my conclusions are wrong and that we can continue rolling blithely along on this terminally ill path of borrow and spend.

E. B. White wrote in Charlotte's Web, "There's no limit to how complicated things can get, on account of one thing always leading to another." That is our world today. My intent is not to frighten or scare, for none of us want to live in a state of fear. Yet if we Americans are to withstand the onslaught of dangers that are at our very doorstep, we best understand what's likely coming straight at us. No one can be sure if any of these dangers will strike nor can anyone be sure they won't, but too many Washington experts agree that the odds are increasingly trouble-some. The only thing we can't predict is how bad it will be and how soon will it hit us.

You decide for yourself, and then prepare accordingly.

1

THE OSTRICH SYNDROME

"Ignorance is not bliss—
ignorance is poverty."
—unknown

I love America more than any other country in the world and it is for that reason that I am speaking out.

The parts of four decades I've been around Washington have led me to one disturbing conclusion: for the most part the American people have no idea what is really happening, especially with respect to the real dangers that lurk as a potential financial avalanche gathers strength and which can (and likely will) have an enormous destructive impact on you and your family. Soon.

America. What a glorious and wonderful notion! The United States of America, the greatest nation on the earth, today or ever, the nation that for over two hundred years has been the hope and the promise and the envy of the entire world. Most Americans think it will stay that way. Oh, there may be problems from time to time, but all in all, everything's okay—the economy is basically stable, and our future prosperity as a nation is assured.

I disagree. The entire United States house of economic cards could be about to tumble. The trends are alarmingly real, the frightening warning signs for a perfect storm of destabilization and crisis are all about us. There are today at least ten major and imminent politico-economic dangers facing our nation. The effects of any one of them will be disruptive; two or three happening simultaneously—a distinct possibility—could trigger a worldwide depression and bring the American economy spiraling down.

That's a pretty radical statement. You may be thinking, who is this guy? An alarmist? A crank? A bomb-thrower from some fringe-group think tank?

Nope. I'm as establishment as they get. I've held senior White House positions for Presidents Gerald Ford, Ronald Reagan, and George H.W. Bush, and I served on the Federal Home Loan Bank Board under President Bill Clinton. In between that public service, I've made a career in business and investment banking. Earlier in my career, I was a police chief. I'm a husband, father, and grandfather, and by no stretch of the imagination a radical or a professional alarmist—at least I hope not.

I am alarmed, though—deeply alarmed. I've worked inside the Washington political system for a long time, and I'm sorry to tell you that it is badly broken. Today's political system is so rife with irresponsibility and intellectual dishonesty (and sometimes plain old dollars-and-cents dishonesty) that it has become incapable of dealing with the problems this country faces.

Which is tragic, because the problems we're facing have the potential to seriously damage (if not destroy) the American economy and our hopes for a prosperous future. I'm not talking about long-term potential, either; I'm talking about things that are happening right now. They aren't things we can sidestep and let our grandchildren deal with.

A MESSAGE OF HOPE

In short, my friends, we're in a fix. And since our elected leaders, Republican and Democratic alike, cannot and/or will not do anything useful to solve it, the only hope is for the crew—you and me, the American   people—to take over the ship and steer it to safety.

And we can. I'm not offering you a counsel of despair; I don't believe in despair. The American people, once they focus their minds and hearts on it, can do anything.

When I talk about taking over the ship, I don't mean let's overthrow the government or run off and start new political parties or hole up somewhere and become survivalists. There's no need for any of that. We have—on paper, and sometimes in practice—the greatest form of government and the greatest society ever created. We just have to do clean up the way they're currently being operated.

There are specific ways to do that, and later on I'll be discussing some of them. First, though, if you're going to steer the ship out of trouble, you need to know where the icebergs are.

THE INSIDE VIEW

Countless were the times when entering the Oval Office or flying aboard Air Force One that I would pause and ask myself "What is a kid from a small western farm town doing here?" Yet one day I realized that everywhere in America is equal, and that everyone had to be from somewhere. But it never ceased to be an honor for me, nor did I ever forget that it was our duty to do our best for the people of America.

As a senior White House official I was bound by rules of secrecy; today those rules don't apply and I am free to speak the unvarnished truth about our national condition, the lurking threats, and America's looming economic crisis.

My view of world-changing events is a Washington insider's perspective, based on what I have seen and heard and know that the American public does not. Top-level Washington insiders are, for the most part, highly intelligent people with access to information unavailable to the ordinary citizen. Whatever they may say in public, they usually know what's going on. The intoxicating power of elected office, however, makes many leaders overly sensitive to public opinion and they say only what they believe the electorate wants to hear. Their private opinions are rarely shared in public—because it would frighten any thinking American.

But we need to hear the real facts and the plain truth even if it hurts, because as a nation we are more vulnerable to pending dangers than any time in the past two hundred years. China is on course to overtake us as the world's premier economic, industrial, and political power; Saudi Arabia could bring down our economy literally within weeks; our so-called ally Russia is a devious and increasingly powerful new player; Iran may ignite a nuclear war; fundamentalist Islamic terrorist attacks may wreak economic havoc on this nation far greater than the trillion dollar impact of 9-11; and the bursting of the so-called "housing bubble", already in progress, will soon create an unprecedented level of personal bankruptcies. And there's more: millions of Americans will suddenly find themselves without their expected pensions; the Social Security System is certain to fail, and all these baby boomers who think their health care and retirement are secure are in for a shocking and frightful awakening. All of which is further complicated by the moral decay evident throughout our American political system.

FOUR BASIC FACTS

The causes of these situations affecting our future national prosperity are rooted in four basic facts:

• Trade is no longer national, it is international. American industry must acknowledge and respect this fact of life, and devise strategies to join the trend rather than try to complete against it.

• Politics is now international—we must learn the skills of accommodation and understanding rather than confrontation. We must recognize that we cannot always have our own way in the world. Our insistence that our way is the right way has led inevitably to the perception in many quarters of the world that America is narrow minded, a bully, and inept at handling complex situations. Our future foreign policy must reverse this dangerous perception.

• We are a country living far beyond our means, at both the personal and national level. We have pursued this destructive course in the face of increasing prosperity in our major world competitors. We have been banking on American industry and the resilience of the American economy to eventually rectify this problem, but they can't.

• Probably the most serious and certainly the most insidious of our problems is a decline in moral values in every branch of our society. There has developed a national tolerance of many unsavory, immoral, and amoral practices by individuals, government, and corporations which must be reversed if our society is to survive.

I spoke earlier, for instance, of intellectual dishonesty in government. It's not that statements of government and monetary officials are overtly untruthful, though sometimes they are, but rather that those in charge at the highest levels are politically expedient and thus selective about how much of the truth they reveal. Some of the truth, usually the most important and unsettling part, is kept from public view.

It doesn't work any more. It doesn't work on the personal and corporate level, either. We must clean up our own act, just as we have to force our government to clean up its act. When I said we were endangered by a decline in moral values, I mean it. I'm not going to preach at you; there are many aspects of private morality (maybe too many) that are publicly debated these days, but that's not what I'm talking about. Honesty, the Golden Rule, and taking responsibility for your own actions aren't controversial. If we can all manage that, we'll come a long way toward sorting out the rest of it.

So this book is a call to arms: let's get control of this ship and steer it away from the icebergs. To do that, we have to do it in a completely nonpartisan way. All the current political nastiness is good for is to keep things the way they are now—and we don't want that. We're on this ship together, and if it goes down, we're all going with it. So whoever you are—whether a Democrat or a Republican, a baby boomer worried about his old age or a twenty-year-old who isn't even sure he's going to have an old age—I'm talking to you.

AMERICA'S IMPERILED FUTURE

Today I worry for America's future, for the country my grandchildren will inherit. Do I find this depressing? Absolutely, because it's all preventable. It is so easy to point out what is wrong but so very difficult to get it right. Today we are an increasingly fragmented society living on borrowed time and borrowed money, a nation potentially on the brink of a perfect storm of destabilization, retreat, disarray, and the complete disappearance of civility.

We live in very difficult and uncertain times, even dangerous times as we face America's looming economic crisis. Our glorious land of opportunity abounds with the complacency of the easy life, all of it enveloped in a virtual roller-coaster ride of societal break down borne of selfish human behavior, an absence of principle-centered morality, exploding government largess, and all too much greed. And maybe with a government in denial, seemingly untroubled by the growing prospect of economic disaster.

Gordon B. Hinckley, an extraordinary American religious leader, says "We're living in a very difficult season in the history of the world... a world marching toward self-destruction." He speaks of "the almost overwhelming challenge that comes with life in our time." These are indeed times of challenge and peril.

The opening of the Berlin Wall came without warning—we did not see it coming. And almost no one foresaw the total collapse of the Soviet Union. Sitting across from Red Square in the Metropole Hotel on a cold snowy Moscow day, I watched in amazement as the Soviet flag ceased to fly and just like that the Evil Empire was no more. Today the world is in turmoil and things may quickly turn out in ways we do not yet see. With each passing day the prospect of economic calamity and a global economic meltdown grows larger and more likely.

Having spent most of my adult life in and around this nation's halls of power, I have grown increasingly troubled by what far too many of our elected officials at all levels of government are not telling the American public. I am deeply troubled by their self-serving theatrical puffery, verbose platitudes, and endless partisan venom, troubled by their often myopic perspective defined and perpetuated by their never-ending pursuit of campaign dollars and their instinct for personal political preservation—their own re-election. Far too many members of Congress, regardless of party, are really more interested in their own political future than the future of the nation, though they would of course deny this. Oh, the hypocrisy of it all! It has been said that the only thing many in Congress stand for is their own re-election. Sure, there are honorable public servants at every level, including some in Congress. But the bottom line is that for most of them, they are driven by their personal desire to remain in office.

This is not to indict all elected "leaders". I was privileged to serve Ronald Reagan, George Bush, and Gerald Ford, and I shall be forever grateful for the opportunity they gave me to serve this nation. All three of these American presidents, as far as I know, were true to their principles and to the country, though it can't be said that everyone in their Administrations steered by that same compass.

For a century and a half our federal government usually managed its affairs soundly and responsibly, but with the advent of World War II came a fundamental change in our personal and federal views toward debt, consumption, and sovereignty that is fast ensuring our ultimate undoing. Sadly, we embraced a misplaced confidence in government to manage every element of our lives when in reality government at most levels has limited ability to manage anything with sufficient competence, except maybe the national defense. The reason for this mismanagement syndrome within all levels of government is due in large measure to the absence of serious accountability—we all have a bad case of the Ostrich Syndrome. It's an unfortunate reality that government at all levels today knows neither spending restraint nor spending reductions, and seems to lack any sense of fiscal prudence and probity.

In ancient days King Hezekiah of Judah was near death, and the prophet Isaiah came to him, saying "Thus saith the Lord, set thine house in order…"(2 Kings 20:1). Tragically, today our national house is anything but a "house of order".

Whether in the Punjabi war zone along the explosive tinder keg of the India-Pakistan border; or in the hate-filled third generation Palestinian refuge camps of Lebanon (where Americans dare not go); or amongst the helpless and dying AIDS victims in sub-Saharan Africa; or in the traditionally pompous yet hollow courts of the United Nations, marked by shrewdness and manipulation and overflowing with an abundance of egotism and classic yet insincere eloquence; or in hush-hush White House meetings; or in countless other experiences in dozens of countries, or airborne aboard Air Force One, or in a host of other off-limits places—I have experienced all this first hand, and what's coming scares the socks off me!

Serving in the White House for three presidents gave me access to a broad array of domestic and foreign intelligence. What the White House (any White House) and the Treasury and members of Congress say publicly is not necessarily what they say privately and internally—

and if they do rarely do they connect all these seemingly disconnected facts. I'm not sure anyone in the market is connecting all these pieces, probably because they don't know most of them, and somebody should be connecting them. This country is in danger, and so are your investments!

Why have so many of us have failed to connect the dots? Simply because few know all the dots and if we did we would fear connecting them because we would see what lies ahead. Too many of us, especially our elected "leaders", are suffering from the "Ostrich Syndrome"— burying their heads in the sand for fear of seeing the lion standing close by just waiting to do us in by ripping off our legs. Instinctively we know there are seriously threatening problems with our economy and government but because our leaders seem bent on a standard everything-is-manageable-not-to-worry course (with little expressed public concern), we want to make ourselves believe all is well, despite the signs.

As I write this it is only days since spending time with several former colleagues who are highly competent and dedicated senior officials in the Bush Administration. They are honorable, sincere, hard-working public servants who see things as they really are—and who privately agreed with my concerns.

Today those in the know sense something ominous and fore-boding on the horizon. Highly acclaimed author James Fallows predicts "an economic meltdown looms by 2016". The world has become so complicated and so interconnected that, for me, it's impossible to be merely optimistic or pessimistic. There is no such thing today as the foreseeable future; it's upon us and with us constantly yet not foreseeable. For those who listen the avalanche is already well within hearing distance, for the world is a very dangerous place. Debts climb on every front, destruction of the environment is at an unprecedented scale in countries around the globe, terrorism and nuclear proliferation threaten on many new fronts, and emerging diseases threaten global pandemics.

In the late 1930's President Franklin Delano Roosevelt knew something was occurring in Europe and the Far East. But there was nothing Roosevelt could do, for the political will to intervene was not there. Today's elected leaders, like Roosevelt, know something is amiss and they must attempt to keep the economic dominoes from falling, yet the political will is not there. As a nation we are sailing in very dangerous waters, and never have I seen so many simultaneous dangers facing the United States of America.

The list of dangers which may soon upend the economy is lengthy: a slowdown in China's red-hot economy, a bankruptcy of General Motors, the growing problem of underfunded corporate pensions, terrorism, housing bubbles and subprime finance, or, more likely, something unforeseen.

As a young man I worked as a sheepherder in the rugged and imposing mountains of Utah. Later I worked as a forest fire smoke-chaser in the magnificent wilderness mountains of Idaho, where on wilderness lookout towers we'd watch rolling storm clouds and lightening become fires of destruction. Occasionally we would see herds of grazing sheep, totally unaware of pending disaster.

The parallels between those sheep oblivious to gathering storms and far too many American citizens are frightening. I was in Moscow, Russia on a dreary wintry day to happily witness the ignominious end of the Soviet Union, yet hardly any saw its collapse coming, just like we didn't anticipate the opening of the Berlin Wall. Today we are like those ignorant sheep grazing peacefully as the storms gather all around us.

In his historically famous speech to the Virginia House of Burgesses in 1775, Patrick Henry noted that it is "natural to man to indulge in the illusions of hope. We are apt to shut our eyes against a painful truth." He continued, "Is life so dear, or peace so sweet, as to be purchased at the price of chains and slavery? Forbid it, Almighty God! I know not what course others may take; but as for me, give me liberty or give me death!"

As Americans we have too long "indulged illusions of hope" and "shut our eyes to painful truth", and allowed ourselves to be enslaved by crises looming large on the horizon. We are the living, breathing proof of the "Ostrich Syndrome", going blithely along with our heads in the sand.

PART
TWO

TEN DANGERS
FACING AMERICA

---------------------------------- 2 ----------------------------------

FIRST DANGER–
A TRIPLE THREAT:
CHINA, INDIA, AND RUSSIA

🕉

> "In antiquity, those that excelled in warfare
> first made themselves unconquerable
> in order to await the moment
> when the enemy could be conquered."
> – Sun Tsu, in *The Art of War*

For over a century, the United States has been the economic power-house of the world. During half of that time—from the end of World War II until the mid-1990s—we occupied that role in the context of a relatively stable economic and political world order. There were disruptions and occasional shifts of allegiance, but overall, changes in America's relationships with other countries tended to be minor and predictable.

But not for much longer. Daily a change of historic proportions is occurring as power and wealth move eastward—to China, India, and Russia, with their two and a half billion consumers.

America's economic leadership is not over yet; at the moment we're still the overwhelming leader. The economy of California, if it were a country, would rank 6th amongst the nations of the world. If

American cities were countries, they'd make up forty-seven of the largest one hundred economies in the world. For now, the combined economies of Los Angeles, New York, Boston, and Chicago have a larger economy than all of China. New York's economy is about the size of Russia's or Brazil, and Chicago's economy equals that of Sweden. America is the world great economic powerhouse, but not for long.

All that is about to change. China and India make up almost forty percent of the world's population, and their economic engines are on fire as they transition their economies from Third World to First World. Never in history has such an enormous percentage of humanity improved their economic circumstances, and it is likely to never again occur. These are times of historic economic and social change.

As the epicenter of power and wealth in the world rapidly shifts eastward to China and India, most predictions are China will become the world's largest economy by 2050 or sooner, but will not remain so for long as India will likely eventually overpower China's economic lead and America's economic reign comes to a dangerous end.

Respected scholar Clyde Prestowitz accurately describes this change in his book *Three Billion New Capitalists: The Great Shift of Wealth and Power to the East*:

> "With the rapid entry of China, India, and the former Soviet bloc nations into the international economy, three billion 'new capitalists' have emerged to compete with America on the world stage. The U.S. has no strategy to deal with these new competitors—and the ultimate losers will be America's workers.
>
> "The second problem is that China and India are rising at a time of a simple yet fundamental imbalance in the global economy: Americans consume too much and save too little while Asians save too much and consume too little. The deep trade and budget deficits reflect and exacerbate these conditions. The nightmare scenario—the economic 9/11—is a sudden, massive sell-off

of dollars," Prestowitz warns, "a world financial panic whose trigger might be as minor, relatively speaking, as the assassination of a second-rate archduke in a third-rate European city."

China, India, Russia, and our southern neighbor Brazil have in the last two decades doubled the global labor force, resulting in unprecedented increases in global output. The new and growing economies of these countries, especially China and India, combine cheap production cost advantages, low wages, tax advantages, increasingly skilled professionals, a new and growing entrepreneurial energy, and enormous consumer markets which enables unprecedented competitive advantages. The migration of American manufacturing jobs to these overseas markets is now being followed by service and technology jobs. Telephone an 800 number for customer service and chances are you'll be speaking to someone in India.

But such rapid change has not come without cultural cost and political strain. Major Chinese cities, especially economically overheated Shanghai, Shenzhen, and Beijing, have become worlds apart from vast impoverished rural areas which remain mired in Third World conditions. Unlike even two decades ago, Chinese living in urban areas today have lifestyles infinitely different from their fellow citizens in rural areas, making these abundant conflicts a considerable challenge for political leaders.

The same is being experienced in India, where religious, economic, and lifestyle imbalances are becoming increasingly pronounced and worrisome. Hyper-growth cities such as Bangalore, Hyderabad, New Delhi, and Mumbai (once Bombay) are increasingly modernized with higher standards of living while rural India falls further behind, resulting in growing political division and economic tension.

The first time I visited the People's Republic of China and India and Russia I was interestingly struck by similar thoughts in each place. Though vastly different, each possesses an enormity of geography, population, and untapped capacity. A quarter century later the enormity of change is almost beyond our ability to comprehend and the future is unclear. But no matter what the outcome, the United States stands to be the big loser in this historic transition and change.

CHINA—FRIEND OR FOE?

Did you know you owe China several thousand dollars? It's your share of the U.S. Treasury bond debt to China. How did this happen to you?

Not much more than a mere quarter century ago, China was a land largely unknown to the West, a vast country and ancient culture frozen in Communist entrapment and isolated from the rest of the world. Diplomatic and trade relationships with the West did not exist, modern conveniences were available only to the designated Party elite and were of poor Russian or Czech or Bulgarian-made quality, and the only Americans who found there way there did so as covert CIA operatives sneaking in under darkness through the back door of remote mountainous borders or by night submarine landings along isolated rocky coastal beaches or smuggled in from British Hong Kong. Even telephone calls from the outside world were outlawed. There was no welcome mat for Americans or any other Westerners. We were enemies.

It has been a quarter century since I first visited China, under the protective authority I carried as an American diplomat. Countless have been the times I have returned since and the change has been so enormous as to be in the category of unbelievable. The differences are almost beyond comprehension and are cause for alarm.

On that first visit to Beijing, or more correctly Peiping, or was it Peking, the dingy airport terminal was a coldly bland concrete hall of poor construction, dim lighting, and absolutely no indications of hospitality. It was less like a major national capital's arrival terminal and more as one would find in a small third world country. But then why build a pleasantly welcoming terminal if there were no welcomed visitors! Hordes of tourists, or any tourists for that matter, were non-existent and the endless stream of American and Japanese and German and French businessmen coming in future days had not yet been invited. Even the thought of a telephone booth or a currency exchange were unheard of.

The main and only highway from the airport to the city was a winding, narrow, rutted two-lane road weaving through never-ending rows of trees planted by cadres of regimented Chinese workers, the people's workers. Along the entire route were drably dressed Chinese men and women walking and riding bikes by the tens of thousands, and in the whole distance from the airport to the hotel we saw but a few decrepit trucks and one car which passed us at a high speed. Only senior Communist party officials and the elite had cars, and they were either colorless Chinese forgeries of 1950's American-made Buicks or of poor Russian and Chinese manufacture. This was a place trapped in impoverished conditions dating back decades, overlooked by progress and development, all evidences of its self-imposed disconnect from the rest of the world.

As a diplomatic guest of the People's Government, I was accorded VIP treatment. Staying at the nondescript and worn Beijing Hotel, at the time China's finest, I felt as though I had stepped back a half century in time. The hallways were dark and dingy, the rooms were shabby and dated. And as far as I could tell I was the only American guest in residence.

When I reached my room my luggage, so thoughtfully collected at the airport by my helpful government hosts, was already in the room. And only that one car had passed us on the drive in from the airport. Oh the efficiency of a government-controlled society. Before leaving the locked bag with my helpers, out of their sight I had weaved a long dark thread through the black zipper just to see if the bag had been opened. Sure enough, the thread was gone. And a thorough search of the room revealed several hidden listening devices. To have a little fun, I said to the U.S. Secret Service agent who was with me, "Oh how I would love a ham sandwich." A few minutes passed when a knock came on the door, and there to my amazement was a bellman with a ham sandwich. Ah, welcome to China.

The sweeping main thoroughfares of Beijing were wide and empty, at least of cars, trucks, and busses. Hundreds of thousands of bicycles but only a smattering of ancient green and gray trucks, some of them three-wheeled, and a handful of cars. Along the main roadways were numerous bland apartment complexes piled high like so much fire wood and just plain ugly Soviet-era government buildings of imposing yet tasteless architecture and shoddy construction, intermingled with countless aging shanties. What few billboards there were advertised encouraging sayings of Chairman Mao and the People's Party. Color and vibrancy were almost non-existent in the buildings, cars, and clothing—everything was gray and fading, with an air of the spiritless regimentation so often seen in Communist countries.

Today everything in China is different—except we are still enemies, though we pretend otherwise. It's not so much that the Chinese are anti-American but are foremost pro-Chinese and yearn to restore what they view as their centuries old rightful place as the dominant world power. Throughout history the Chinese have viewed the rest of the world with a blend of amused tolerance and irritated silence, but always with the same goal—to achieve their own purposes. This is a concept totally at odds with the American experience, and those who have not lived or traveled in China view the Chinese attitude as one of hostility. This is not so—it is something far more dangerous and effective: they wish to use us to further their own goals, and I would say they are doing so very effectively.

Returning to Beijing some years later with then-President George H.W. Bush, the changes were astounding—at least the visible part.

The texture, the feel, the mood is different. Gone were dowdy Soviet-style architecture hotels, replaced with steel and glass skyscrapers as China races toward global economic dominance. Chinese cities, like Beijing and Shanghai, are places in hurried transition and housing about 400 million with populations expected to double by 2020.

And that dilapidated airport terminal is gone. A spacious modern replacement was constructed to celebrate the 50th anniversary of Chinese Communist rule. This bright and airy terminal, built at a cost of $1.1 billion, is a welcome replacement for the former facility and is three times its size, and like the rest of the world puts emphasis on passenger comfort. Luggage is inspected by laser scan technology; computer-aided aircraft guiding systems, security equipment, and information display boards are world-class. The terminal has 63 escalators, 51 elevators, and 26 moving sidewalks. Weary travelers are today able to stay in touch with the world using multimedia payphones, and there are ATMs and auto cash exchange machines that accept American credit cards!

And you paid for it all, whether you realize it or not.

Lately, however, there have been growing concerns about China's true interest and intent; the enormous trade imbalance is raising security concerns as is China's ravenous pursuit of energy sources from such disagreeable governments as Venezuela. Since President Richard Nixon opened the door and established our relationship, American foreign policy toward China has been in a continual state of uncertainty and confusion whether we view China as friend or foe. Of late we seem more unsure than ever.

Maybe it's the flowery television reports on China that give us a false sense of a "new China." While two decades of robust economic reform has awakened the capitalistic interests of many in this Communist country, China is not an open and free society—as evidenced by Microsoft and Google's recent willingness to delete such words as "freedom" and "democracy" from their search engines in

China. China still embraces a core value system that is against all that we stand for.

Still, in our illogical fascination with all things Chinese, American companies continue investing in China. One example is America's third largest bank, Bank of America, which recently agreed to pay $2.5 billion (of stockholder's money) for a 9% stake in state-run China Construction Bank. Yet Chinese banks are burdened with pervasive corruption and debts so deep that since 1998 the central government has been forced to inject more than a quarter trillion dollars into its banks.

What are we thinking?

THE GROWING CHINA THREAT

Talk to the managers of Wal-mart and they will tell you China's meteoric economic growth is good for the U.S., a source of inexpensive consumer goods for American customers and a potential 1.3 billion Chinese shoppers market for American goods. But talk to those who understand the deeper purposes and global ambitions of China and it becomes suddenly apparent why China is a threat to us. Last year Robert Zoellick, then Deputy Secretary of State, posed a serious question: "Picture the wide range of global challenges we face in the years ahead—terrorism and extremists exploiting Islam, the proliferation of weapons of mass destruction, poverty, disease—and ask whether it would be easier or harder to handle those problems if the United States and China were cooperating or at odds."

Quite simply there is no bilateral relationship of greater importance than between America and China, a relationship accurately described by President George W. Bush as "complex". The relationship is unusual, often insincere and always questioning, and tentative at best, yet we continue to outwardly attempt the façade of friendship. In 1979, China's late leader Deng Xioping impressed many Americans by donning a Stetson cowboy hat at a rodeo in Texas. Years later in Beijing, after a lengthy clandestine effort by the CIA to learn his shoe size, obviously a Chinese state secret, President George Bush gave Deng a pair of Texas cowboy boots. And the dance continues.

To understand China is to understand something altogether foreign to American thinking. As countries go ours is just an infant, whereas to the Chinese a century is but a moment in their 5,000 year history. Americans value honesty and candor, China values neither. Their system is corrupt, businesses are corrupt, bribes are essential, and they will always cheat—at least in our way of thinking. To them it is all about winners and losers and to win someone must lose. Since Deng Xiaoping opened China to the outside world in the late 1970's, China has transitioned from a disintegrating dynasty to an emerging superpower as it has outwardly pursued its place as a world-class competitor in every sector yet perpetuating its mistrust and suspicion of the outside world and foreigners.

Today China, with nearly one quarter of the world's population, is a serious economic threat to the United States, as enormous trade imbalances with the U.S. allow it to churn out an exceptional 9% to 10% GNP growth rate each and every year, yet our numerous apprehensions remain mostly unaddressed. America is a great power and China seeks to be one, and because a collision is possible we cooperate. During the decade of the 1980s foreign direct investment in China totaled $20 billion, a number that expanded 23 times to $450 billion in the years 2000-2003 and now exceeding the U.S. in foreign direct investment.

China is "attacking" us on every front, a menace to our national security. Today China produces more steel than the U.S., Europe, and Japan combined, and all of it's done with government subsidies and U.S. technology. Some years ago I visited a factory in China that made athletic shoes, complete with a U.S. brand label but they were all forged knock-offs for export. Today its technologies they're stealing, not only gym shoes. Germany's respected Spiegal magazine actually questioned in print if China is "the beginning of an economy based on thievery?" Reporting on a German trade mission to China, German Foreign Minister Frank-Walter Steinmeier said German business executives are "really incensed about China's growing large-scale theft of ideas and patents, trademark and product piracy. Fully 70% of all illegal copycat products come from Asia, and most of that comes from China, in what has mushroomed into a $300 billion market," says Spiegel. They steal our intellectual property. Only 297 of 170,000 patents granted in the U.S. in 2002 went to China; it's easier to steal it and copy it. Then they sell us cheap goods which we purchase with more debt; they fund that debt by capturing the sale of U.S. government bond debt.

While 300 million Americans were complacently snoozing, few took notice last year when the U.S. government named our "friend" China as the Number 1 threat to global security. The Department of Defense and the Commission on U.S.-China Economic and Security Review, a bipartisan Congressional review panel, identified Beijing as a major threat to U.S. national security, pointing out China's mounting military power and its use of predatory economic strategy for "competitive advantage over U.S. manufacturers." Also noted was what many economists view as the significantly undervalued Chinese currency, and that through camouflaged entities "U.S. investors may be unwittingly pouring money into black box firms involved in activities harmful to U.S. security interests."

Expressing concern about China's developing military strength, the Department of Defense budget indicated China will have "the greatest potential to compete militarily with the United States," and that "China's methodical and accelerating military modernization presents a growing threat" to our security interests in the Pacific.

In past years our defense concern has been focused primary on China's threat to Taiwan, but the Pentagon now says China's military expansion makes it "capable of prosecuting a range of military operations in Asia well beyond Taiwan".

In recent years China's military expansion and modernization has been more than significant. The U.S. estimates that over 700 mobile short-range ballistic missiles are now aimed at Taiwan and annually increasing by about 100 missiles. Taiwan split from the mainland in 1949 yet China insists it remains part of China and is on record saying that should Taiwan formally declare its independence, China will use military force, as recently authorized by law, to regain control of the breakaway island nation. Chinese General Zhu Chenghu, Dean of China's National Defense University, blatantly stated they will launch nuclear weapons at "hundreds" of American cities if we assist Taiwan in defending itself from Chinese military attack. A Pentagon report revealed that China has 20 nuclear warheads that can reach almost all of the United States.

There is also serious concern about China's rising production of missiles and weapons of mass destruction, some of which has been wholesaled to Iran, North Korea, and other nations openly hostile to the U.S. China is rapidly expanding its own Navy with 20 new submarines and 20 new amphibious lift ships, which China says are to ensure passage through its strategic sea lanes and prevent the U.S. Navy from snatching China's imported oil. A recent Pentagon report noted that "China does not now face a direct threat from another nation. Yet, it continues to invest heavily in its military, particularly in programs designed to improve power projection." China is conspicuously building a military that far exceeds its defensive requirements, with defense spending increases in the double-digits and it now ranks third in total defense spending behind the U.S. and Russia, improving its military with sophisticated high-tech weaponry.

"The People's Liberation Army is moving very quickly to adopt practically every information-related aspect of military technology that the U.S. is pursuing at this time," according to Rick Fisher, vice president of the International Assessment and Strategy Center in Washington. The United States-China Economic and Security Review Commission reported to Congress that China's technology position is "raising the prospect of future U.S. dependency on China for certain items critical to the U.S. defense industry as well as vital to continued economic leadership."

Simultaneous with its buildup of military might, China today has the world's third-largest spy network after the U.S. and Russia. Here at home we are vulnerable: in addition to China's diplomatic missions and nearly 3,000 commercial offices, the government estimates there are more than 100,000 students from China abroad in the land, many of whom are sure to be spies snatching every piece of information for the People's Republic, especially technologies and nuclear secrets. Chinese companies proclaim independence and private ownership but in the final analysis are an extension of the government.

On my first visit to China with President George H. W. Bush I was struck by their heightened attention and pervasive worries about Russia, a fellow Communist nation but China's militarily arrogant neighbor. The Sino-Soviet relationship was completely strained, yet today the two have developed an expedient relationship as reciprocal rascals, and last year the two nations staged joint military exercises for the first time since the cold war. Chinese armaments targeting U.S. aircraft carriers, including advanced cruise missiles, were supplied by Russia, and together they are the leading suppliers of advanced weaponry and arms to the unscrupulous nations of Iran, Syria, Cuba, Libya, and North Korea. It now appears that to quench its thirst for oil China may even trade advanced weapons to rogue nations for oil.

And yet because China controls hundreds of billions of our national debt and because we buy more than 40% of China's exports to satisfy our extravagant consumer wants, we maintain an outwardly cordial yet deceptive and misleading relationship while at the same time China enhances its military might targeting the United States. America's recent Trade Representative Rob Portman, a respected former colleague, is unusually candid about the relationship: "Our U.S.-China trade relationship lacks equity, durability and balance," When the Soviet Union collapsed in 1991 China immediately stepped in to fill the void and is now our main geopolitical threat. On every front they are accelerating. Nowhere has their newfound power been more prevalent than in the world's commodity markets. China's natural resource thirst for oil, gas, and minerals such as copper and uranium is unquenchable, driving up commodity prices worldwide. This year China is consuming over 30% of the entire world steel production, with its steel import demand increasing more than 20% annually; domestic production is increasing even faster.

And in the process China is bringing irreparable destruction to its environment. Two decades of reckless mining, farming, and logging practices have obliterated millions of acres of grassland and forest—all to fuel its dramatic industrial output and enhance its position of power in the world. The Gobi Desert is increasing in size at a frightening pace; several thousand lakes and rivers have dried up. Industrial waste has made water in five of China's largest rivers too toxic to touch. Chinese officials estimate 600 million rural Chinese drink contaminated water.

Air pollution grows worse each day. Where in the cities and countryside bicycles were the primary means of transport, they are being replaced by cars. Today China has slightly more than 1 million cars—in fifteen short years that number will be 160 million cars! And 75% of China's energy is produced by burning coal. Visit Beijing on a winter day and note how many people must wear protective breathing masks. Follow the winds currents and see where that pollution ends up: in the U.S.A.

CHINA'S EXPANSIVE GLOBAL PRESENCE

While funding the American consumer society China is simultaneously bloodlessly and strategically planting its flag in countries all around the world. Chinese "companies" now operate the Panama Canal and the nuclear bomb inspection service in the Bahamas for containers bound for the U.S., and are constructing the port in Gwadar, Pakistan, to name just three. To satisfy its unending oil and gas needs, China's in bed with such outlaw nations as Myanmar and Sudan and with countries adverse to U.S. interests, especially Cuba, Venezuela, Sudan, and Iran, reported offering arms for oil.

In Latin America, leftist Brazilian President Luiz Inacio Lula da Silva, vocally anti-American, named China as Brazil's "most promising business partner." Brazil exports soy and iron to China, and China returns with chemicals, machinery, and electronics—and enormous amounts of illegally copied products—all the while curtailing U.S. prestige and influence. Similar cozy relationships are being nurtured by China with our two leading opponents in Latin America, Cuba and Venezuela, where defense forces are now using Chinese air-defense radar and soon Chinese weaponry. Venezuela, our fourth-largest supplier of oil, has an avidly anti-American President, Hugo Chavez, who last year ended a four decade military relationship with the U.S. and says "Maybe we'll have to buy Russian or Chinese planes to defend ourselves."

China is also aggressively seeking to purchase operating energy companies around the world, such as its aborted attempt to purchase California Unocal for $18.5 billion. It's buying of energy assets around the world, especially in Latin America and Africa, is so alarming that senior diplomats from Japan, Australia, and the U.S. recently met just to discuss China's "energy diplomacy."

FUNDING OUR CARELESS DEBT

Because of the imbalance of trade (the Chinese sell vastly more to the rest of the world than it does to them), China has accumulated an enormous foreign reserve surplus — a trillion dollars and counting, more than 70% of it in U.S. dollars. Looked at from one angle, this is not such a bad thing; the Chinese willingness to buy and hold our Treasury bonds.

Unfortunately, this ties the fate of the U.S. economy directly to China. If the Chinese decide to stop buying our Treasury bonds, or start selling off the ones they hold now, it would put severe downward pressure on the dollar.

China, far more disciplined than the U.S., has captured a strategic advantage that is now a dangerous hazard and impossible to readily repair. Recognizing our recent federal deficits and allowing Congress to keep spending, China has invested hundreds of billions in U.S. dollar assets—more than 70% of China's $770 billion in foreign reserves—a number expected to reach an unbelievable trillion dollars by the end of 2007.

Our national government has grown dependent on China to finance American consumers and our deficit by buying our Treasury bonds. But what will happen to our economy if they stop? It may already be happening. Early this year China announced it would begin moving away from the U.S. dollar and U.S. Treasury bonds, instead diversifying its foreign exchange reserves into other currencies, potentially raising havoc with our economy and achieving the counsel of former Chinese Premier Deng Xiaping: "Bide your time. Build your capabilities. Defeat your enemy without firing a shot."

Our American appetite for inexpensive consumer goods has a hidden price the shoppers at Wal-Mart don't see. Our record bilateral trade deficit with China, which has almost doubled in the last four years, passed $200 billion last year, and we can't blame it all on China.

It's because of our failure to save and our excessive spending by every segment of our society. The easy tendency to blame the Chinese for unfair competition because of artificially low currency and cheap labor is a cop-out for American failure of fiscal self-control.

Because we must find a way to pay for our excessive government borrowing and our uncontrolled consumer debt spending, we have allowed ourselves to become prisoner to China and its policies. China didn't contribute to our deficit, they merely funded it—and along the way slowly strangling our economy and leading to our ultimate economic ruin and collapse. We have met the enemy and it's ourselves.

INDIA—THE NEW TIGER

India, land of the tiger, is China's neighbor and because it lives for the time being in China's shadow many are unaware of this growing threat. But do not ignore India, a democracy which today is a confident rising power emerging from that shadow to become an important 21st Century player in global business, trade, and politics.

Though its economy is about 40% the size of China's, India is the sixth-largest economy in the world and is in an accelerated pursuit of global power. India is a country in transition, from the India of yesteryear's colonial vestiges and painful poverty to the India of the future seeking to define itself amidst newfound (albeit regional) economic growth and prosperity. Over half of India's 1.1 billion people are under age 25—that one quarter of the world's population under age 25—and 80% are under age 45. This youthful energy is made ever more complex by its 17 major languages and 22,000 dialects, many diverse cultures, and religious diversity that are never far from the surface of conflict. India has the largest Muslim population of any nation but so far al-Qaeda hasn't made a toehold, though it is a growing nuclear power with unsettled border conditions with Pakistan and China.

At the stroke of midnight of August 15, 1947, India broke free from British colonial rule and became an independent nation. Ever since, Independence Day is celebrated on that date with ceremonies and festive cultural events throughout the nation. I once found myself in India on Independence Day and planned to attend an event for the Prime Minister in a large stadium. Shortly before the starting time a bomb exploded, rocking the ceremonies bleachers and creating instant chaos. Needless to say I did not hang around to hear the politicians' speeches (which are the same in every country). Just the day before I had traveled north from the bustling city of Amritsar on a rutted road crowded with cars, trucks, motorcycles, bicycles, tractors, and elephants to the India-Pakistan border, there to "watch the war" in much the same manner as Abraham Lincoln rode a carriage to the Maryland countryside to "watch" the Civil War. It is amazing that a country so large in land area and population, so rich in educated people and natural assets would have such seeming instability, decrepit infrastructure, chronic electricity shortages, widespread poverty and pollution, a devastatingly rapid spread of AIDS, and a well-deserved international reputation for its mass bureaucratic ineptitude. (Once when visiting India I began to wonder if their national slogan was "Please stand behind the yellow line!") Yet India's thrilling future is only now awakening.

Much was said in the last presidential campaign about outsourcing of American jobs, which is precisely why India and China, where people will work for far less than in the U.S., are rising stars on the world stage. For decades India's greatest problem has been its teeming population but today that has become its greatest asset, expected in the next 20 years to add more people to its workforce than any other country. Since 1991 when India abandoned decades of Soviet economic influence, India's economic reforms have resulted in average growth of 6 percent per year, and economists anticipate even higher annual growth for at least a decade. Add to that one distinct advantage over China: India's pulsating workforce is generally well educated and they all speak English, the primary reason why some of

American largest corporations have relocated call centers there.

The southern city of Bangalore has become world famous for its exploding information technology industry, fast becoming a world leader in quality and unbeatable pricing where engineering graduate schools churn out highly educated computer specialists by the tens of thousands and where the industry is so hot that wages in some technology sectors are increasing by 25 percent a year. India is now rapidly expanding its industrial prowess into the textiles, biotechnology, chemical, and pharmaceutical industries as it solidifies a growing global reputation for its highly educated technical competencies.

India's challenge will be to expand this education and employment growth to other poorer regions of its enormous landmass where population growth is exploding and where 36% of the population still cannot read or write. Our challenge is how American industry will compete with this new and dangerously competitive force.

While East Asian countries experienced booming growth for the last twenty years, India has undergone deep cultural changes making it slower than the "Asian tigers" but poised for sustained strength and power. Just how fast India will become that global economic force will depend upon how India overcomes the political implications of the long-simmering religious differences that exist within the subcontinent. In the meantime, India has launched a massive 15-year project to improve 40,000 miles of crumbling national highways, something that will further energize commerce in one of the world's fastest-growing economies.

RUSSIA—AWAKENING DANGER

The snowy muddy December days in Moscow were cold and damp as the Soviet Union came to its ignominious end, brought down by the crushing and unsustainable weight of its discredited doctrines, excessive military, artificial economy, and the fabricated illusions of power and strength. The great Soviet Empire, more fragile than we realized, was no more. Sitting in my hotel room across from Red Square I frequently looked out the unwashed window to see if the Soviet flag were still flying atop the Kremlin, like everyone else a bit anxious as to what might occur next as Soviet society simply withered. The year was 1991. Long accustomed to falsehoods, Soviets doubted their leaders, their government, their newspapers, their God, even themselves. The Soviet Russia of breadlines and empty shelves had ceased to be a superpower and was in danger of simply imploding under its own weight into countless ancient regional ethnic conflicts.

As the Soviet Union ceased to be a superpower, so did Russia. No one was sure what course nuclear-armed Ukraine would take, let alone the Muslim former Soviet republics such as Kazakhstan, Uzbekistan, Tajikistan, and the others. Festering ethnic feuds made its future unclear, its economy in shambles, its spirit deadened, its history marked by tens of millions of deaths in civil war, a revolution, two world wars, famine, plagues, and seventy years of lies, purges, secrecy, and brutal Communist repression and tyranny.

Moscow was a mess. Surrounding Red Square were buildings once stately but now dingy, darkened by years of pollution from belching trucks, busses, and cars. At the Moscow Airport I—an American no less—walked unchallenged into the control tower and counted 140 Aeroflot airliners grounded for lack of fuel. Outside of Moscow, traveling through still and lonely countryside and passing small farming villages and collective farms was as if time had stood still. Heat from wood burning fires, little or no electricity, one telephone in the middle of each village. Modern Russia had ended at the Moscow city limits.

Returning a few years later as an American delegate to a Russian banking conference, I found Moscow still gray and grimy, but alive with a new filth and new riches: prostitution on Red Square, well armed mafia bosses, well connected corrupt politicians, former party officials now profiteers with a get-rich scheme mentality, a country lacking any central leadership and fast moving toward chaos and social disintegration, reportedly less than 20% of the people paying their taxes, and AIDS running rampant. Asking the chairman of Russia's largest bank how much capital the bank had, I was taken aback when he said he didn't know; if the bank needed money he "called the treasury and they printed some and sent it over."

Now the whole nation was a mess, a nation in despair. Skilled engineers were working as dockworkers, medical doctors unpaid for months on end, school teachers going hungry—while the former nomenclatura diverted foreign aid and tapped the federal treasury for their own profit, openly selling munitions and military material. People actually missed the secure crime-free guaranteed-income days of the Communists, many ready to trade freedom for security and yearning to return to the days of Russian supremacy.

Throughout its history Russia has existed as a cultural island between East and West, a unique blend of the two but never either. Russia courts favor with the European Union, yet Europe has been her natural enemy for centuries. Russia is establishing new friendships with China, yet in eastern Russia the big concern is China as large numbers of Chinese are illegally migrating across the Amur River.

When the Cold War ended in the collapse of the Soviet Union, a disgraced and humbled Russia stood on the sidelines economically and politically powerless to influence world affairs. No longer; spurred by rising oil revenues and 50% oil production increases its economy has expanded by two-thirds in the past five years, and Russia's proud sense of self has reawakened.

"Russia is emerging from a 20-year cycle of decay, and it is rebuilding a strong central state in a way that future historians will probably decide was inevitable," says Thane Gustafson, a professor of politics at Georgetown University. "In America, we just never thought Russia would recover and begin to throw its weight around."

We were wrong. Today, Mother Russia is a dangerous second-rate country with substantial nuclear capacity, vast undeveloped oil and natural gas reserves, and an awakened longing to return to its former status as global superpower. As the Russian military deteriorates and its nuclear stockpiles are quietly walking off, its leaders are playing a cagey game of statesmanship as they retrench toward authoritarianism and brutal central control, returning media repression and assassinations and poisonings in an ever-more insidious political culture. The assassination attempt on Victor Yushchenko, the opposition candidate elected President of Ukraine in 2004, was a reminder that political freedom was not alive in the Russian sphere of influence. The Soviet Union is dead but the Russian bear is regrouping and reasserting itself. President Vladimar Putin, with whom President Bush has admirably attempted a diplomacy of personal friendship, is busy consolidating the key elements of power—politics, media, economics, and its vast untapped energy resources—under Kremlin control, and using that control of energy to leverage autocratic Belarus and penalize democratic Ukraine. Quietly in the making is either a new and dangerous Russia-China alliance or a Russian-Iranian axis—either scenario presenting a grave danger to the United States and Europe. Simultaneously, they are aggressively leaning on Central Asian countries to oust American military forces.

POTENTIAL LIMITING FACTORS

In all three of these countries, there are factors that may limit or at least slow their development as great powers. For Russia, one such factor is the tendency toward autocracy and centralization of power. While they have oil and gas reserves, for instance, the Russians lack the experience and capital to develop these energy resources themselves. In the 1990s, therefore, Russia entered into licensing agreements with a number of global energy players, among them Royal Dutch Shell, Total,

ExxonMobil, and BP. On the strength of those agreements, these companies have invested billions in oil and gas fields and pipelines in Russia.

Now that those investments are beginning to bear fruit, the Russian government is using a highly selective application of (otherwise largely ignored) tax and environmental laws to force the Western companies to sell controlling interest in the projects to the quasi-state-owned firm Gazprom. (Gazprom itself, incidentally, was created by what most observers regarded as the outright confiscation of the private firm OAO Yukos.)

In the short term, this is a victory for President Putin: he now has control over the nation's energy supply. In the long run it's disastrously ill-advised. Capitalism—the Chinese may have to learn this the hard way as well—is fundamentally based on trust. If there is no protection of law—if contracts are not enforceable in something resembling an impartial court—that trust cannot exist. If you can't trust somebody to keep their word, you aren't going to risk your money on a business deal with them. The Russians are showing themselves to be massively untrustworthy, which means that the flow of external capital into Russia will eventually stop.

Russia also faces serious public-health and demographic problems. Due to a very low birth rate, a very high mortality rate, short life expectancy (a Russian male born today will be lucky to see his 60th birthday) and numerous deaths from unnatural causes, the population is declining precipitously. Now at 143 million, it is expected by some experts to drop to 120 million by 2050, which may be too few people to control the vast Russian landmass. The Russian government is aware of this but is doing very little about it. One solution for this problem used elsewhere, the encouragement of immigration, is pretty well out of the question. The Russians, as witnessed by their behavior toward Chechens, Georgians, Ukrainians, and other neighbors, are rather xenophobic; they would not welcome, in fact would not tolerate, a significant influx of non-Russians.

Compounding all this is the AIDS situation; Russia has one of the fastest-growing rates of HIV/AIDS infection in the world. Transmission began there primarily through the sharing of needles by intravenous drug addicts, but is reported to have crossed over to the general population, where it is spread by sexual contact.

China is also facing a growing AIDS problem, but its problems in this regard—and the potential danger it faces—are dwarfed by what's going on in India. India has a very high infection rate, has an estimated 5 million HIV/AIDS cases (the number in China is about 750,000), and is in a widespread state of denial. Homosexual activity is so taboo as to be virtually unmentionable among both devout Hindus and devout Muslims, and there are senior, otherwise responsible politicians in India who flatly refuse to acknowledge either the infection rate or the enormous number of cases.

AMERICA IN THE NEW WORLD ALIGNMENT

All those issues, however, will not stop the formation of a new global alignment; they may slow it down, but that's all. For now, our foremost concern is, how long can the U.S. economy keep leading the global economy? How long can we continue to finance such a mammoth trade deficit? How long will the world, especially China, remain content to keep financing our debt? What unforeseen event or crisis will cause them to flee the dollar?

Sooner or later, somebody's going to answer those questions. We'll like it a lot better if we answer them ourselves than if we wait for somebody else—almost certainly the Chinese—to answer them for us. China, India, and Russia, together and separately, are an unstoppable juggernaut; add Brazil and it really gets dangerous. While the U.S. has long had a distinct historic advantage in terms of superior education, entrepreneurial flair, visionary innovation, quickness to respond, nimble business ingenuity, and market leadership, we can no longer take our position in the world for granted. We will have to compete, and compete effectively.

OUR FUTURE WITH THESE RISING POWERS

It's confusing. Their sisterly disputes notwithstanding, China and Russia are strengthening new bonds of military alliance, allied against the United States. If China attacks Taiwan, as many predict it will, the U.S. is bound by treaty to militarily assist Taiwan; Russia will back China. Yet sometimes our strategic interests align: most of China's imported oil must travel through the Malacca Strait between Malaysia and Indonesia, as do the oil imports of Japan, Taiwan, and South Korea—each our close allies.

The National Intelligence Council in its report "Mapping the Global Future," forecasts that in 14 years the world economy will be as much as 80% larger and China and India will rival the U.S. for global economic supremacy. Much of this growth will occur because of high-speed internet technologies, which simultaneously will accelerate the spread of radical Islam. Paralleling this economic growth is the considerable and concerning expansion of military power. One misstep between China and Taiwan or India and Pakistan, potentially involving nuclear weaponry, and the world will irreparably change.

China views itself as the rightful leader of the world; its overarching goal is to reclaim that ancient stature. China views the rest of the world with a mixture of amused tolerance and irritated silence, always mindful of their common goal—to pursue their own purposes. This is a concept totally at odds with the American experience, and those who have not lived or traveled in China mistakenly view the Chinese attitude as one of hostility. It's not—it's far more dangerous and effective: they wish to use us to further their own goals, and are doing it very effectively. Last year Chinese diplomat Chen Yonglin defected to Australia. Able to then speak freely, he reminded us of the words of

Great China Leader Deng Xiaping, " 'Bide our time, build our capabilities." What that means is that when the day is mature, the Chinese government will strike back.

Former U.S. Secretary of State Henry Kissinger once said, quoting George Washington, that "countries do not have friends; they have interests." No where on earth are America's interests more concerning than in China, India, and Russia.

3

SECOND DANGER–
AMERICA'S DEBT
TIME BOMB

✦

"The deficit problem is a
clear and present danger to the
basic health of our Republic."
—Ronald Reagan

World War II ended just prior to my birth. My father had been a
decorated bomber pilot in the Army Air Corps, my mother a
lookout spotter for invading Japanese aircraft along the Pacific coast-
line. Those were America's glory days, basking in a rich sense of
national invulnerability and invincibility.

"When [Franklin Delano] Roosevelt entered office, having chided
the Republicans before him for spending too much money, the federal
debt, after 143 years, had grown to $19 billion," writes Bill Bonner in
Empire of Debt. "Roosevelt—in just four years—borrowed almost as
much money as all the dead presidents who came before him. He and
members of Congress at the time were disturbed about it, but ideas

arise as they are needed. The big spenders needed an idea that would permit huge new levels of government debt. They soon found it: a government, unlike an individual, can borrow and spend indefinitely without fear of bankruptcy."

But they were wrong. Sooner or later, a government—yes, even the government of the richest nation on Earth—can spend itself into trouble. And we have.

For my entire lifetime America has been the world's economic superpower. Dire predictions that it would cede that supremacy to the Soviet Union, Germany, or Japan never came true and the dollar became the world's primary currency of choice, of trade, and for central banks. But today the United States is on a precariously slippery slope toward bankruptcy and losing its historic position of leadership privilege in the world. University of Arizona economist Gerald J. Swanson, writing in *America the Broke*, argues that runaway government and personal spending are leading the richest and most powerful society in history toward "fiscal Armageddon." Isabel Sawhill of the Brookings Institution equates the widening abyss between what the government spends and takes in to a "category 6 fiscal hurricane."

After two hundred years of reasonable fiscal stability, balanced growth, and global economic leadership, in little more than a quarter century the United States has ceased to be the world's biggest creditor nation and is now the world biggest debtor nation. No nation in the history of the world has had so much debt, and we should be ashamed of ourselves. Every few years, after the requisite political sound and fury, Congress casually again increases the federal spending limit and away they go with more spending.

The total value of every asset in America, owned by every American and by every company, added together is about $50 trillion. Currently official U.S. debt is about $37 trillion. But add to that the present dollar value of all other federal government liabilities, including interest, and America is broke.

In 1938, J. Reuben Clark, the distinguished former Undersecretary of State and Ambassador to Mexico, delivered an eloquent insight and warning about interest:

"Interest never sleeps, nor sickens, nor dies. It never goes to the hospital. It works on Sundays and holidays. It never takes a vacation. It never visits nor travels. It takes no pleasure. It is never laid off work, nor discharged from employment. It never works on reduced hours. It never has short crops nor droughts. It never pays taxes. It buys no food. It wears no clothes. It is unhoused and without home and so has no washing. It has neither wife, children, father, mother, nor kinfolk to watch over and care for it. It has no expenses of living. It has neither weddings, nor births, nor deaths. It has no love, no sympathy. It is as hard and soulless as a granite cliff. Once in debt interest is your companion every minute of the day and night. You can't shun it or slip away from it. You cannot dismiss it. It yields neither to entreaties, demands, or orders, and whenever you get in its way or cross its course or fail to meet its demands, it crushes you."

And this debt cost is crushing us. Apparently no one in the federal spending circles gave any heed to his prescient counsel. In fiscal 2004, just one single year, the Congressional Budget Office reports our federal government paid $159 billion in "net interest" costs alone—more than the combined total spending for the Departments of Agriculture ($20.7 billion), Commerce ($5.8 billion), Education ($55.7 billion), Energy ($23.3 billion), Housing and Urban Development ($30.4 billion), and the Environmental Protection Agency ($8.4 billion), which combined spent "only" $158.2 billion.

Our American debt clock continues to tick and the debt is ever more crushing. Depending on which source you believe, the U.S. national debt now stands at approximately $9 trillion, roughly

$30,000 per citizen. Add to that a variety of "off book" federal, state, and local government debts, consumer debts, real-estate debts, and the nation's future financial obligations, and the total government debt exceeds $44 trillion. How much of that is your share, and are you prepared to divvy up?

And just in case you aren't sure, a trillion is 1,000 billion!

Each of our six children learned as teenagers that spending on dad's borrowed credit card was fun and easy. Americans and our government are spending in that same easy manner, all of it made even easier by a flood of cheap foreign capital, mostly from Asian banks intent on expanding their countries' exports to American consumers. As a nation we now import more than we export. Then those exporting countries, especially China, India, and Japan, use much of the cash earned from this imbalanced arrangement to purchase U. S. Government debt in the form of "Treasuries" at about $40 billion per month, all of which merely postpones the inevitable reckoning day of national bankruptcy.

The longer we finance our personal and government spending excesses, the more we increase the inevitability that the American dollar will cease to be the world's primary currency standard. And then what happens to you and me if that occurs?

Asian leaders, especially in China and Japan, think long term, very long term: they think in terms of generations. Not so in this land, where near-sighted American politicians think only in terms of election cycles and where self-enriching executives think only in terms of quarterly earnings and their personal job preservation and stock appreciation. This absence of foresight and vision may just result in one of several seemingly unthinkable scenarios.

Our trade deficit in effect sends more than $700 billion annually to other countries. In large measure American and global economic stability depends on them keeping much of that money. Should they begin to quickly shed dollars we would have immediate turmoil in the world's money markets. What happens if foreign investment in the United States dries up? What happens if China and Japan, and others, quit buying several hundred billion dollars worth of U.S. Treasury bonds each year?

Suppose Chinese and Japanese and other Asian banks decide the return on their investment is nearly worthless. Our Federal Reserve has Washington crank up the money printing machines to pay the interest, the dollar falls, and inflation surges. Foreign investors turn in their dollars for other currencies, likely the euro, and the world's largest economy collapses. This scenario is possible but not immediately likely, at least I hope not.

But what happens if OPEC (Organization of Petroleum Exporting Countries) nations stop using the dollar as reserve oil currency and replace it with another currency, again probably the euro. Devastating currency devaluation would immediately follow.

China, Japan, Korea, Taiwan, Thailand, Singapore, Indonesia, and a host of other nations whose economies depend on exports will immediately cease to purchase U.S. debt instruments. So who then funds our uncontrolled spending? No one, and very soon thereafter the stock market collapse will follow. And our drunken government continues its spending, now obligated by countless senseless entitlement programs and future obligations and off-book liabilities. And the American consumer, upon which our economy has come to depend, continues to spend. This is a scenario that may well lead to a repeat of the Great Depression.

For several years American consumers have been on a spending binge, thanks to unusually low interest rates and easy borrowing. Credit cards come uninvited in the mail; retail stores offer credit even when we don't ask. We have become a nation of financed spending, and signs abound that we have spent too much.

Though interest rates have remained comparatively low, except for consumer credit, the percentage of Americans' disposable income devoted to paying off debt is now at record levels. As interest rates continue to rise, many American households will find themselves in a financial bind. One fourth of all home mortgage debt and over one quarter of consumer debt is now "adjustable". Because American consumers have burdened themselves in recent years with more adjustable-interest-rate debt than ever in history, the carefree American consumer is today more vulnerable than ever before to interest rate increases. As rates rise, so do monthly payments. Families will become increasingly cash tight, or even cash crippled, and their care-free credit card spending will eventually cease.

But the American consumer is not alone in its spending habits. Our federal government, the one you and I elected, has been on a spending binge financed by an explosion of public debt. The 2006 federal budget is the largest in our nation's history, estimated to be 2.77 trillion dollars; two years before it was $1.9 trillion. The federal deficit was "only" $319 billion for the budget year ended September 30, 2005 and the deficit for the 2004 budget year was $413 billion. And some economists believe war costs in Iraq and Afghanistan and the 2005 hurricanes will add $1 trillion more over the next decade.

What's happening? A study by the respected Cato Institute concluded that total federal government spending increased thirty-three percent in President George W. Bush's first term, making him the biggest spender since Lyndon B. Johnson's Great Society spending of forty years ago. So much for Republican fiscal conservatism.

Peter F. Drucker is known as the most respected thinker on management in the world. Recently he wrote: "The U.S. government deficit... is fast becoming the sinkhole of the world financial economy. The persistent U.S. deficit creates a persistent deficit in the U.S. balance of payments, which make both the U.S. economy and the U.S. government increasingly dependent on massive injections of short-term and panic-prone money from abroad."

Government officials have said that government debt in the hands of the public and foreign governments, at $4.5 trillion, is not inordinately high in an $11 trillion economy. True maybe, unless there is some unforeseen and horrific shock to our economy. Regardless, the rate of growth of that debt should be worrisome to all of us. Obviously it isn't to Congress and the Administration, which last year added a drug-benefit to Medicare which adds billions of unfunded liability to the already nation-sinking federal debt.

The apparent nonchalance about the growth of spending and debt has whirled out of control. As a nation we seem preoccupied, maybe even enthralled, with the latest televised broadcast of another Southern California high speed police chase or a national "news alert" for a missing teenager in Kansas—all while we ignore the weightier matters destroying our financial house.

In 1789, Thomas Jefferson wrote to James Madison saying that "No generation can contract debts greater than may be paid during the course of its own existence." Yet we just keep on spending, federal budget deficits are out there as far as we can predict. The Congressional Budget Office forecasts deficits every year through 2015. Even former Federal Reserve Chairman Alan Greenspan recognizes that "in the end, the consequences for the U.S. economy of doing nothing could be severe," and the approaching retirement of 78 million baby boomers will put "massive strains on the country's finances."

OUR SPENDTHRIFT GOVERNMENT

The United States of America is technically bankrupt and yet, like the legendary drunken sailor, just keeps spending and spending. Congress has passed laws which define bankruptcy for the rest of us, but apparently not for themselves. The Employment Retirement Income Securities Act (ERISA) and other legislation established accounting standards for American businesses, and if those same standards applied to the federal government it would be required to declare itself bankrupt. That will be the day! Those in the know peg the total value of all land and property in the U.S. at the beginning of this year at $48 trillion, but the unfunded federal liabilities are way past $70 trillion. For any company that is insolvency and you'd be out of business.

With impunity our squandering political leaders are ransoming our future. In our family are, so far, a dozen grandchildren, and thanks to Congress each of them came into this life already more than $156,000 in debt, the estimated debt that every one of us owes the federal government. How did this happen to us? Just add up the annual budget deficit and the national debt accumulated over the past century and the promised but unfunded commitments like my Medicare and Social Security payments. The burden on your grandchildren and mine just continues to grow and grow as Congress spends and spends. Spending by our elected federal government in just the past five years has increased a gigantic 34.7%. Since 2001 discretionary spending has increased 49%!

But it's even worse than official figures reflect. The federal debt is now approaching $9 trillion—that's public record—about $30,000 for every man, woman, and child in America. Since 2000, the federal debt limit has grown almost $3 trillion and because of record level budget deficits another increase in the debt limit will be necessary next year. Even more frightening, as Paul Harvey says, is "the rest of the story." For that gargantuan federal budget debt does not factor in the biggest federal debts, including the vast Social Security and Medicare obligations that will soon come due for 78 million retiring baby boomers.

The Heritage Foundation's Brian Riedl, a top budget analyst, explains the deficit this way: "Right now the federal government spends $22,000 per household—the highest since World War II, adjusted for inflation. We tax about $19,000 per household. That's an annual budget deficit of about $3,000 per household."

But we will pay in other ways as well. All this accruing government debt will result in higher interest rates that you and I will be forced to pay. Respected federal budget analysts Alice M. Rivlin and Isabel Sawhill of the Brookings Institution anticipate that the cost of a 30-year mortgage of $250,000 will increase $2,000 a year in higher interest costs alone, adding up nationally to a massive surcharge penalty.

For three decades government spending, with very few exceptions, has continually added to the federal debt. Since the turn of the century, tax cuts coupled with enormous new federal expenditures rather than offsets in spending reductions have resulted in a veritable explosion of public borrowing.

And now it's time to pay the piper. If our political leaders fail to reform various federal entitlements such as Social Security, Medicare, and Medicaid, then the choices are either unbearable tax increases, elimination of almost all federal programs, or budget deficits large enough to sink the U.S. economy. One recent study found that the only way to prevent the avalanche is an immediate one hundred percent increase in every citizen's taxes, or an immediate fifty percent reduction in all benefit programs. It's beyond thinkable, a one hundred percent increase in everyone's tax bill! It's equally unthinkable for a fifty percent reduction in most federal programs. But the inevitable is upon us.

Plain and simple, America is going broke—the painful and probably unavoidable consequence of decades of spendthrift elected officials.

Add to that the federal costs associated with 2005's hurricane disasters, which some analysts estimate could reach $500 billion dollars, and the costly military spending in Iraq and Afghanistan, and the federal deficit continues to worsen for the foreseeable future.

When Ronald Reagan took office the national debt reached $1 trillion, an amount that Reagan termed "incomprehensible." Oh yeh? Today the national debt is $8.7 trillion and growing every day. Of course that doesn't include personal debt or $1.7 trillion in state and local government debt which is just as real and deadly. Our federal government has borrowed more money in the last two presidential terms than in all the years of our national history up to that time combined! You are one of nearly 300 million Americans responsible for that debt and you should be outraged! I certainly am!

That's not all. Sorry, you actually owe more because that's not the true total federal debt. When you include unfunded entitlements for Social Security and Medicare, the federal debt is now in excess of $44 trillion, expressed in today's dollars, or nearly three quarter of a million dollars for every family of four in the nation. But that's not really the true federal debt either, because it does not include future federal civilian and military pensions and other so-called "contingent" liabilities. It is beyond comprehension.

Add to that the rapidly rising debt obligations of state and local governments, corporations, and individual and family debt—and the indebtedness exceeds $60 trillion! Rounded out it heaps over $1 million in debt on every family in the country.

Some political leaders say things are improving, that the federal government reduced its bloated budget deficit from $412 billion in 2004 to $313 billion in 2005. All over Washington politicians were seen patting themselves on the back, congratulating themselves on sound budget policy and public spending.

Don't join in with their hollow applause. Senator John McCain, speaking at a gathering of the Concord Coalition in New York City, said, "No one's sounding alarms. We don't want to make any tough decisions." He was joined by former Senator Warren Rudman, who warned of a coming iceberg. "For people currently alive, we have $50 trillion to $65 trillion in unfunded liabilities," referring to Social Security and Medicare. And he warned that if politicians delay dealing with this shocking disparity, "we'll crash into the iceberg and see if we can float."

The late Senator Everett Dirksen once said, "A billion here and a billion there adds up to real money." It seems as though no one in Congress today remembers that, as they have raised the debt ceiling 50 times in the last 40 years.

Last year's projected deficit of "just" $313 billion is all smoke and mirrors. Once again our irresponsible federal representatives in Washington resorted to magic so they could tell the voters back home they were reducing the deficit. What they failed to tell us is that they raided the already bankrupt Society Security System for $173 billion in surplus funds last year. However, the $173 billion obligation to future retirees didn't go away; all Congress really accomplished was growing the true annual federal deficit for last year to almost $500 billion. Even based on Congress' funny numbers they expect the federal budget deficit to total $1.6 trillion over the next five years!

"Our nation's financial condition is much worse than advertised," said David M. Walker, the U.S. comptroller general, when asked about the Administration's rosy budget forecasts. "We're adding debt at near record rates. Our long-term deficit has worsened significantly," said Walker, "and our long-term liabilities and commitments have increased dramatically. We face a demographic tsunami which, unlike most tsunamis, will never recede." This national financial problem is serious, long-term, and maybe unfixable.

As my generation retires, Social Security surpluses will quickly dwindle and vanish, and then this program, like most other federal programs, will slide into the red. And that is but a small piece of the pie, as Medicare, Medicaid and health care costs continue to soar.

If Washington can't discipline itself, Walker said, interest rates will rise, investment will decline, and foreigners will own more and more of America's assets. On trade and foreign policy matters, we are already "losing our leverage" with China and other economic powers, Walker said, "because they hold part of our mortgage." "If we do nothing, by 2040 we may have to cut federal spending by more than half or raise federal taxes by more than two and a half times to balance the budget."

But maybe the danger is upon us already. Isabel Sawhill, senior fellow and vice president at the respected Brookings Institute, not known for conservative thinking, warns that federal "deficits will become unsustainable when baby boomers begin to retire in 2008 and are poised to boom out of control a generation hence, wreaking having on today's younger Americans."

For a century America has enjoyed the singular privilege of being able to borrow what we want—now at roughly $782 billion this year—mostly in our own currency. Countries heavily in debt usually have to borrow in a foreign currency, yet we continue to borrow in dollars. Because foreign lenders continue to carry more of the risk, credit-hungry America can afford to be less prudent.

But $782 billion a year—more than six percent of GDP—is nothing but reckless behavior. The federal government deficit was $413 billion, or 3.6% of GDP, in 2004. By some estimates, America's deficits will average about 3.5% of GDP over the next decade. By 2014, the Brookings Institution projects America's public debt will amount to 55% of GDP. By 2030, on present trends, debt could reach 139% of DGP. Is there no end to this insanity?

Federal spending is out of control, no matter which party is in power. Growth of federal spending has averaged 6.4% annually since 2000, primarily because there is no political will in Congress to address escalating entitlement costs. Today in Washington there is massive spending, minimal accountability, and pathetic results. But more bad news lies ahead: things are forecast to get progressively worse. The number of Americans 55 and older is expected to grow from 67 million in 2007 to 97 million by 2020. At age 59 one becomes eligible to begin collecting certain Social Security and other retirement benefits. Beginning in 2007, more than four million so-called "baby boomers" (those born between 1946 and 1964) will start turning sixty each year. As these baby boomers begin to retire, every analysis of federal health care and retirement benefits anticipates federal costs will skyrocket.

The Congressional Budget Office recently reported that Medicare costs are growing faster than they have in a decade, and that does not include the expensive new prescription-drug benefit package that recently went into effect.

What about the highway bill recently approved by our spendthrift Congress, which will cost $286.4 billion over the next four years? The Committee for a Responsible Federal Budget cited nearly 6,500 "pork barrel" projects worth a record $24 billion. Talk about Congress working to keep itself in office!

Based on current spending proposals and expected trade deficits, the United States will borrow an unprecedented $1 trillion this year alone, mostly from foreigners.

But the Feds are not alone in their spending recklessness. State and local governments increasingly look to federal assistance to fund their increased spending, rather than the more politically courageous pattern followed for years of either cutting spending or raising taxes locally. It seems today everyone wants the federal government to pay. State and local government spending was $6,214 per capita in 2005—up about $675 since 2000 in inflation-adjusted dollars, according to an analysis from the Bureau of Economic Analysis and the Census Bureau. And you guessed it: the biggest factor in the increase was Federal money, accounting for one-third of the rise. Borrowing ranked second. Regrettably, and following the disastrous federal example, political courage and common sense have been lost at the local level too.

After meeting with then Federal Reserve Chairman Alan Greenspan, the Minister of Finance for France, Thierry Breton, quoted Greenspan as saying "'We have lost control.' That was his expression. The United States has lost control of their budget at a time when racking up deficits has been authorized without any control (from Congress),' Breton said. If Greenspan says "we have lost control," maybe it is time we became justifiably frightened.

President Bush has submitted a federal budget for the coming year that totals spending of $2.77 trillion—equal to roughly one of every five dollars produced by the U.S. economy. This budget will result in yet another significant deficit, projected to be $354 billion. Independent analysis shows that absent major change the federal healthcare spending alone will cost as much as one in every five dollars in the economy by the middle of the century, creating deficits five times the size of today's.

Even without a crisis, the progressively growing mountain of federal debt has a caustic and destructive impact on the economy that's destroying the foundation that supports up our country. As the debt grows ever larger, the stability and safety of our economic foundations erode away ever faster. It seems Congress has never heard or read the words of Winston Churchill, who said "I contend that for a nation to try to tax itself into prosperity is like a man standing in a bucket and trying to lift himself up by the handle."

BORROWING TO FUND THE UNITED STATES

For years many economists have said only foreign investment is preventing fiscal Armageddon. Foreign investors have been enamored with American assets, American Treasury bonds, American consumers, and the resulting flow of their funds into the United States has allowed the federal government to borrow without constraint. During the 1990's and the early part of this decade, America's brisk economic growth and higher yield returns have also attracted private foreign investors at unprecedented levels. Congress has managed to succeed at its two primary priorities: spending more and more (while maintaining taxes at lesser levels) and keeping themselves re-elected. They've accomplished this through financing the deficit with foreign money, and can continue this fatal financing as long as foreign investment keeps coming.

They seem to overlook that important reality that government spending must one day be paid for, and the only way that bill gets paid is through tax revenues—either taxes today or taxes tomorrow. Over two hundred years ago George Washington, father of our country, gave counsel that was wise then and wise now, and which Congress has failed to give heed. "Avoid foreign entanglements" he cautioned. Government has sold our future to "foreign entanglements", ransoming future generations by selling treasury bonds to those "foreign entanglements" who have purchased so much U.S. government debt that they could destroy our economy at their desire.

By anybody's standards $3 trillion is a gigantic amount of money, and that's how much the United States now owes foreign creditors—an amount equal to about 25 percent of our national GDP. In 2004 our net international indebtedness increased by $500 billion, in just one year. Writing in the Wilson Quarterly, Robert Aliber describes the level of risk this presents: "It's international indebtedness has been increasing at an annual rate of 16 percent, while its GDP has been growing at a six percent rate. In the long run, international indebtedness simply cannot increase more rapidly than GDP. If it did, foreigners would, in theory, eventually end up owning all the assets and securities in the United States."

The United States has enjoyed the unusual and rare home-court advantage of having its own currency as the world's financial standard. It has allowed our government to borrow in the same currency it prints, a privilege enjoyed by very few nations. Foreign producers export their products to us, and we pay for them with dollars. Then those foreign businesses, usually through their central bankers, quickly invest in dollars, primarily by buying U.S. government bonds, and the money is right back here where it started. But this comfortable process may not likely continue much longer.

Subtle and not-so-subtle changes in how foreign capital views America are increasingly evident as our enormous debt dampens their confidence in the American government's ability to service debt, in the

American economy, and thus in the American dollar. Recent quarters began to see private foreign investors reducing their spending for American assets, though their central banks continue heady investment in American treasuries.

But the time will come, and no one knows precisely when, that these foreign lenders will slow their investment in American assets. What if it happens suddenly? Such questions are continually studied by federal economists, and some scenarios are downright frightening. As foreign investment decreases, interest rates will rise, possibly sharply, as the government seeks new buyers of its debt. As interest rates soar, consumer spending will fall sharply and quickly and personal bankruptcies will escalate. And as consumer spending plummets, those nations who are exporting massive amounts of consumer goods to the United States will experience a corresponding loss of revenue, with the resultant reduced ability to invest in the United States. Consumer spending falls even more, the stock market tumbles, inflation increases, and recession or worse is seriously upon us.

China and Japan have led the nations of the world in being remarkably robust in buying U.S. Treasury securities. It's an insular circle where they export their manufactured goods to us, Americans buy their goods which in turns drives their economic growth, and they use that revenue not necessarily to better their society but to buy American debt, so that the process can begin all over again. This year China will "loan" the United States $300 billion. The central banks of China and Japan now hold nearly $1 trillion of U.S. government debt in the form of Treasuries. Have you even pondered what would happen if they decided to dump those Treasuries on the market? The shock to our economy would be severe, widespread, and lasting.

The annual report of the "central bankers' bank", the Bank for International Settlements (BIS), outlined several for concern, foremost of which were excessive consumer debt and inflated housing prices in several nations. The BIS actually expressed its concern that these two factors could cause severe global economic strains. And if these risks worsen, central banks either squeeze their investments in the U.S. or get crushed by the coming avalanche.

Another unusual dynamic has also been that several developing areas are experiencing surpluses, including much of South America, Africa, and the oil-rich Middle East, and this foreign liquidity must be invested somewhere. It is both embarrassingly absurd and a pathetic indictment of our national culture and policy that the world's richest nation now depends on the savings of the world's poorest! We Americans buy all kinds of stuff we can't afford and China, India, and other countries, instead of building infrastructure and improving quality of life they build factories to produce what their own citizens can't afford, and the whole world economy supposedly moves happily forward.

How long foreign investors will continue to buy U.S. Treasuries debt to pay for our federal and consumer debt is anyone's wild guess. One thing is for sure: the future is less certain regarding Japan, and China lacks the needed sophistication in its maturing financial systems and its currency is not convertible, so they continue to stockpile U.S. dollar reserves which sit in their central banks. They are not unmindful that as the value of the dollar declines so too does the value of their reserve holdings, and thus lately China has begun to diversify into other currencies, especially the euro. China, as are other governments, is also increasingly mindful of its domestic obligations.

The world for China, India, and others is rapidly evolving as their internal demographics change more than any time in history and as their cities and urban areas experience explosive growth. In two hundred years the percent of the world's population living in urban areas has changed dramatically, from a tiny 3% in 1800 to nearly 30% in 1950 to 50% today. There are now five urban areas which have more than twenty million residents each. Twenty-four cities have populations of more than 10 million, and sixty cities more than five million, and 150 cities have in excess of 2.5 million people.

Today there are more Treasury bonds owned by foreigners than at any time in history, Japan being the largest buyer and China now in a strong second position. This foreign ownership gives these two nations, one of questionable true friendship toward us, an interest in domestic budgetary priorities and decisions. Have we surrendered?

The crash of 1929 began when foreigners pulled out of the U.S. market, and any unanticipated bump could trigger it again at any time.

The man recognized around the world as America's most savvy investor, Warren Buffett, is troubled by the $10 trillion of the U.S. economy now owned by foreigners. "If lots of people try to leave the market, we'll have chaos because they won't get through the door," Buffett told Forbes. He believes that the dollar dropoff "could cause major disruptions in financial markets." Morgan Stanley's chief economist Stephen Roach laid it out in even more disconcerting language, saying "America has no better than a 10% chance of avoiding economic 'Armageddon.'"

DERELICT GOVERNMENT POLICY

Our misguided national policy of current-account deficits requires the United States to attract $3 billion every single business day. That is a lot of money annually. Should a dollar crisis occur, and many experts predict it soon will, the instant result will be higher interest rates, and gone is the capacity of the twin underpinnings of our current economy: excessive consumer spending and the overheated housing market.

Add to that the demographic pressures ignored for far too long by our elected public policy makers—such as the massive unfunded liabilities of Medicare, Medicaid, and Society Security—and the likelihood of a horrific outcome is substantial.

Former Federal Reserve Chairman Paul Volker, not known for being an alarmist, gives a probability factor of 75% for a major U.S.

financial crisis within the next few years without a significant shift in public policy. Another respected economic thinker, Stephen Roach, Morgan Stanley's chief economist, isn't as conservative as Volker. Roach pegs the probability at a whopping 90%. These are incredible odds for a very difficult road ahead. The fiscal environment America faces today is more perilous than at any other time in modern American history. Without some major changes, the rushing fiscal avalanche will bury us in an economic calamity the likes of which no nation has ever experienced.

In the past two decades the United States has weathered corporate corruption and the resultant loss of unprecedented personal and pension wealth, the Russian crisis, the Black Monday stock market crash of 1987, multiple financial crises in Asia and Mexico, and two recessions. We have been through rocky days, but how long we will have the capacity and good fortune, and maybe in the words of George Washington "the hand of providence," is now in serious question. American's economic environment is more hazardous than at any time since the Great Depression, the result of failed, reckless, and politically expedient policies.

Daily we seem enamored by and glued to the stock market as a national barometer. Yet it is filled with examples of failure and loss. When telecom Global Crossing was flying high, fueled by thoughtless investments by millions of Americans, its founder Gary Winnock walked off with $730 million. And then Global Crossing exploded, and American investors lost $2.5 trillion in market value. That's real money! The liquidation of Enron, WorldCom, Quest, Tyco, and Computer Associates—all victims of corrupt management—wiped out nearly half a trillion worth of corporate debt.

Is this risky for America? Absolutely! In 2000 over half of all American households were "in the stock market". And of them, nearly half counted the majority of their wealth in shares of public companies. Oh such misplaced faith.

WAR COSTS OF IRAQ AND AFGHANISTAN

President James Madison, our fourth president, wrote in Political Observations in 1795 words that speak truth to us today: "Of all the enemies to public liberty war is, perhaps, the most to be dreaded because it comprises and develops the germ of every other. War is the parent of armies; from these proceed debts and taxes... known instruments for bringing the many under the domination of the few... No nation could preserve its freedom in the midst of continual warfare."

Simply stated, war is costly. And the United States is today immersed in a very costly war not of its choosing, a war where our enemies are committed for the long-term. This year the United States will spend more for military costs that all the rest of the world combined, and Defense Secretary Robert Gates has asked Congress to approve nearly $190 billion for war costs in 2008.

As of this writing, the U.S. has spent well over $300 billion on military operations in Iraq and Afghanistan, costs accounted for not in the budget but "off budget." The cost of continuing operations exceeds $100 billion annually. Add to that the long-term costs such as interest payments on war debt and military personnel costs such as war-caused disabilities that will continue for many years and the total cost of the war is today estimated to exceed $1.3 trillion. Two research studies released earlier this year predict the true cost to the U.S. economy over the next decade could be anywhere from $657 billion to $2 trillion for the Iraq war alone." And that money has to come from somewhere, from you and me.

Because of the misguided persistent deficit spending policies of the federal government, estimated to exceed several hundred billion dollars this year alone, as a nation we must borrow to pay for the costs of this war—burdening future generations of Americans with over $1 trillion in additional debt, and most of it owed once again to Asian countries. Some analysts estimated that federal spending for war in

Iraq and Afghanistan and Hurricane Katrina will cost every American household an additional $12,000. Our elected leaders keep on spending, and you and I are the ones who must someday pay.

And these federal deficits just continue. Brian Riedl, budget analysis for the Heritage Foundation, predicts, much because of these war costs, the federal deficit will grow to $500 billion in 2008 and an astonishing $873 billion in 2015. Even more troubling, Riedl warns "even these estimates could prove overly optimistic."

TRADE DEFICIT

For every one dollar of product that the United States sells abroad, it buys $1.60 worth of imports, most of it consumer goods. We don't have to spend very many dollars to be quickly in serious imbalance.

We set a new record in 2005 as the trade deficit hit $725 billion, having risen every year since 1991. This year American consumers spending generously and without restraint as they fuel the economy will add another $750 billion or more to the ever-growing trade deficit. Some analysts frightfully predict the trade gap will top $1 trillion annually by the end of 2007. These costs are then financed by the government through borrowing, and thus accruing not only more debt obligations but additional interest cost obligations as well. This burgeoning trade deficit reached a new all-time high last year: $726 billion. By definition we are borrowing these amounts from abroad.

One-fourth of the deficit is with just one country—a $202 billion trade gap with China. Aggravating these matters, this gap is financed largely by the Chinese state banks' ownership of U.S. debt. These same Chinese state banks are weighed down with enormous numbers of non-performing loans. Should those loans start to fail, the result for the U.S. and world economies could be devastating.

Though China and Japan have large current-account surpluses, the world leader is no longer Asia, but the oil exporting nations including OPEC countries, Norway, and Russia. The oil exporting nations could this year alone reap a bounteous harvest of $700 billion just from selling oil to foreigners. The International Monetary Fund estimates that oil exporters' current-account surplus could reach $400 billion, further weakening the USA's position in the Middle East and elsewhere. In Saudi Arabia alone, their current-account surplus is expected to exceed $100 billion this year, equaling an amazing 32% of their GDP. And where are those dollars going? Increasingly to Europe, where Europe's share of OPEC's imports has climbed to 32%, compared with America's 8%—just one more thing endangering the dollar.

FOREIGN DEBT TO THE UNITED STATES

As a member of a United Nations delegation staying in Kenya's finest luxury hotel operated by its corrupt government to impress international travelers, I visited Kibera, an impoverished and dangerous ghetto section of Nairobi, the capitol city of Kenya, about the size of Manhattan's Central Park. It is the largest and poorest slum in Africa with a teeming population of over 800,000 residents, half of whom are under the age of 15. Most have come from the rural areas of Kenya in search of evasive opportunity. Covering an area of six hundred acres of mud and filth, a putrid brown stream of decomposing sludge meanders through its center. We couldn't find it on any map because Kibera is an illegal camp, yet it's home to at least one third of Nairobi's exploding population. Nearly half of Nairobi's nearly three million people live in slums.

Home to five of Kenya's six largest native ethnic groups, in addition to a Muslim group, there is hunger and disease and squalor and filth and poverty, fetid open sewers running down grimy dirt alleys with diseased rats scurrying everywhere. Water is sold by private profiteers who lay hoses in the dirt and charge double what people pay for water outside Kibera. Approximately 80% of all youth aged 16-30 years in Kibera are unemployed, and the U.S. Centers for Disease Control estimates that over 20% of the population is HIV positive. Needless to say, this vast and squalid slum wasn't part of our government-sponsored itinerary.

As we began to walk the rutted narrow dirt paths, our nostrils filled with the overpowering stench of rotting garbage and countless wood cooking fires and recently caught fish and raw human excrement. Street kids seemed to roam everywhere, bewildered youngsters searching for food or trouble, or both.

Our anxious American Embassy guide was increasingly frightened, as this is a place "white faces" do not visit. I doubt if the Kenyan government visits either. It's a dangerous place with no apparent law and obviously no order—it's even too dangerous for Nairobi's corrupt police. Muggers and thugs abound, and our guide was worried. Night was soon approaching. The slum itself seemed to be crawling, and it was apparent we had overdone our stay.

That night as we attended an elegant government-hosted dinner in sumptuous and opulent surroundings, not five kilometers from Kibera, the enormity and complexity of Africa's economic challenges hit squarely home.

Across the continent of Africa on its western coast is the tiny diamond-rich nation of Sierra Leone. To Pedro da Cintra, the Portuguese explorer who visited the coast in 1460, the coastal mountains looked like lion's teeth, so he named the country Lion Mountains—Sierra Leone, in Portuguese. In 1792 slaves freed by the British navy were brought from Nova Scotia to found the colony of Freetown, now the country's capital and the largest city with an official population of two million and an added unofficial population of hundreds of thousands, maybe even another two million, of refugees from Sierra Leone's barbaric civil war.

I visited the large national hospital in the capital city and found conditions shockingly appalling. The fading paint-chipped pharmacy stood bare of medicines, dedicated physicians lacked even rudimentary equipment, conditions were bleak and dreary. A nurse lay dying of a disease readily treatable by prescription medications in the U.S. Conditions were unspeakable and unnecessary.

Nearby, we later stopped at one of countless scrapboard shacks covered with rusting corrugated roofs, "home" to a sickly and aging man speaking a tribal dialect we did not understand. He had no family, no retirement income, and no apparent means of support. His limited home "furnishings" consisted of a grimy woven matt on the dirt floor, where we sat, yet he was pleasant and warm in welcoming us into his humble home. Through our interpreter we spoke of life and hope and survival, and I asked how he planned to take care of himself in his old age. He looked at me and with a child-like honesty and hopeless candor said "I have no way. I shall die."

Such expressions are not unusual in Africa or in much of the so-called Third World, where 1.2 billion people live on less than $1 per day. The International Monetary Fund and the World Bank have now designated thirty-eight countries too poor and too indebted to repay their onerous debts and deserving of debt forgiveness. These thirty-eight countries owe a combined $42.5 billion to the World Bank, $10 billion to the African Development Bank, and $5 billion to the International Monetary Fund. Annual interest payments in over two dozen nations exceed what they spend for education and health care.

Not only are these government debts unpayable, but these governments service these debts only because their lenders loan them more money to repay the old debts. This is debt insanity in its highest measure, done to make bad loans look good and it's commonplace throughout the developing world.

The majestic beauty of Africa is found not only in its remarkable nature and plentiful wild animals, but equally in its seven hundred million people. From the slopes of snow-capped Mount Kilimanjaro to the sun-drenched white powder beaches of Tanzania to the unspoiled plains of the Serengeti to the desolate deserts of the Sahara, Africa is an extraordinary continent. Yet its future has been mortgaged by corrupt and incompetent governments led by bungling politicians and merciless dictators devoted to stuffing their secret numbered Swiss bank accounts. In many countries of Africa, per capita income is below levels reached in the 1960's and life expectancy is declining.

Jeffrey Sachs, director of The Earth Institute at Columbia University, and labeled "the most important economist in the world" by The New York Times Magazine and "the world's best-known economist" by TIME magazine, says that tropical Africa is simply too poor to grow. Geographically disadvantaged, it attracts little capital to sustain its growing population and is too impoverished to save and thus create its own capital. The results of that poverty are high rates of disease; it accounted for 85% of 1.2 million malaria deaths last year and 75% of the 3.1 million AIDS deaths last year. Some estimate an African dies every three seconds from poverty-related illnesses. Some 30,000 Africans die everyday, maybe more.

But fiscal ineptitude is not limited to Africa's 53 countries and the developing world. The independent European Court of Auditors refused to certify the financial accounts of the European Union for the eleventh year in a row, citing errors of legality and regularity. It is either magic or it's deceptive accounting for the U.S. to incur enormous mounting liabilities from these nations when we know they will never ever be repaid.

WASTED FOREIGN AID

The United States of America commendably and generously leads the nations of the world in so-called foreign aid contributions, and has done so for decades. As Senator John McCain said in the well of the Senate in 2003: "America is great not because of what she has done for herself, but because of what she has done for others." Our record of aid to others is without peer.

A United Nations analysis in the mid 1990's of U.S. and European foreign aid found that the United States had spent $1.2 trillion (of your tax dollars) on aid and yet all seventy recipient countries were worse off today than they were in 1980—and forty-three nations were worse off than in 1970. Since 1960 the industrialized world has pumped a staggering $450 billion in aid into the forty-eight nations of sub-Saharan Africa, the equivalent of six Marshall Plans. Yet Mallam Nuhu Ribadu, chairman of Nigeria's Economic and Financial Crimes commission, reported recently that nearly $400 billion in African aid had been "squandered" between 1960 and 2000. Doug Casey, an interesting economic thinker and classmate of Bill Clinton at Georgetown University, says "Foreign aid might be defined as a transfer of money from poor people in rich countries to rich people in poor countries."

Some U. S. government studies estimate that 80% of aid funds lent between 1970 and 1996 flowed out as capital flight in the same year; this amounts to about 40% of Africa's privately held wealth. Even so, last year political leaders of eight wealthy nations, including the United States, pledged to double their aid (with your tax dollars) to the region by 2010.

And what is there to show for this enormous outlay of money, most of it from the United States? Next to nothing. Through our foreign aid assistance programs we have attempted to court those nations and buy their friendship. And to what real end?

After decades of generous foreign aid, Africa, for example, is still trapped in poverty. So where did all this aid go? More often than not the dollars ended up in the secret bank accounts of dishonest government officials, their crooked cohorts, and violent warlords who devote their energies to strategizing on how to get even more aid rather than how to develop their destitute countries. The number one problem facing Africa today is not AIDS or any of its other extreme health challenges, but corruption. A striking example is Zimbabwe's corrupt President Robert Mugabe, a vicious murderer who has destroyed his own country's economy through the vast taking of highly productive privately-owned farms now unprofitably operated by Mugabe's loyal cronies, and through an "urban renewal" project that has left several hundred thousand people homeless.

Of course corruption is not limited to Africa; it is epidemic and worldwide. Our relatively naïve American understanding notwithstanding, in most nations of the world, especially in Africa, the Middle East, and South America, theft, dishonesty, fraud, corruption, and even murder are customary for government. A 2004 World Bank study on global corruption found that bribery is a trillion-dollar business, "causing far more wealth to flow from poor countries to rich countries than the poor countries receive in foreign aid." On top of that, an estimated $1.5 trillion in 2001 (latest figures available) went into money laundering, much of this facilitated through our inept foreign assistance programs.

Is it any wonder that so many people around the world regard us with derision and contempt, that so many consider us the Great Satan? We offer what we hopefully intend to be relief and comfort to countries suffering calamities and hardship throughout the world, and so much of it ends up in the pockets of corrupt leaders.

Trinidad, Bolivia was founded in 1686 by Padre Cipriano Barace on the shores of the Mamoré River. It's a difficult place to reach, about 500 miles by a rubble and broken asphalt road from the city of Santa Cruz, or easier by air, which we did in an unmarked U.S. Drug Enforcement Administration aircraft. Its remoteness contributes to its success as a cocaine production center, where violence and brutality are a daily part of the drug trafficking life. The climate is tropical and humid, and one feels like he has stepped back a century in time.

Walking along a dusty street in Trinidad, a Bolivian leader gave me his perspective on U.S. foreign aid. "You Americans just don't understand. You want everyone to love you so you give us your money but you don't care about how we feel. You always want to change everything about us. You condemn us for producing cocoa, but you forget that we produce it for America! You should remember that most people in the world don't have the advantages you have."

Our vast and generous foreign aid gifts notwithstanding, human suffering is at unprecedented levels in many countries around the world. Hundreds of millions continue to suffer the abuse and corruption of the privileged power class and to live in abject squalor and hunger. Our foreign aid hasn't produced many results, and leads one to ask the question, "What would the situation be if we had never sent anything?"

A MOUNTAIN OF CONSUMER DEBT

We're under siege in this country from the credit card companies. In 2003, they mailed over 5 billion offers for credit cards. My grandparents did not own a credit card; if they didn't have cash they didn't make a purchase. Today our children live in another world; if they want it, they buy it, on credit cards. Today, Americans spend more than they earn, as if they can run up debt forever. American households are swamped and sinking under an incomprehensible amount of consumer debt—which grew to $2.16 trillion in late 2005, up from $2.07 trillion one year earlier and $1.64 trillion just five years ago. And we're paying more for that privilege of irresponsible spending: the average variable-rate credit card now charges interest of 14.2%, up from 11.9% last year. Three out of five American families can't pay off their credit cards each month, and the revolving part of our credit card debt, the part we don't pay off every month, now exceeds $700 billion! Total consumer debt is now over $7,100 for every person in America, not including mortgage debt. The average college student owes $2,800 on credit cards, not including student loans. The personal debt of Americans in 2002 was equal to the gross national products of Russia and Great Britain combined. And last year the estimated average credit-card debt per U.S. card-holding household was an astounding $9,312.

Simultaneously, as consumer debt has grown personal savings have plunged. Twenty years ago, the personal savings rate averaged 9%. Ten years ago, our rate of savings had dropped to 5.2%. And now, according to the San Francisco Federal Reserve Bank, since 2000 it has averaged an abysmal 1.9%. And the savings rate had now declined to below zero—the U.S. personal savings rate in 2005 was a dangerous –0.4%, and our net international investment position now exceeds $3 trillion in the negative. By comparison, in economically soaring China the personal savings rate nears 25%, and may be as high as 40% of the national income. Were it not for their personal savings and their government's willingness to buy U.S. treasury bonds, all denominated in U.S. dollars, our spree of debt spending could not have continued.

At the same time, we are spending the equity in our homes. Today we have a smaller equity share overall in our homes that at any time since the 1950s. Last year, the most recent year for which data is available, American consumers spent $20 for every $19 they earned.

In 1987, the average American family owed $28,892. By 2005, the debt average had rapidly risen to $101,386 for every family in the nation. Household debt doubled to more than $10 trillion between 1992 and 2004, adjusted for inflation. Americans had $2.1 trillion in consumer debt at the end of 2004, double what it was ten short years earlier. Credit cards accounted for an estimated $1.75 trillion in purchases in 2005, compared with an estimated $872 billion on debit cards, according to The Nilson Report.

Youthful spenders (ranging from 18 to 24 years old) now purchase over half of all spending on credit and debit cards, earning them the unbecoming title "Generation Plastic" or "Gen P." Day after day the mail contains enticing invitations from credit-card companies that woo them with low "introductory" interest rates which just months later triple when they're a day late making a monthly payment. So to solve that problem the youthful consumer opens another enticing letter and signs up for another low-interest-rate introductory "special", transfers his balance to get the bonus frequent flyer miles, and starts the process all over again—only with an ever higher balance owing. Then when that becomes too onerous they negotiate for an interest-only long-term payment plan that years down the road leaves them still owing the burdensome original amount.

The number of American men and women hanging on by a financial thread because of excessive burgeoning consumer debt, most of it at exorbitant interest rates that used to be illegal because of usury laws, grows ever higher. And with that the danger of a widespread consumer breakdown and collapse grows ever more real.

NOW WHAT?

My first presidential campaign was when I was five years old, walking with my mother as she campaigned door to door in our neighborhood for General Dwight D. Eisenhower. "I like Ike" was the motto, and I still like Ike—for when he was President the United States was the world's biggest creditor nation and it remained so until 1980. Remarkably, in the few short intervening years the United States of America is now the world's biggest borrower nation. There has never been such a gigantic reversal in financial history, and today we are drowning under staggeringly mammoth, almost immeasurable debt—a sure prescription for disaster.

American households are overstretched to the breaking point, worn down and worn out by the burdens of debt. State and local governments are exhausting sources of tax revenues to sustain their undisciplined spending. The federal budget deficit is out of control.

But there is no end in sight to this debt spending, and our only way to fund our government deficits is to continue recklessly drawing on surplus savings in other nations, especially from Asia. And out of necessity we will also continue to finance our consumer-driven trade deficits with foreign borrowing.

Our tragic pattern of debt spending and chronic government deficits is eroding the pillars of American prosperity. Like termites quietly eating away the wooden foundation of a home until it one day collapses, our national course is no different. As George Maynard Bush writes in the Economist, "Given too much license to roam, Congress [will] soon reach the economy's outer frontiers—and carry right on over the edge."

The last time Washington repaid any of its debt was nearly a half-century ago, in 1960, and then it only paid $1 billion.

When will our excesses come to an abrupt halt? There is growing vulnerability, for Treasury bonds, for the dollar, for the stock market, for inflated housing prices. Intelligence sources in Dubai tell us several Middle East central banks are laying the groundwork to switch reserves from the U.S. dollar to the euro. Syria has already abandoned the dollar for the euro. With the housing bubble bursting or when consumers stop spending or other nations stop buying U.S. government debt, or some combination of the three, our economy will slide quickly into very difficult times.

And you will get the bill. This land of unequalled opportunity has become a land of epidemic indebtedness and our generous government will take more and more of your money just to pay its debts. American's second president, John Adams, said "There are two ways to conquer and enslave a nation. One is by the sword, the other is by debt." It's happening, and not by the sword.

Remember, you're not just a consumer; you're a citizen. It's said that on the day the founders of this country finished writing the Constitution, in the summer of 1787, Benjamin Franklin emerged from the closed, guarded Pennsylvania State House where the Constitutional Convention was taking place, and was accosted by a man on the street who said, "Doctor Franklin! What have you given us?" "A republic," Franklin responded, "if you can keep it."

Notice he didn't say, if your fearless leaders can keep it; he said, if you can keep it. It's up to us to take responsibility for our own fate, and demand that our representatives take responsibility for the nation. And that means we have to get out of debt. It may take a hundred years, but it will never happen it we don't get started now.

4

THIRD DANGER–
AMERICA'S
BANKRUPT SAFETY NET

✿

"The federal government is on an
imprudent and unsustainable path,
worse than advertised."
—David M. Walker

In a small countryside farming village in Russia I visited a pharmacy.
Like the dismal hospital in Freetown, Sierra Leone and like Old
Mother Hubbard's cupboard, the cupboards and shelves were bare.
Medicines simply weren't available. Such conditions of course could
not exist in the United States. Or could they? For generations we have
depended on promised government and corporate benefit programs to
care for the financial and health needs of our aging citizens. But our
illustrious safety net is failing.

Testifying before one of five national hearings conducted by the
Congressionally created Citizens Health Care Working Group, David

M. Walker, Comptroller, Government Accountability Office, called federal health spending "an unsustainable trend" that will break the economy if it's not reined in. He went on to say that this long-term fiscal hole could be resolved IF our country has "real average annual economic growth in the double-digit range every year for the next 75 years." That kind of sustained growth has never happened in the history of this or any nation, and it's highly unlikely to start anytime soon.

- $26 trillion: Current level of underfunded liabilities for Social Security and Medicare.
- $44 trillion: Current total federal debt with the inclusion of Social Security and Medicare liabilities.
- $53 trillion: Government estimates of Social Security and Medicare underfunded liabilities by 2008.
- $77 trillion: Estimates of total retirement debt including underfunded liabilities. [SOURCE: CATO INSTITUTE]

"An unsustainable trend!" "Break the economy!" What statements! Either we are turning a deaf ear or a blind eye to this growing and ruinous danger or we are simply asleep, I'm not sure which.

THE AGE OF OLD AGE

We're getting older and the industrialized world is aging. In 2000, roughly 10% of the world's population was sixty years old or older—the highest percentage in world history—a number that will grow to 22% by 2050. By 2030 in industrial power nations Japan and Italy, both vital partners of the United States, 20% of the population will be sixty-five years old. In the industrialized world, there will be two old people for every child by 2050.

In important Western Europe, the median age of the population is progressively rising, as fertility rates drop below the 2.1 children per couple needed to sustain population growth. The birth rate is now 1.4 in Germany, and even lower in Italy and Spain. From 1970 to today, ten million German children we would have expected in another era were not born, and thus are not available to join the work force in twenty years.

The result of this unwise strategy is adding massive costs to government health care and retirement spending in countries around the world. In the U.S., Medicare, Medicaid, and Society Security have in forty years more than doubled as a share of federal spending and will continue to grow, according to the Congressional Budget Office's "intermediate" projections. In 1966, they accounted for 7% of federal spending. Next year it is expected to be 43%, and in 2046 55%—reducing to dangerous levels all federal funds available for all other federal needs.

Since 2001, federal spending has increased a whopping 33% to almost $2.5 trillion—or $22,000 for every American household. Worse yet, discretionary spending in those same few years has increased 49%. Unreformed entitlement programs are now at almost 11% of GDP and are expected to double in the next decade. One of the primary causes in this expected growth is Medicare drug spending, which is expected to add $8.1 trillion in unfunded liabilities over the next seventy-five years.

Already Social Security, Medicare, and Medicaid are costing the taxpayer $1.1 trillion per year, almost 40% of the federal budget. Economist Robert J. Samuelson, writing in the Washington Post, referring to this problem as an "economic death spiral" said, "The great danger of an aging society is that the rising costs of government retirement programs—mainly Social Security and Medicare—increase taxes or budget deficits so much that they reduce economic growth."

MEDICARE

A wildly costly federal program that's draining the treasury was launched by President Lyndon Johnson and Congress in 1965, Medicare is supposed to provide federally funded insurance to seniors. It is supposedly self-funded through a Medicare tax: 2.9% on all income earned by American workers, half paid by the worker and half paid by the employer. (Self-employed people pay the entire 2.9%.) In return the government provides seniors with medical insurance (Medicare Part A) which pays for hospital and hospice care, and for a small premium "supplementary medical insurance" (Medicare Part B) which pays physicians' fees and outpatient care.

Medicare spent $309 billion in 2004. Premiums covered only one-fourth of the costs of Medicare Part B. And you, the taxpayer, paid the other three-fourths from general federal revenues. The federal government spends almost 3% of the nation's total economic output on Medicare, and it is rapidly growing worse. As baby boomers retire and require more and more of advanced health care, in the next forty years Medicare jeopardizes the federal treasury. Medicare spending will nearly quadruple to almost 10% of gross domestic product, and in seventy-five years to more than 13.6% of GDP. By 2079, it is estimated Medicare alone will consume one-eighth of the U.S. economy. The Government Accountability Office now projects unfunded Medicare obligations of $27.8 trillion over the next seventy-five years, others project those unfunded liabilities to total $68 trillion—six times the unfunded liabilities of Social Security.

And now along comes another costly Medicare program, this time the prescription drug plan (Medicare Part D) which began last year. Medicare's own trustees have determined the cost of this program to be $8.7 trillion over the next seventy-five years. As Heritage Foundation Policy Analyst Bob Moffitt writes: "The drug benefit itself imposes staggering new unfunded liabilities on future generations. These cannot be honored without huge deficits, huge tax increases, or slashing other programs."

Who will pay for this?

FINANCIAL DANGER

Senator Hillary Rodham Clinton has often spoken of "a health care crisis in America." There is no health care crisis in America, at least not yet; American health services are among the best in the world. What we do have is a health care financing crisis in America. 10% of the population consumes 72% of health care expenditures. America provides $34.5 billion a year in free health care for the uninsured, outside of the Medicare system, according to the Urban Institute. Government at all levels in America directly pays for 45% of health care spending, with Medicare paying one-third of all hospital fees and 20% of doctors' fees.

Medicare's own trustees now recognize that Medicare benefits promised to current and future retirees Medicare are already unfunded an astronomical by $29.7 trillion. The most recent Medicare trustees' report shows that in just one year the long-term cost of Medicare's unfunded obligations soared roughly $2 trillion. A huge part of that was the debt for the drug benefit portion which shot from $8.1 trillion to $8.7 trillion.

Yet amazingly, in its self-claimed wisdom and with obvious political cowardice, both the executive branch and Congress continue to postpone dealing with this bulging crisis. Medicare's spiraling costs cannot continue forever—because you and I and the rest of America simply cannot afford it.

MEDICAID

President Lyndon Johnson and Congress also generously created Medicaid in that same blindly bighearted year of 1965 as a joint federal-state program to pay health-care expenses of the American poor, a noble but ill-conceived idea. Congress tells the states who to cover and what services to provide, and the states are free to expand either or both at their pleasure. Today Medicaid serves forty-six million poor Americans and is just one more government program that Washington either has no idea how to pay for or they know and don't have the political chutzpah to fix it, so they just keep borrowing and borrowing and heaping the bill that will one day come due on the backs of our children and grandchildren.

And the burdensome costs just keep rising, and you are paying for it. This fiscal year, Medicaid is expected to cost the federal government $193 billion and the states an additional $145 billion. Testifying before the House Committee on Energy and Commerce, U. S. Health and Human Services Secretary Mike Leavitt said, "Over the next ten years, American taxpayers will spend nearly five trillion dollars on Medicare in combined state and federal spending." In addition, the Medicare prescription drug benefit is projected to cost an additional $1.2 trillion! Ah, the politics of federal largess that we as a nation simply can no longer afford. Add to that as baby boomers age, by the year 2030 just Medicaid's nursing home expenditures are projected to reach $130 billion per year.

The Congressional Budget Office labels Medicaid as one of the foremost causes of the growing disaster in federal spending over the next few decades. The program is expected to cost $338 billion in this fiscal year, up $80 billion, or about 31%, in just the last three years. If current trends continue, federal Medicaid spending alone will increase from 1.5% of GDP today to an expected 4.5% by 2050. Over the next 10 years, the Medicaid program is projected to cost $2.6 trillion, but it's beyond me where Congress thinks it will find the money.

And the feds are killing the states. Washington pays nearly 57% of the program's costs, but has left the fifty states holding the tab for the balance and governors are crying foul and demanding relief from

Washington. For example, South Carolina Governor Mark Sanford has sought federal authority to implement radical changes in Medicaid in his state, which now costs South Carolina taxpayers more than $1 billion a year, or a whopping 14% of their penny-pinching state budget. That percentage is projected to double in just ten years, and South Carolina is not alone.

SOCIAL SECURITY

Social Security was launched in 1937 as the most far-reaching government program ever created. Beginning in 1940, participants age sixty-five and older could for the rest of their lives collect a monthly retirement payment from the government.

Speaking at the signing of the original Social Security Act, President Franklin D. Roosevelt said, "The civilization of the past one hundred years, with its starting industrial changes, has tended more and more to make life insecure. Young people have come to wonder what would be their lot when they came to old age. The man with a job has wondered how long the job would last."

Nearly seventy year later another President, George W. Bush, made an extraordinary admission to the American public about the financial stability of Social Security, saying it "is on the road to bankruptcy" and will be "unable to pay promised benefits to future generations." Today young people also wonder what will be "their lot when they came to old age."

When Social Security began there were forty-two workers for each beneficiary; today there are less than 4 workers per beneficiary and by 2030 there will be 2.2 workers per beneficiary. Because today's workers pay for the benefits of the retired workers, as baby boomers retire and live longer Social Security will spend far faster than its funds, creating massive shortfalls. By Social Security's 90th birthday, payouts already cost 110% of contributions.

People depend on the "guaranteed" benefits of Social Security. As envisioned by President Roosevelt, Social Security was to be the primary source of providing financially for seniors lacking sufficient savings to sustain themselves. Today, an astounding 80 to 90% of all seniors rely upon Social Security as their prime source of income. But the problem is even deeper: Social Security is the primary income for nearly five million widows and widowers, five million disabled workers, and nearly four million children of deceased workers.

Today Social Security is broke. Social Security took in $657.7 billion in taxes in 2005, and paid out $501.6 billion in benefits, a healthy margin allowing for a build-up of undistributed reserves for future needs. But alas, once again Congress and the administration spent the $156.1 billion surplus on other things.

As a result of this myopic politically-motivated strategy, the Government Accounting Office says Social Security faces $3.7 trillion in unfunded liabilities over the next seventy-five years caused by the retirements of seventy-eight million baby boomers starting this year. Others calculate it is now underfunded by $23 trillion, causing a deficit by 2018. Social Security becomes technically insolvent by 2042, according to estimates from the Cato Institute.

But by far the worst of the projections came in 2004 directly from Social Security and Medicare trustees, who estimated the unfunded benefit liabilities in today's dollars at an incomprehensible $74 trillion dollars.

FISCAL IRRESPONSIBILITY

In recent decades Social Security has collected far more in payroll taxes than it paid in benefits, and these surpluses were intended to be held by the government "in trust". However, Washington politicians once again played the foolish federal spending shell game, tapping the surplus "trust" piggybank to help fund such federal programs as education and defense—in order to hide the honest amount of the federal deficit. Social Security actuaries, in their February 2005 report, expect Congress to repay $1.7 trillion previously borrowed from the program's trust fund to pay for other government programs. I wouldn't count on Congress.

Starting in 2018, payroll taxes will collect less than benefits to be paid out, and the trust funds will need to be tapped. But Congress already spent those trust funds, so what solutions remain? The options are limited: raise taxes, cut spending, or borrow trillions more.

Can older and aging Americans survive? One out of two older Americans has no pension. And they have little money: one-third of those 65 to 74 and nearly half of those 75 and older have incomes of $18,000 or less for an individual, and $22,000 or less for a couple.

Those expecting, indeed depending on, the government for "guaranteed" Social Security benefits are in for a sad day.

Former U.S. Senator Zell Miller sums it up with painfully clarity: "The current dollar 75 year unfunded liability in Social Security and Medicare is $51 trillion. The total household wealth in America is less than $44 trillion. If you took every asset from every American and applied it to our retirement programs, it would cover only 80 percent of the shortfall."

A recent study by Joseph Antos of the American Enterprise Institute and Tracy Foertsch of The Heritage Foundation frighteningly found that to just pay all the Medicare benefits promised to current and future retirees over just the next ten years, Congress will have to impose a $2.7 trillion tax increase on American workers and businesses, beginning immediately.

Does Congress think we are nuts?

PENSIONS ARE BROKE TOO

CORPORATE PENSIONS

More than half of American workers, 68 million, are currently enrolled in employer-based retirement plans, and those plans are failing like never before. Today, private pension plans are underfunded by a total of $450 billion, according to the U.S. Secretary of Labor. That's almost half a trillion dollars! According to the Associated Press, "Pension plans of the 263 companies in the Standard & Poor's 500 index offering defined benefit [pension] plans went from being over-funded by $280 billion in 1999 to being underfunded by $165 billion last year." In simple language, that means they are short $165 billion in being able to pay what is already obligated to their pensioners.

This is a mammoth and growing danger. The shortfalls are astonishing. Of the 369 S&P 500 companies that offer pensions, 311 do not have enough money in their pensions to cover their obligations. The massive shortfalls are astounding. For example: Ford Motor $11.7B, Exxon-Mobil $10.1B, General Motors $8.6B, Boeing $6.7B, IBM $5.8B. Let's look at four "respected" American industrial behemoths.

General Motors:

In my growing up years my father was a General Motors car dealer, and all my life I've known GM's unofficial and somewhat arrogant business motto: "What's good for GM is good for America." Not anymore, because General Motors can't sell enough cars and trucks to buy its way out of its employee and retiree healthcare and pension costs, which will total nearly $6 billion this year. In 2004, GM paid $3 billion into its retirement health trust fund—three times its earnings. In 2005 it lost $10.6 billion. Not good sustainable business.

For most of a century General Motors has been an undisputed worldwide king of business, earning a certain deserved bluster and smugness. As a member of the President's Export Council I witnessed this arrogance of power firsthand, and came to appreciate that GM's place and impact in the American economy is undisputed. Listen to how GM's CEO Rick Wagoner sums it up: "GM is the canary in the mine shaft," meaning that GM is so large, so powerful, that whether it sinks or swims in dealing with its overwhelming problems could suggest the future of American industry.

Long a world leader in auto sales, GM controlled 50.7% of the U.S. market in 1962. Today its share is half that at 25.4% and the company's losses are in the billions. Recently GM announced plans to cut 25,000 jobs and close factories. A key factor in the decline of this giant is its costly employee and retiree benefits.

In 1961, General Motors committed to pay 100% of the health premiums for workers and their families, and retired workers were added soon thereafter. Forty years later those obligations, now more than $50 billion, are killing the company. Current employees are outnumbered by retirees more than 3 to 1. Health care alone is expected to cost GM a staggering $5.6 billion this year. The company, with a U.S. workforce of 150,000 (and declining), must provide health care for a total of 1.1 million workers, retirees and dependents, though it has agreed with the United Auto Workers leadership to rescind $1 billion worth of health-care benefits for its retirees. Its future pension fund liabilities are $89 billion and its health care liabilities are about $77 billion, for a total obligation of $166 billion. GM reports $20 billion in the bank and Wall Street values the company at about $17 billion. Those numbers just don't add up.

Add to that competition. While General Motors spends about $1,520 on health care for every car it produces, arch rival Toyota spends less than $400 and is poised to surpass General Motors as the world's largest automaker. Then factor in as much as $12 billion in potential benefit liabilities caused by the failure of Delphi, its auto parts unit, and the $4.4 billion it lost in its purchase of Fiat, and GM's "junk" debt rating is understandable.

The American automobile industry health care obligations total more than $95 billion dollars.

Polaroid:

Polaroid employees had $300 million in retirement funds in Polaroid stock, which was worth around $60 in 1997. From then until Polaroid filed bankruptcy in 2001, while workers were prohibited from selling any shares, the stock fell to just nine cents per share, and the retirement of six thousand Polaroid workers was wiped out.

Northwest Airlines:

Northwest Airlines pensions are underfunded by almost $4 billion, according to CEO Doug Steenland in testimony before the U.S. Senate. The company has also filed for bankruptcy protection (on the same day as its rival Delta Air Lines). The company said it had nearly $17.92 billion in debt and is losing money at the rate of $4 million a day. Northwest also has $2.5 billion due to its underfunded pensions in the next two years.

United Airlines:

UAL Corp, parent of United Airlines, has filed for bankruptcy. In the process, United jettisoned its underfunded pension plan—underfunded by $9.8 billion, the largest pension-plan default in U.S. corporate history.

COULD IT HAPPEN TO YOU?

Yes it could and it may!

There is an old saying about things not being worth the paper they're written on. Such is the case with corporate pensions in America today. Traditional pensions, which promise a guaranteed monthly payment at retirement, are called "defined-benefit plans." Last year companies dumped 1,381 defined-benefit plans, and though most were fully funded so that workers will receive 100% of their benefits, 192 were "distressed" and workers may lose all their promised retirement benefits. Yet tens of thousands of American businesses and nearly 75% of America's 500 largest corporations provide defined benefit pensions.

Every day the pension crisis in the United States is worsening. For many companies such as General Motors their pension and health obligations actually exceed the company's total worth as measured by the stock market. But that is even misleading, because this corporation's other debt obligations may be first in line for payment.

Most pension funds hold investments in stock, and must liquidate stock to pay obligations. Two-thirds, or $1 trillion, of the $1.6 trillion held by defined-benefit plans is currently invested in stocks. As baby boomers retire and pension funds must liquidate stocks to pay benefits, a negative impact on the stock market could result. And America is not alone in its pension crisis—similar problems exist in Latin American and Europe. British Airways, for example, owes almost half its $6.1 billion market value to its pension fund.

In 1980, 35% of American workers earned a pension; today that number is less than 20%. In 1985, American businesses provided more than 112,000 pension plans; more than 80,000 of them no longer exist. And nearly half of all Americans say they have less than $25,000 saved for retirement.

The number of corporations to shed their pension plans just keeps mounting. Most recently IBM, a perceived mainstay of American business stability, announced that in 2008 it would freeze pension benefits for 117,500 U.S. workers. Will your pension be next? No one is safe as American investment bankers and stock managers restructure and shed long-standing employee pension funds.

CHURCHES TOO

Yes, even churches are in financial trouble. The Roman Catholic Church, for example, has tens of thousands of nuns now over age seventy, resulting in an extraordinary financial shortfall confronting the

Church. Add to that an unfunded future liability of $8.7 billion for nuns, priests, and brothers still serving in the Church, and it's expected to worsen to more than $20 billion by 2023. To put this in perspective, this unfunded financial burden far exceeds all costs from the clergy abuse scandal which by themselves has bankrupted many dioceses.

STATE & LOCAL GOVERNMENT PENSIONS

You work for a state or local government and you think your pension is safe? Think again. Barclays Global Investors' analysts say American public-employee pension funds are short $700 billion, a number exceeding what all state and local governments collected last year in all taxes combined. Wilshire Associates, an investment advisory company, studied sixty-four state pension systems and discovered that fifty-four of them were underfunded by a total of $175.4 billion. The situation is even more severe at the municipal level.

So who is going to pay for this deficiency? You are! In the last ten years state and local governments have borrowed approximately $30 billion just to fund a portion of existing pension obligations, and there is no relief in sight. Because raising taxes is unpopular with voters and cutting costs is unpopular with government employees (who also vote), many jurisdictions are resorting to pension obligation bonds where governments borrow against hoped-for future revenues and investment returns.

Recent studies found that more than 2,000 different states, cities, and agencies owe more than 16 million state and local public employees and 6 million retirees $2.37 trillion. In 2003 alone, states and municipalities spent over $46 billion funding these generous plans, according to the National Association of State Retirement Administrators. Even with such colossal funding, the largest state and city funds were still short an estimated $278 billion in 2003. Said another way, this deficiency is about 20% of all state and municipal tax revenue. Calculated using the more conservative formula used by private pension funds, the true shortfall is more than $700 billion. Only a major taxpayer-funded bailout will solve this ruinous financial disaster the states and municipalities have created.

But believe it or not, the problem for states and cities is yet even worse. Very few disclose the amount of retirees health care benefits they have promised and they tend to be more generous than private plans. The amounts are unknown but are measured in the tens of billions of dollars, most of which is not yet funded. Acknowledging the rapid rise in medical costs, these unfunded obligations could grow to hundreds of billions. In Maryland, for example, the state spends $311 million annually on health insurance for retired state workers. But following a recent order from the Governmental Accounting Standards Board, total Maryland obligations for health costs for retired state workers were found to $20.4 billion and the state must now set aside nearly $2 billion annually—a six-fold increase.

Every state is struggling to meet its pension obligations. For years, New York State enjoyed low pension payments, but in 2004 cities and counties across the state got a rude awakening: pension contributions jumped as much as 248% in one year. Unlike the private sector, state and local pension plans continue costly guaranteed benefit plans, costing taxpayers ever more to meet unfunded obligations. For example:

Illinois has the worst problem of any state, where the unfunded pension liability was estimated last year at $43.1 billion—nearly double the state's budget. Illinois' five state pension funds are $35 billion underfunded, yet the entire annual state general operating budget is only $43 billion. Illinois owes $2.6 billion this year and within five years that will reach $4 billion annually, compared to the $5 billion it spends on public education.

California's economy is the eighth biggest in the world. Yet each of the state's two major pension funds has a deficit of more than $20 billion. The state will pay $3.5 billion into pension and health benefits for retirees this year, almost triple what it paid just three years ago. The state Legislative Analyst's Office expects that to climb another $1.1 billion over the next five years.

New Jersey's State Health Benefits Program this year will spend $1 billion for active workers and an additional $900 million for retirees. By 2010, the state will spend more on health care for retirees ($2.3 billion) than for active workers ($1.8 billion), and has $58 billion in unfunded retiree health care obligations.

In Michigan school districts, the most rapid growth of expenditures is for pension and retiree health costs, an expense that will double to 20% of payroll costs within three years. This is similar in school districts all across the country.

And to make matters worse, public pension systems are for the most part free of the regulatory oversight governing corporate plans.

MUNICIPAL PENSIONS

The chickens are coming home to roost in thousands of cities and towns all across America, where local governments have been granting medical and retirement benefits to police officers and firefighters and street workers—without keeping tabs on the total cost. Those cities and towns too are now in deep financial trouble, where obligations to public pension plans are straining local coffers to the breaking point. Several of the seemingly most healthy cities are in dire condition. For example:

San Diego, the nation's seventh-largest city, today teeters on the brink of bankruptcy. It has an extraordinary pension deficit of at least $1.4 billion. And because of political corruption and official incompetence, independent auditors refuse to certify the books and thus the city is prevented from further borrowing.

In Philadelphia, the City of Brotherly Love, the city's three large pension funds were deficient $2.6 billion at the end of 2003, even after city sold $1.2 billion in pension-obligation bonds in 1999.

Pittsburg is worse. In 2003, the police pension plan had enough assets to cover just 33% of promised retirement benefits, only after Pittsburg sold $302 million in pension-obligation bonds between 1996 and 1998.

In New York City they estimated 2004 pension costs at $650 million; they actually were $2.46 billion. The Independent Budget Office predicts by fiscal 2007 pension contributions will be almost $5 billion, a whopping 12% of the $40.5 billion budget.

In the City of Angels, Los Angeles Mayor Antonio Villaraigosa acknowledges a "450 million deficit in just five years, and that's assuming that there is no catastrophic event or recession." Primary contributors: employee health care and worker's compensation costs increased by more than $215 million between 2002 and 2006; and the city must contribute another $200 million to the pension system next year just to keep it solvent.

On top of all that, the estimate of the cost of already promised retiree health care is simply unknown by anyone. Best estimates are in the tens of billions.

As the pension crisis deepens, states, counties, cities, towns, villages, school districts, water districts, even cemetery districts all across America—and the elected politicians who run them—will be forced to reduce services or raise taxes or borrow, which once again pushes obligations to future generations. But reducing pension benefits takes political courage, may be politically unacceptable, and in some jurisdictions even prevented by law as public-pension retirement benefits are frequently guaranteed by state constitutions.

Those politicians continue to be extra generous with your tax dollars. The Census Bureau says 90% of state and local workers have a more costly defined-benefit pension with a guaranteed payout, as opposed to only 24% of workers in the private sector. The Employee Benefit Research Institute found that state and local government wage and salary costs are 40% greater than the private sector, and its employee benefit costs are 60% greater. Oh my.

PENSION BENEFIT GUARANTEE CORPORATION

Though millions of Americans depend on the Pension Benefit Guarantee Corporation (PBGC), most have never heard of it. Today it represents another little-known but economically deadly deficit. Created by Congress in 1974, the PBGC is a federal corporation established to supposedly protect the pensions of over forty-four million American workers and retirees in 30,330 private single-employer and multi-employer defined benefit pension plans. Though it receives no funds from general tax revenues, it is a creation of Congress and it is an agency of government—and like most government agencies charged with our long-term wellbeing it is in a financial pickle. Though the PBCG is not technically backed by the U.S. Government, its government status and its fiscal health could necessitate a multi-billion dollar taxpayer bailout.

One reason for this is that in recent years, courts have granted authority for many large corporations—often for reasons of business strategy—to terminate their retirement plans. These include such corporate household names as United Airlines, US Airways, Bethlehem Steel, Kaiser Aluminum, Huffy bicycles, Big Bear supermarkets, Polaroid, West Point Stevens, and others who walked away from their obligations and dumped them on the PBGC.

They make the mess, we clean it up.

So far American workers are the big losers in all this, but it could soon become the entire American taxpaying public. Five years ago, the PBGC operated with a $10 billion surplus. By 2004, the surplus had become a $23 billion deficit, and this year some estimates expect that deficit to exceed $30 billion. But the true picture is far worse: Depending on how one calculates the unfunded deficiencies of PBGC plans, either it exceeds $450 billion or $600 billion if the plans of unionized workers who work for more than one business are included. The PBGC admits that it is already exposed to $108 billion in pension losses.

Enron's employees lost over $1 billion in their insolvent pension plans; so did people who worked for WorldCom. The collapse of those corrupt businesses has consigned thousands of Americans who thought their retirement years were secure to a retirement standard of living marked by misery and financial despair.

Another major company to default on its pension obligations is United Airlines, which through the shrewd craftiness of a bankruptcy filing transferred responsibility for the pensions of 120,000 workers and retired workers to the Pension Benefit Guaranty Corporation—because United's new investors had no desire to assume pension liabilities of almost $10 billion. Obviously the workers who made United the great airline that it once was just don't matter.

In the airline industry United is not alone in its pension woes. Delta, Continental, Northwest, and American each have massive operating losses and now must compete with pension-free United, sufficient incentive for them to unburden themselves of their $40 billion pension obligations and pass them along to the government too.

What about the automotive sector? In that market sector alone, the PBGC says the pension commitments and obligation to its workers and retirees are underfunded by between $45 billion and $50 billion. Several auto parts companies, such as Delphi Corp. with its underfunded pension obligations of perhaps $5 billion, are now in bankruptcy and will surely jettison billions more in pension obligations to PBGC. It just keeps adding up.

If you listen carefully to what government officials say about this growing mess and its potential to burden the taxpayer, the numbers are a moving target.

Steven Kandarian, Executive Director of PBGC, gave this statement to the Senate Committee on Finance in March 2003:

"During Fiscal Year 2002, PBGC's single-employer insurance program went from a surplus of $7.7 billion to a deficit of $3.6 billion—a loss of $11.3 billion in just one year.... In addition, we estimate that the total underfunding in the single-employer defined benefit system now exceeds $300 billion, the largest number ever recorded."

In a speech last year, Labor Secretary Labor Secretary Elaine Chao estimated underfunding of private defined-benefit pension plans at $450 billion. That's almost half a trillion dollars! Who's going to bail out that problem? A defined-benefit plan is a pension that supposedly "guarantees" workers a fixed monthly amount in retirement, and those workers and their families plan their retirement based on those "guarantees". Secretary Chao said the financial consequences for companies with defined-benefit pensions could be "very bad."

And here things get sticky. Yes, PBGC is a government corporation—standing behind the pensions of 44 million American workers and retires in nearly 31,000 private-sector defined benefit pension plans—but its obligations are not "backed by the full faith and credit of the United States government." At least so far, no federal tax dollars are appropriated to PBGC; it is theoretically self-funded. As more and more pension plans go bankrupt and PBGC lacks funds to cover those obligations, what happens to the pensions of those American workers?

OUR RETIREMENT FUTURE

With the number of Americans over age 65 doubling by 2030, our nation faces bankruptcy if this reckless state of affairs is not soon addressed. If it's not too late. As millions of baby boomers start to overload Society Security and Medicare and Medicaid systems, and thus the U.S. Treasury, many economists are starting to argue it is already too late. Alan Greenspan, recently retired Federal Reserve Chairman, was more blunt: "As a nation, we may have already made promises to coming generations of retirees that we will be unable to fulfill."

The costs are astronomical. As USA TODAY noted, "In 2004 alone, federal spending on Medicare and Social Security increase[d] $45 billion, to $789 billion. That one-year increase is more than the $28 billion budget of the Department of Homeland Security." Add baby boomers to this mess and the direction we're headed becomes not only glaringly self-evident but alarmingly frightening.

How deep is the hole? So deep no one is certain of where the bottom really is. The federal government cautiously estimates $53 trillion of unfunded liabilities (in current liabilities) by 2008 in private and other government pension systems, Medicare and insurance coverage. But it's far worse than the government wants to acknowledge. Total retirement debt, including enormous unfunded liabilities, is more likely approaching $77 trillion.

In addition, about 28 million U.S. households do not own a retirement savings account of any kind. Only 11% of all Americans have retirement savings of $250,000 or more.

What is certain is that there is a fiscal avalanche bearing down on this nation with growing momentum and burden that is sure to send millions of older Americans, especially aging women, into poverty. Without fundamental, sweeping, and drastic solutions—which will require new attitudes and intensity of political courage—there simply is no acceptable or workable solution.

5

FOURTH DANGER –
RADICAL ISLAMIC
EXTREMISM & TERRORISM

✸

"From my perspective,
the terrorists are racing and
we are somewhere between a walk and a crawl."
—Sam Nunn, Former U.S. Senator

I ts sleek baby-blue and white fuselage gleaming brightly in the
brilliant morning sun, Air Force One rolled down the runway for
takeoff from Berlin, Germany. She quickly gained altitude and banked
toward the Atlantic and home. As I sat in regal luxury and secure well-
being looking out the windows at western Europe quickly fading, my
mind filled with a sense of pride in the U.S.A. and in recognition of
our unmatched superiority as a nation of intrepid strength, infinite
capacity, and courageous spirit. At the end of an exhausting trip to
several former Soviet republics where the vestiges of Communism
were everywhere evident amidst the colorless decaying buildings and

tattered people, the thoughts of American dominance and supremacy and I suppose invulnerability were much on my mind—after all, we'd defeated the Soviets and won the Cold War without firing a shot!

We live in a country that in the words of George Washington has been "favored by the hand of Providence." We have also experienced extraordinary good fortune and had the isolating protection of two oceans. For two hundred years, and especially in the last century, we've lived with a sense of invulnerability because of those two oceans, with our enemies far away on other continents. It was a time before American airports were populated by armed soldiers and metal detectors, a time before planes were hijacked and flown as suicide bombs into towering office buildings. The day of our invulnerability is over and our luck is running out. The war and the terror that were on the other side of the world are today a war targeting the United States and our allies, determined to destroy this nation and every free democracy in the world. Any nation not Islam is their target. Danger is omnipresent.

America is the most powerful nation in the history of the world. She is the wealthiest nation ever, with an overflowing abundance of material goods, plentiful natural resources, a bounteous food harvest unequalled anywhere on earth, and a supremacy of military might and power unmatched at any time ever before. It is that very power and plenty that scares much of the world and kindles a flame of hatred and envy.

The world sees America through the pervasive negativism in television news clips, sensationalized by Hollywood in its recent efforts to undermine public policy through its distorted films, and as a result of intentional distortions by some foreign media. And what they see is an inaccurate portrayal of our richness in material things, our poverty of spiritual goodness. The America that through generations was a beacon of hope and example to the world, a bonfire of envy, is today in much of the world becoming a firestorm of perceived injustice, a growing blaze of loathing and violence. We have treasured our invulnerability, and today it is an illusion of history.

Not long after the violent demonstrations in Seattle against the World Trade Organization, an ambassador to a Middle Eastern country, who must remain nameless, told me that we Americans are an arrogant and ignorant people. "Why", he asked, "do you feel it necessary to police the world, to come to the rescue of every troubled place, to flaunt your wealth and moral-less culture, to think you are somehow superior to the rest of God's children?" He went on to express his puzzlement at how we Americans never seem to understand the depth of anti-Americanism, that people around the world equate globalization with American economic occupation, our sordid sexual immorality and homosexuality with hypocrisy, and our opulence with hedonism. His view was that the WTO protests were no different than the anti-American demonstrations in the Philippines or Indonesia or the firebombing of McDonald's in France, that they were a sign of the times, an omen of things to come, and not isolated and inconsequential events. It was a chilling assessment.

And he was at least partially correct that today for the most part we remain blissfully ignorant of the depth and intensity of loathing and the constancy of threats. Washington has reached an apparently hopeless stalemate of partisan gridlock at the same time as the United Nations has evolved into an incompetent, impotent, and corrupt puppet of anti-American diplomacy. Our supposed allies the Russians are helping Iran become a nuclear power and North Korea too is close to maybe a dozen nuclear bombs. Iraq remains unsettled and unsure. But what about the "independent" terrorists? National Intelligence Director John Negroponte chillingly testified before Congress that nearly 40 terrorist organizations, insurgencies or cults have used, possessed, or expressed an interest in chemical, biological, radiological, or nuclear agents or weapons, calling such terrorist threats the "top concern" of U.S. intelligence services.

Bill Joy of Sun Microsystems says it more forcefully: "I think it is no exaggeration to say we are on the cusp of the further perfection of extreme evil, an evil whose personality spreads well beyond that which weapons of mass destruction bequeathed to the nation-states, on to a surprising and terrible empowerment of extreme individuals."

The world has become a very dangerous place and it is only a matter of time before America is attacked again, this time conceivably involving weapons of mass destruction, including cyber. "It may be only a matter of time before al-Qaeda or other groups attempt to use chemical, biological, radiological or nuclear weapons," said then-CIA Director Peter Goss in even more frightening terms. John Negroponte, National Intelligence Director, is equally blunt: "Terrorism is the pre-eminent threat to our citizens, to our homeland, to our interests and to our friends."

The United States of America and the modern Western world are at war with Islamofacism—the first time in American history when we've been at war with an enemy we can't identify. The oft expressed term "war on terror" is a misnomer for terror is merely a tool of war. The real war is not so much a war "against" someone or something, but a war "for" freedom, liberty, and our cherished way of life. Islamic fanatics don't want peaceful coexistence; they want to eliminate us in a firestorm of terror. We have for too long consistently underestimated the enemy, too long been ignorant of our adversary and too long blissfully persistent in our American arrogance. As we watched in horror at the collapse of New York's World Trade Center, we witnessed live shots in a war that has changed the world and given us a worrisome fear of future terrorist attacks. The war on terrorism is a new kind of war, and I wonder and worry whether Congress and the American public have the stomach for what it will take to win this lengthy and costly fight. Will the 21st century become the century of terrorism?

President George Bush and former British Prime Minister Tony Blair have responded with courage and clarity, and whether or not we agree with their actions (I do) we must applaud their resolve. This is manifest evil intent on destroying us—because of who we are and what we believe. Daniel Patrick Moynihan, a distinguished former U. S. Senator and U. N. Ambassador, expressed it well: "We are assailed because of what is right about us. We are assailed because we are a democracy." Every American, indeed every freedom-loving person in the world, needs to ask themself what would life be like if they succeed.

We face a grave threat to the very values of liberty, freedom and democracy. What lies on the horizon is danger in the extreme, and if we fail to meet these multiple asymetrical threats straight out and head on, the consequences will be nothing short of catastrophic.

CATASTROPHIC THREATS

In spite of the fact that since September 11th Congress has appropriated nearly $180 billion to protect America from terrorism, the feeling won't leave me—the feeling that there's an imminent threat out there, something far more devastating that we have yet known. This year Congress will spend at least $50 billion on homeland security, roughly $450 for every American household, and I still sense "it" is coming. Adds Michael Scheuer, a former CIA analyst who pursued Osama bin Laden, "I don't think it's even started yet."

With unusual candor the bipartisan 9/11 Commission made clear the seriousness of the "catastrophic threat" America faces, spelling out that an attack of even greater magnitude is now possible and even probable. "We believe we are safer today... but we are not safe," the Commission said.

In the 1980s, terrorists of the violent Irish Republican Party attempted to assassinate Britain's Prime Minister Margaret Thatcher and her entire cabinet in the British seaside resort of Brighton. They succeeded in blowing up the hotel but failed to kill their targets. With frighteningly prescient truth the terrorists declared: "Today we were unlucky. But remember, we only have to be lucky once. You will have to be lucky always."

I once experienced terror first hand, sort of. Representing President George Bush, I strolled uncomfortably through the sleepy wintry farm fields near the village of Lockerbie, Scotland. I was struck by the stillness and tranquility, the pastoral and picturesque setting of the idyllic Scottish countryside where only days before bodies had simply fallen out of the sky unannounced and without warning, hurtling to earth amidst working farmers and destroying forever the peaceful calmness which was their lives. Eleven townspeople were killed in Sherwood Crescent where the aircraft's wings and fuel tanks hurtled to earth raining fire and fury and death.

Without warning Pan Am flight 103 had been exploded out of mid-flight by radical Islamic terrorists using C-4 explosives sent from Libya, the same C-4 explosive used in the Berlin discotheque bombings. Until September 11th, 2001, this was the worst act of terrorism against American civilians ever.

Here I witnessed the evil brutality of state-sponsored terrorism first hand. Speaking with an emotionally shattered farmer, he tearfully described airplane parts and human bodies "falling from the sky like rocks, just coming out of no where. Bodies of men and women and children were crashing all about. Some were still seat-belted into their aircraft seats. People were dead all around me, in my field. It was horrible." And then, overcome with anguish because of the barbaric destruction he'd witnessed over the last few days and unable to speak further, like a ghost he just drifted away. I stood in his raw dirt field and looked heavenward at the blue sky where the passengers of Pan Am 103 had done nothing to deserve this horror, and I struggled to understand what twisted and distorted thinking could prompt such senseless evil.

For terrorists, the rules and the thinking are wholly different. There aren't any rules, traditional rules of engagement are no more, and there are no values—only destruction and murder and death. Islamic extremists don't think in a Western way. This is the first time we've had an enemy who unilaterally embraced their own death as a means of achieving their own ends. This is an enemy different than we have ever known. These are fanatic zealots blinded by their false righteousness who hate America, hate freedom, and hate all religions but their own. Gone are the stagnant days of a two superpower contest. In their place are regional conflicts between hapless developing nations, misguided rogue states who disdain accepted standards long embraced by the civilized community of nations, and state-sponsored or religious-sanctioned terrorism where individuals wreak death and horror. The danger of a lone terrorist bringing nuclear, chemical, or biological destruction to America is today a very plausible probability.

The war in Iraq and American military presence in Afghanistan, both perceived by many in the Middle East as an occupation, aggravates false beliefs that America is at war with Islam, intensifying jihadist passions and resolve. This is not a war of religions but it is a war of values and liberty, and the United States is engaged in the fight of its national life with a terrorist network about which we all know far too little.

In the White House designated officers are authorized varying degrees of security clearances, and with those levels of clearance come classified briefings about national security, threat assessments, security issues such as foreign weapons development and nuclear proliferation, and a whole range of festering foreign policy concerns facing the United States.

I remember well the first time I saw Mount Weather, a special facility unacknowledged as a "Continuity of Government" (COG) facility containing an underground bunker designed to house vital elements of the American government in the case of nuclear attack or other catastrophic incident. Supposedly operated by the Federal Emergency Management Agency (FEMA), the 434 acre secret mountain location at the north end of the stunning Shenandoah Valley is protected by heavily armed guards and conspicuous for its towering razor wire-topped chain link fences plastered with bold warning signs. Much of the facility is underground and is equipped with everything necessary for a self-sustaining government in exile. A similar secret facility long existed underground at the Greenbrier Resort as an evacuation site for Congress. When I was at Mount Weather I was told the place does not exist, but hey, I saw it. In years past it was long assumed the non-existent site would be used in case of a Russian nuclear attack on America; today the likelihood of use has expanded to countless possible causes.

There remain so many unknowns. Threats to American security come in every imaginable shape and size. Terror organizations and rogue nations may be developing resources and weaponry of which we know little or nothing. Unknown future events could unfold more quickly that we anticipate—literally overnight—and faster than our national ability to respond.

But there are some things we do know. America's enemy number one, today, is Islamic extremism and fanaticism—not Islam per se—centered in several nation states but found worldwide. The tools they will use and the risks and the threats to America have worsened and cannot be taken lightly. I have observed the rushing surge of extremism and fanaticism increase during the nearly thirty years I have been in and out of the White House, and it is approaching this nation like a lethal avalanche, filled with murder and destruction, ominously crushing down a mountainside and gathering power and momentum along the way.

There is common ground and great good in Islam, but the diabolical objectives of these radical aspects are two fold: first, to unite the rest of Islam and second, to overtake the world. As Americans we cannot treat Islam as a single enemy. If we fail to engage with Islam in sharing common values and building understanding, then we risk pushing the rest of Islam to unite with its worst side.

102

ISLAMIC EXTREMISM

For an American, understanding the radical Islamic fundamentalist mind is difficult at best. Based on our traditionally Judeo-Christian system of moral values, our modern standard of living, and our rules of civilized society, fanatic Islamic extremists to us appear crazed and in some ways they are. According to Marwan Abu Ubeida in TIME magazine, "The only person who matters is Allah—and the only question he will ask me is, 'How many infidels did you kill?'" In their perverse and intolerant view we Americans are infidels, and infidels are to be killed. Women are no better than cattle, merely property to be owned or disposed of, and women not "of the faith" are considered impure and evil. A religion that transforms reasonable men into perverted killers willing, indeed anxious, to exterminate women and children and destroy villages and towns and whole nations—this is a dangerous irrationality that must be taken with utmost seriousness.

They interpret Muhammad in the Koran as having promised them they would control the world, constantly reaffirmed because the education in much of the Muslim world consists almost exclusively of memorizing the Koran in the context of their political agenda and radical interpretation. Hamas terrorist leader Khaled Mashal said it clearly: "The nation of Islam will sit at the throne of the world. The Arab and Islamic nation is rising and awakening. Tomorrow we will lead the world." Every failing is blamed on the "infidels" who embrace "modernity," and the mullahs teach that attacking western "infidels" pleases Allah (God). Sacrificing their lives is even better, and they are taught they go straight to heaven where countless virgins await. It's no wonder there are tens of thousands or hundreds of thousands, maybe millions, of faithful young Muslim men anxious to engage in holy battle.

The squalid Chatilla refuge camp in Beirut, Lebanon, a training ground for terrorists, is one of the most depressing places I have ever visited, and one of the few times I have known bone-chilling fear. Several thousand Palestinians are housed there, some of them since 1948, many of them second and even third generations to be born in the camp. Feelings of hopelessness in Chatilla are pervasive, poverty and deprivation are everywhere, and anger is palpable, anger at Jews, at America. There were many small homemade memorials for young men from the camp who joined the jihad to annihilate Jews, Christians, and everything western and modern, and sacrificed their own lives. Everyone I spoke with was devoted to victory against the infidels, and there will be no cease-fire.

Their hatred they say is fueled by what they view as the illegal taking of their homeland by the Jews in 1948, but their hatred is deeper, darker, and more evil than this, and it has nothing to do with Iran or 9/11 or Bush. Sipping cold water with a reasonably hospitable group of camp residents in a strangely uncomfortable psychological minefield, the people I met in Chatilla spoke admiringly, in religious phraseology and ferocious tones, of suicide bombers and praised terrorist groups who provide the funds.

We were then driven in a beat-up Mercedes on an intentionally confusing and circuitous route through bombed-out Beirut to the headquarters of the terrorist group Hezbollah where we were thoroughly searched by hateful young men and escorted into a dreary room adorned only with a large photo of Ayatollah Khomeini, and soon received by the Hezbollah leader. After lecturing us that the United States is a terrorist nation, he spoke of unthinkable things; the more catastrophic the terror, the more infidels killed, the better.

Like a spreading cancer that quietly progresses through a diseased body, they intend to kill us. They spoke of Jihad, and although they may be fanatical minorities, there are millions of them, extremists for whom terror and revenge is their new devotion. This isn't a military battle, it's a religious and cultural one and the worst is still to come. Singapore leader Lee Kuan Yew succinctly described the problem: "If the jihadists win there, I'm in trouble here."

Westerners wrongly think only in terms of "the Middle East" or the "Arab world". We tend to think the conflicts there are fought over oil, yet wars have been fought there for centuries before the discovery of oil, mostly between Arab tribes and factions. Those historic factions still exist but today are united in a focused hatred devoted to crushing Israel and its "godless" American benefactor. The majority of Arabs are today under age 30, a foreboding demographic that will bring about sweeping and troublesome change in coming years. In the 30 years between 1970 and 2000, Muslims made up 26% of world growth, and in one generation the lesser-developed Muslim nations became as populated as developed nations.

Today the world of Islamic extremism is no longer solely the Middle East—but India, Pakistan, Afghanistan, the heavily Muslim former Soviet republics in Central Asia including Tajikistan, Uzbekistan, Kazakhstan, and more. Today it is also Indonesia, the world's fourth largest country located thousands of miles from the Middle East, growing portions of the Philippines, and much of North and East Africa including Egypt, Morocco, Libya, Algeria, Nigeria, Kenya, Sudan, Yemen, Somalia, and others. The fastest growing religion in Europe is now Islam, the largest number of immigrants flooding into Western Europe are Muslim, and the Balkan states are a hotbed of Islamic turmoil. Seeds of Islamic restlessness have been planted in South America, Russia, and yes, even in the United States. This potential for twisted extremism is global, a worldwide crazy-quilt of believers increasingly joining together in a misguided worldwide determination to destroy the United States of America and our allies who cherish the values of human life, democracy, freedom and liberty.

There is no doctrinal obligation in the religion of Islam to obliterate modernity, to kill Americans or destroy America. To peoples suffering with long-term deep-rooted regional economic hardships who already have a misperception of American injustices and dominance, zealous Muslim fanatics preach a totalitarian religion of confusion and distortion with the goal of making Islam the world's dominant religion. The Wahabbis in Saudi Arabia and the mullahs in Iran preach that for the Arab world to rise to its rightful role requires the eradication of every Christian and Jew. These fanatics are a small but influential fraction of Islam who are the worst danger to unite all of Islam in waging the jihad holy war against America and our friends, not to conquer lands but to conquer civilization, wiping out our business, technology, science, religions, culture, values—our every way of life.

Speaking last year at a global security conference in Germany, then U.S. Defense Secretary Donald Rumsfeld issued a warning about a growing "global extremist Islamic empire", saying that violent Islamic extremists "seek to take over governments from North Africa to Southeast Asia and to re-establish a caliphate they hope, one day, will include every continent. They have designed and distributed a map where national borders are erased and replaced by a global extremist Islamic empire."

The global spread of Islam has made the United States more economically vulnerable that at any time in our national history, as we watch Islamic extremism and terror spread from the oil-rich Middle East across North Africa to the oil-producing costal nations of Africa. Nigeria, a bitterly corrupt country that's 50% Muslim, is already our fifth-largest source of oil, and the Gulf of Guinea will provide 25% of our oil in the next decade. Without oil and the vast riches they produce most Middle Eastern nations would be nothing more than unproductive sand, powerless in the modern world. But they have those riches—we're buying their oil!—and they're using those riches to inflame the deprived masses of Islam in anger and terror against America. The Soviet Union collapsed because there were no values, no beliefs, no faith or religion, no ideology of substance; the Muslim world has all that, and in greater measure that we do today.

We each remember the morning of September 11, 2001 and the unspeakable horror that unfolded in New York City and Washington and in rural Pennsylvania, and in our own hearts. Though the objectives of terror were achieved that day, as a people and a nation we rose to the occasion and did not surrender to fear, but our way of life has forever changed and we live in a far more precarious world. The growing danger today is very real and the cost and consequence of ignoring the peril is too horrible to contemplate. A nuclear, chemical, or biological attack in those 9/11 cities or elsewhere in America, no longer an unrealistic possibility, could kill millions and almost overnight devastate our economy and send the entire world into a global depression.

As Islam foments a worldwide holy war, our only hope is to help those in Muslim countries who for centuries have lived in tyranny, bloodshed, bigotry, disease, poverty, and darkness of knowledge to establish understanding and democracy where such notions are historically unprecedented. In the meantime we would be wise to heed the wise counsel of Thomas Jefferson two hundred years ago: "The price of freedom is eternal vigilance."

STATES OF DANGER

Historically threats and dangers to America have come from sovereign nations with contradictory or competing ideologies who we met first at the negotiating table and failing that then on the field of battle. And with the exception of the wars against the British two hundred years ago and at Pearl Harbor, those battlefields were in distant lands, never on our American homeland. Our enemy today knows no such civilized discourse, no conventional rules of engagement, and the battlefield for Americans and American interests is here at home and everywhere.

Not one Islamic country is a democracy, not one, and right now the only small hope for an Islamic country to become a democracy lies in Iraq. Our enemy today is extremist states governed by unscrupulous thugs and religious fanatics, terrorists linked to revolutionary hate groups, and whatever deadly weapons they may possess, most especially nuclear, biological, chemical, and electromagnetic pulse bombs. If you don't understand this deadly potential, stay tuned; I'll tell you about it later. In the abbreviated vernacular of the military and news media, this weaponry is now commonly known as WMDs, weapons of mass destruction—for that is what they do.

CONFLICTED SAUDI MONARCHY

While the threat posed by Islamic extremism is global, there are about a half dozen trouble spots that pose acute—and in most cases, worsening—problems. One of the most worrisome is Saudi Arabia.

The first time I flew over Saudi Arabia I was struck with the expanse and nothingness of its vast sand deserts and that the only reason the country was even noticeable on the world scene was what was beneath that desolate sand: oil. Giant amounts of oil—25% of the world's known reserves. Were it not for oil the entire country would be irrelevant but instead its founding family is rich and powerful.

The ultra wealthy House of Saud, the ruling royal family of Saudi Arabia, finds itself in an increasingly untenable position with two unsatisfactory alternatives. They're supposedly a strategic partner and ally with the United States and yet they firmly embrace Wahhabi Islam—it's their state religion—positions that are inherently in conflict. Much of the success of the House of Saud has been its ability to adeptly navigate compromises while appeasing the more radical religious elements of its society. Now the Saudis can please no one as the long simmering fundamentalist displeasure with Western cultural influence is about to boil over, and this has profound implications for the U.S.—because the safety and presence of the United States in the Middle East and the strength of our economy depends on the stability of the House of Saud.

It was only a few years ago that the Soviet Union seemed stable and solid. The Berlin Wall was in place, the iron curtain was permanent, and Communist states were resilient. Or how about our Middle East friend Mohammed Reza Pahlavi, the Shah of Iran? In surprisingly fast order the Shiites rebelled and the Shah and his monarchy were gone, replaced by Islamic extremists. For the Soviet Union and Iran, there stability was nothing but a fragile façade.

The House of Saud is every bit as much a fragile façade, neither stable nor safe and its days are numbered. Abundant oil dollars, religious homage, and no political opposition which have kept the 7,000 or so princes of the royal family in power and extravagance since the nation's creation are now its undoing as the twenty-three million subjects tire of the royal excesses. This at a time when per capita income has plunged from more than $28,000 in 1981 to less than $7,000 today, when their standard of living has steeply declined, government provided benefits are reduced, taxes have increased, and 25% of those under age thirty are unemployed. The country's population, with one of the fastest growth rates of any country, has nearly tripled in a quarter century and today is overwhelming young and restless, and heroin from neighbors Iran and Afghanistan is a seriously growing problem.

In Saudi Arabia, Islamic theology is paramount. "The reason is that religion is the law," says Prince Amr ibn Muhammad al-Faisal, the grandson of King Faisal. "It permeates the culture. It is rooted in the history. It is part of the DNA, if you like, of the Saudis."

As part of their longtime strategy the Saudi Royals have funded religiously extreme Wahabbism, the most radical sect of Islam, and to position Saudi Arabia as the leader of the Arab world they have exported this extremist ideology. Long a relatively inactive sect, when the House of Saud conquered the holy cities of Mecca and Medina and created the Saudi monarchy Wahhabism took root. Controlling these holy shrines gave the Saudis enormous influence in Islamic thought. When oil was discovered beneath their barren desert lands, they ceased to be an irrelevant backward nation and all of a sudden had sufficient wealth to aggressively spend billions (estimated to be as much as $4 billion annually) spreading their Wahhabi message and its accompanying terror. A Saudi Royal decree declared there are "no limits... put on expenditures for the propagation of Islam," and the results are alarming: the Wahhabi dogma of intolerance is the central ideological belief and inspiration of Osama bin Laden and his murderous followers.

Those Wahhabi forces are now part of the undoing of the Saudi Royal Family as disdain for the Royals' westernized habits grows amongst the religious and lower classes, making it ever more difficult for the Royals to maintain commercial and military ties with the U.S. and Europe. Theirs is a nation of conflicts: modern communications and nomadic tribesmen, religious police who enforce mandated personal prayer, advanced technology and religious police who allowed school girls to burn to death rather than escape in immodest clothing, and a close relationship with the U.S. and a simultaneous institutionalized abhorrence for Israel. Wahhabi fundamentalism views the U.S. and its influences as evil and corrupting, and the Saudi Ministry of Religion is run by Wahhabis who promote their extremist doctrine worldwide, funding schools, mosques, and community centers where the curriculum is limited to memorizing the Koran and its extremist interpretations. Thousands of Wahhabi schools are filling the minds of impressionable young children with notions that democracy and modernity are evil, pernicious, and impede the glorious divine destiny of Islam to rule the world—all part of the plan of the Great Satan. For over forty years Wahhabi religious zealots have controlled Saudi education, teaching only rigid Islamic beliefs.

Realizing its growing and precarious instability amongst its own subjects and in the Arab world, the Saudi Royals are subtly distancing the Kingdom from the U.S. on many key issues, including terrorism, as they publicly embrace Wahhabi influences. Even a free society with a democratic government in Iraq would be perceived as a grave threat to the House of Saud.

In so many words, the House of Saud (and thus our ally Saudi Arabia) has funded its own downfall and is in serious peril as Islamic fundamentalists grow stronger daily, openly accusing the House of Saud of gross mismanagement of their country's wealth and condemning its cozy friendship with the infidel U.S. Even with enormous oil revenues government debt was 100% of GDP by 2000 and the government budget deficit is approaching $200 billion, having operated at a deficit in twenty-one of the last twenty-two years as the infrastructure ages, oil reserves decline, an acute water shortage is ignored and worsens, unemployment exceeds 20%, and the secret national budget is spent by the Royals as if it were their personal account. Without oil revenues the entire country would implode; it may anyway.

The new 81 year-old King, with five family factions breathing down his neck competing for power, faces an insurmountable dilemma: improve conditions in his kingdom without upsetting Wahhabi leaders essential to the powerbase of the House of Saud. Walking a tightrope as they dangerously play both ends toward the middle, many of the Royals continue to bankroll al Qaeda and other terrorist groups. Several princes are known to be aligned with the Rabita Trust, a so-called charity blacklisted by the U.S. Treasury for terrorist connections. Yet such financing notwithstanding, the overthrow of the perceived pro-Western House of Saud is now a primary extremist goal.

Though American officials keep up the public charade of close bilateral friendship, in fact Saudi Arabia is no longer trusted.

Senior Administration officials tell me—very much off the record —they distrust the Saudis because of their continued financial support for Wahhabi extremism, their tepid utterances toward U.S. actions concerning Iran, and especially for their hollow lip-service in stopping the financing of terror.

If the House of Saud collapses, and many in the know say time is running out, not only does the Middle East instantly become more thorny and perilous but the world oil supply is endangered. A quarter of the world's known oil reserves rest under ancestral Saudi soil—an indispensable ingredient of the world economy. In the last year world demand and oil dependence (see chapter on oil) has raised Saudi oil revenues by over 50%, to more than $160 billion. All it takes is another oil embargo or an overthrow of the House of Saud and our economy turns upside down. Saudi Arabia is estimated to have about $600 billion invested in the U.S., the largest investment of any nation. What if they abruptly decide to sell, something which could almost happen almost immediately if the House of Saud falls?

Short-sighted policy has allowed us to become dependent on an unstable windblown nomadic desert country immersed in extremist Islamic teachings but rich in oil we so desperately need. Suffice it to say, the risk for the United States is nothing short of acute; the avalanche is coming.

IRAN AND ITS MADMAN

"Americans are the great Satan, the wounded snake." These are the vile words of Ayatollah Ruhollah Khomeini, a radical Shiite cleric critical of the Shah of Iran and who, in 1979, led the Shah's overthrow and supported the hostage taking of 52 American diplomats, held captive for 444 days. This led to over twenty-five years of Islamic revolution in Iran and has made Iran an outcast from the community of nations.

One of the youth leaders in capturing those helpless Americans was later identified as Mahmoud Ahmadinejad. This fanatic is today

Iran's madman President, next door to Iraq and a maniacal zealot who views himself as the defender of Islam. Though not a majority view in Shiite belief, Admadinejad and his ruling buddies are part of a growing Islamic faction dedicated to securing worldwide Islamic rule through the coming to earth of the 12th Imam, a messiah-like figure long believed as prophesied to return to rule the world.

Labeled by President Bush as one of the "Axis of Evil", Iran is an antagonistic and dangerous nation of considerable concern to the United States, in fact our most dangerous foreign policy issue today. Leaders of the Iranian Guardian Council are quoted as saying "we must prepare to rule the world." Late last year Ahmadinejad, in maliciously anti-American and anti-Israel speeches where he threatened genocide he prominently referred to Israel as a "disgraceful blot" that "must be wiped out from the map of the world." This is a voice of grave danger speaking, especially in view of Iran's secret twenty year pursuit of nuclear weapons, a voice that is rallying and radicalizing the Muslim world toward apocalyptic scale destruction and death, and Iran with its nuclear weaponry may not have the tools to deliver such destruction.

Iran is across the Persian Gulf from Saudi Arabia and also has some of the world's largest oil and natural gas reserves. So are they really so aggressively buying nuclear power plants from Russia to provide nuclear power, as they say? For two decades they've been hiding nuclear activities and refusing to fully cooperate with the International Atomic Energy Agency. It makes no sense other than the obvious: they're building nuclear bomb plants dispersed around their country, assisted by our "friends" the Russians, and are widely believed to be within a couple of years of being able to produce nuclear weapons. At a large rally in early April their demented president, surrounded by ruling mullahs, announced "Iran has joined the nuclear countries of the world. The nuclear fuel cycle at the laboratory level has been completed." So far we've found no way to stop them, and Iran has boldly stated that if any nation interferes with its nuclear power program it will cut off supplies of its oil and gas. Some think the United Nations will resolve this growing threat, but if history holds it's doubtful the U.N. will have the moral courage to act decisively.

In language reflective of Iran's threat to world security, Secretary of State Condoleezza Rice says "Iran is a troublemaker in the international system, a central banker of terrorism." Iran is supporting evil terror networks like Hamas, Hezbollah, and Al-Nakbah. After the infamous American Embassy capture, Iran used these and other terror groups to conduct terrorist attacks around the Middle East. It is known to finance terror against Iraq and Lebanon, but as it rushes to perfect nuclear weaponry the eradication of Israel (our ally) remains its primary objective.

Options for a peaceful solution are fading quickly as America is faced with a likely but undesirable military solution. Iran is known to have at least 24 hidden underground nuclear sites, minimally vulnerable to air strikes. At best a military air strike would damage or destroy Iranian air defenses and infrastructure but would only slow their nuclear weapons development efforts—but the immediate and painful result would send oil prices soaring over $120 or more per barrel. Any use of military ground forces in Iran would mean the deaths of mostly Shiites, and that will provoke the Shiites in Iraq and beyond.

There is no easy fix to this growing danger. Nonetheless, the world must at all costs prevent Iran from achieving nuclear weaponry. To ignore this risk is to endanger vital American security interests in the Middle East and at home.

MAVERICK NORTH KOREA

For a small bankrupt Asian country of political isolation and wretched misery, North Korea manages to be a surprisingly large threat to peace and the economy. Much like the schoolyard bully, the most frequently used adjective to describe North Korea and its leadership is "belligerent." Few people realize how thorny and complex and treacherous is the frightening task of containing North Korea and its irrational megalomaniacal leader, Kim Jon Il, a sadistic and tyrannical madman who has said: "If we lose, I will destroy the world." And his lackey Foreign Ministry is just as menacing, saying "Pre-emptive strike is not the monopoly of the United States."

Though chronic food shortages have abated somewhat, chronic malnutrition still affects 37% of the population. In 1998, three million people died of hunger as the dead went unattended in the streets. Energy is in constant short supply, and North Korea is a country in deep trouble with indications that collapse may be imminent. Yet before that happens, the insane leader has said "One is pleased to see the bugs die in a fire even though one's house is being burned down."

Son of the now deceased Great Leader Kim Il Sung, the "Dear Leader" is a one-man Communist tyranny where every element of his "Hermit Kingdom" depends on his demented personality. A member of the Axis of Evil known for selling armaments to corrupt governments, North Korea seems to ache for confrontation with the U.S. as it consistently refuses to end its nuclear weapons program—which it threatens to use and then denies it has, yet it ejected inspectors and continues making plutonium. The Institute for Science and International Security estimates it has so far enough plutonium for as many as three to nine nuclear weapons.

Meanwhile, thousands of American soldiers stationed in South Korea have been repositioned miles away from the border because we believe North Korea has an estimated 12,000 artillery pieces and rocket launchers. Our ally South Korea, next door with 50 million people and an economy important to the U.S. fears that if North Korea collapsed more than 2 million people would flood south, overrunning the small and stable democracy. The Chinese, who share a 300-mile-long border with North Korea, harbor similar concerns. And as if all this weren't enough, senior officials in our Treasury Department believe North Korea has for over ten years counterfeited billions of U.S. $100 bills and flooded the world with them in an effort to destabilize the U.S. economy.

Though small in size, uncontained North Korea constitutes a grave and growing potential danger for America.

DOUBLE-DEALING PAKISTAN

Since my first visit to Pakistan I have sensed it's a country of mounting population relatively calm on the surface but with seething underlying instability and tension between Punjabis, Pakhtuns, Sindhis, immigrants from India, and non-Muslim religious minorities. With a mostly rural population estimated at 165 million people coupled with some of the most dense urban cities in the world in Lahore and Karachi, Pakistan is the ninth most populous country in the world and more than half of its population is below age fifteen and nearly one-third is below age nine. The implications of these demographics are worryingly frightening as increasing numbers are taught extremist ways and hatred for America, and the long-term potential is horrific. Pakistan is a difficult nation governed by corrupt civilians and successive military regimes and with all the ingredients of turbulence and instability, a constant military alert against India its larger nuclear neighbor, and nuclear weapons. All in all it's a prescription for disaster.

Dr. Abdul Quadeer Khan is a national hero and the acknowledged father of Pakistan's nuclear program, and with nuclear India crowding its borders he has probably prevented, for now, a nuclear exchange between the two. But the story of Pakistan's nuclear might doesn't end there. Last year in a major intelligence revelation, sources disclosed that Pakistan, led by Khan, secretly exported uranium enrichment technology to pariah nations North Korea and Libya and perhaps others including Iran to strengthen their nuclear weapons capacities. North Korea and Libya are sworn enemies of the United States.

We first discovered the business deal when U.S. operatives intercepted a German ship carrying nuclear weapons production parts bound for Libya. Libya quickly confessed and fingered Pakistan as the source and named Khan as the seller—for $100 million. Intelligence operatives also learned that Khan's Pakistan group also sold technical know-how and components for nuclear weapons to North Korea and Iran, both members of the Axis of Evil.

Pakistan and the United States proclaim a close and united relationship in the fight against terror. Pakistan's current president, General Pervez Musharraf, walks a wobbly tightrope in simultaneously satisfying anti-American religious factions and the forces of moderation. Despite his denials to the contrary, it seems obvious to me that nations fighting terror don't help build up the nuclear weaponry of nations committed to terror. It's a very dangerous game Pakistan is playing.

PALESTINE, THE NON STATE

The growing tsunami of extremism is against peace in the Middle East. There are simply too many in the Arab world who believe anything short of the total destruction of Israel is failure. Such was the universal sentiment of the Palestinians old and young that I spoke with in the squalor-filled and crowded Chatilla refuge camp, where Palestinians lived almost like animals in long-neglected and cramped housing because they had no other choice. Every problem whether real or imagined was blamed on the Jews who had stolen their homeland and they wanted it back, no matter the cost—as their passions and resentments seethe.

As I listened to their propaganda, it was clear their telling of history was biased and distorted—but to them it was real, enveloped in hatred almost impossible to truly comprehend. They were pawns in the war against the Zionists with their discontent and hatred fueled by corrupt leaders and constant anti-Semitism. These were angry and unreasonable people for whom "peace talks" and "negotiations" were so much far-away vacant chatter. To see them dance in the streets on 9/11 was not surprising; we will yet see much more dancing and celebrating.

It was both astounding and startling to me as mothers proudly shared photos of their martyr sons, blown to paradise in their suicide bombing attacks. Their younger brothers and sisters—young boys and girls—were being trained with religious and political ideologies to do the same, all in the name of Allah. Yet their fellow Arabs I met, while they pretended concern for their Palestinian brothers, in reality didn't care about them but about using them to inflame hatred and violence against Israel and America.

In the West Bank and Gaza, where 50% of Palestinians are under the age of fifteen, the average Palestinian family earns less than $1500 a year. My grandfather used to say that idle hands are the devil's workshop, so the devil must have a whole factory complex going in Palestine where nearly 50% of men in the West Bank and 70% of men in Gaza are unemployed, with time for self-respect to vanish and hatred to fester. Those children who attend overcrowded schools internalize a daily regimen of hatred of Jews and a call to revolution.

Former Palestinian Authority President Yasser Arafat devoted his life to destroying Israel and passionately seeking to create a new Palestine state, pleading the cause of "his people." Yet when he died it was estimated he had diverted $1 billion into his personal Swiss bank accounts. Obviously for him the glory of Islam had provided him a way to line his pockets as he spewed his venomous hatred.

The resolution of the "Palestinian question" is intricate, convoluted, and complex—both the Palestinians and the Jews merit a place to call home—and it's become even more so by the election of Hamas terrorists to the Palestinian governing authority. They live in a place that has known more conflict over history than anywhere else in the world, and it continues today—where every day the mosques spew forth poisonously hopeless messages calling for a permanent revolution against the Jews. This is an ancient quarrel for which there is no ultimate winner, only death and destruction. Whatever solution will appease the Palestinians will provoke the Israelis, and no matter what is proposed the United States ends up targeted in the crosshairs of a likely conflagration involving all the Middle East. For us it is a no- win scenario.

DISORIENTED EUROPE

If you think of Europe as an Anglo-Saxon heartland, you're missing a sea-change throughout the continent. An estimated 20 million Muslims now live in Europe, a number that will likely more than double in the next 20 years as Islam, after centuries, reverses the conquest of Europe. Many scholars now describe Europe as "Eurabia," a new outpost of Islamic invasion. National allegiances and sovereign territories defer to Islamic ideology, including radical dogma, often inhibiting free speech and the tenants of democracy. Recent widespread riots across France and the furor over a single Danish editorial cartoon show the vulnerability of Europe to the ferocious religious beliefs and doubtful assimilation of the new Muslims citizens.

Fouad Ajami, a distinguished scholar, describes this conquest: "These are the burning grounds of the Middle East and North Africa hurling their disinherited young people across the Straits of Gibraltar to an aging European continent."

Things seem to be worst in France, where 10% of the population is already Islamic. At the current rates of immigration and reproduction, in fifty years France, Italy, and other European countries may have an Islamic majority. The Balkan states of Serbia, Bosnia, and Montenegro, each seeking admission into the European Union, further alter the historic mix in favor of Islam.

For two hundred and twenty-five years, the nation states of

Europe have for the most part been America's key military and diplomatic allies, and remain essentially so today. With a few noteworthy exceptions of misguided European adventures we have generally stood side by side in world conflicts and in the world courts. This alliance, paid for at enormous cost of life and resources and which has long been essential to U.S. national security and global stability, is under attack, not by invading armed forces but by an equally dangerous invasion of legions armed with dangerous ideologies swearing allegiance not to any nation state but to a religion.

The European Union is an alliance of 27 nations and has the capacity and muscle to be the greatest single economic trading bloc in the world. But instead Europe is marching at double-time toward an uncomfortable day of decision and confrontation. As millions of Muslims cry insensitivity toward their faith, millions more native Europeans resent both this characterization and the Muslim desire for domination. Here two civilizations are on a collision course: native (mostly-Christian) Europeans and Muslims, Europe's second-largest religion. So far, traditional Judeo-Christian values are loosing.

WEAPONS OF TERROR

The United Nations Special Commission (UNSCOM) was charged with finding and destroying weapons of mass destruction in Iran. The principal in charge was Richard Butler, an Australian diplomat and United Nations weapons inspector who in his book about that impossible task described in penetrating clarity the dangers of the weapons of terror:

"The greatest threat to life on earth is weapons of mass destruction—nuclear, chemical, biological. These weapons do not exist in nature. They have been made by man, generally as the result of sophisticated research, and complex, costly processes. The community of nations has recognized this threat; indeed, perhaps the most important achievement in the second half of the twentieth century was the weaving of a tapestry of treaties designed to contain and then eliminate it."

Speaking to graduating cadets at the U.S. Military Academy at West Point, President George W. Bush said "The gravest danger to freedom lies at the perilous crossroads of radicalism and technology. When the spread of chemical and biological and nuclear weapons, along with ballistic missile technology—when that occurs, even weak states and small groups could attain a catastrophic power to strike great nations."

"The greatest threat to life on earth." "The gravest danger to freedom." "A catastrophic power to strike." Such incredibly strong language cannot be ignored.

NUCLEAR ANNIHILATION

It's a secret long buried by the CIA that a Soviet nuclear submarine attacked the United States. On March 7, 1968, a rogue Soviet sub with the apparent goal of tricking the U.S. and China into nuclear war launched a Chinese-made nuclear missile against the island state of Hawaii. Miraculously the missile imploded, destroying the submarine and sending its crew to their watery grave. With absolutely no warning we came within seconds of the unimaginable nuclear destruction of an American city. As U.S. intelligence operatives unraveled the failed attack they recognized the probability of national panic and the consequences for the economy if the incident were revealed. To this day, the CIA has never publicly acknowledged the attack and records remain classified top secret.

Nothing could be more devastating to our country or our economy than a nuclear attack on an American city. Imagine al-Qaeda detonating such a device—it's our worst national nightmare but no longer so far-fetched. Officials of the International Atomic Energy Agency are on record saying known terrorists including Osama bin Laden and al-Qaeda have been "actively looking into acquiring a nuclear weapon and other weapons of mass destruction," and the 9/11 Commission said that bin Laden wants to accomplish another "Hiroshima." This time it would be in the United States.

The impact of a nuclear bomb attack on New York City, obviously a prime target, is so far-reaching as to be incalculable. Beyond the human death toll the entire city—the financial capital of the world and the major port area of the Northeast—would be uninhabitable for probably fifty or more years. Stock markets would collapse and disappear, our American banking system would breakdown and fail, trillions of dollars would evaporate, and the shock wave would kick the world economy in the teeth.

Common sense tells us undeniably the safest prevention is to harden the security of the hundreds of nuclear weapons and materials facilities around the world—some of which are secured by chain link fence and a guard vulnerable to bribes—yet while terrorists are urgently using every strategy they can think of to get nuclear weapons we're dragging our bureaucratic feet. Senator Richard Lugar, then Chairman of the Senate Foreign Relations Committee, says "The war on terrorism will not be won until every nuclear stockpile, wherever it may be in the world, is secured and accounted for to stringent and transparent standards."

So just where do terrorists lay hands on nuclear weapons? Most vulnerable is Russia, where the Federal'naya Sluzhba Bezopasnosti (Russia's Federal Security Service) has uncovered intelligence that terror cells are actively planning to target Russian military nuclear and biological weapons arsenals.

Through treaty verification we have learned that the Soviet Union had a least 10,779 nuclear warheads and as many as 13,000 non-strategic nuclear weapons—and not all of them are accounted for. Some have gone missing. Senator Sam Nunn observed that "Never before has an empire disintegrated while in possession of 30,000 nuclear weapons." In addition to weapons the Russians have enormous amounts of enriched uranium and plutonium—an estimated 600 metric tons of fissile material—which could be stolen and used in nuclear weapons or radiological dirty bombs, and several governments are known to have seized stolen enriched uranium or plutonium. The rebel Russian province Chechnya is known to make "surface-to-air missiles" available in the marketplace.

Since Russia is at present too poor to secure either its weapons or nuclear materials, our government is spending about a half-billion dollars annually to pay the bill. At the current pace Government officials expect the project to take at least until 2012 and the 9/11 Commission said it could take until 2018. Less than two-thirds of nuclear warhead storage sites are now secured. If only half of the nuclear material in Russia has been secured, that leaves over 300 tons of fissile material unsecured, enough for more than 15,000 nuclear weapons. It's no wonder the 9/11 Commission gave the government a "D" grade.

But Russia is not alone. More than one hundred facilities scattered around the world are known to have sufficient highly enriched uranium to build a bomb, and we should expect that terrorists know about each one of them. Nuclear materials are difficult to make but relatively easy to steal, and even easier to transport and detonate. Weapons experts caution that a small amount of highly enriched uranium is enough to make a suitcase-size bomb as powerful as the bomb that leveled Hiroshima. Though we're spending billions to prevent just such a thing the Congressional Research Service points out, "scenarios for smuggling a nuclear weapon across unguarded coasts or borders are similar to smuggling bales of marijuana."

To be sure, our government is trying to make our borders and ports more secure though officials acknowledge they have a very long way to go. Before 9/11 border inspectors were looking for drugs and smuggled consumer goods; today they are increasingly equipped with new technologies in a heightened alert for nuclear weapons. Each year over 9 million seaborne containers enter the U.S.; where Customs used to inspect 2% they now inspect many more. High sensitivity vehicle monitors have been deployed on the Canadian border where today over 90% of tractor-trailers and 80% of passenger vehicles are checked for nuclear weapons.

But grave risks remain. Last year, physicists working for the Department of Transportation decided that terrorists were "most likely to use highly enriched uranium (HEU), not plutonium." If terrorists decided to shield the weapon, it would emit virtually no radiation whatsoever. So much for border security, and our enemies have the money and the will born of their religious core to succeed.

CYBER TEROR

Even as recently as a decade ago the notion of a terror attack in the cyberspace world was unthinkable. The concept was even unthinkable. No longer. Today we live in the new "Information Age" where terrorist cyber attacks are not only possible but rank high on the probability list.

Consider how reliant you and I have become on interconnected computers for every element of our lives, from the grocery store checkout to our ATM cash machine to getting a boarding pass for a flight—every element of our lives is controlled by computers, making them an inviting target of terror. But even more concerning than our personal conveniences are every control system for every component of our critical local and national infrastructures (drinking water, sewer removal, telecommunications, electricity, natural gas transmission, airlines, trucking, emergency ambulance and fire services, even police services), key finance industries (such as insurance, banking, and stock markets), and mission-critical military systems—they are all computer-driven and extremely vulnerable to those who are technically sophisticated and inclined toward mischief or terror.

What is the likelihood of such an attack? War games entitled "Exercise Eligible Receiver" carried out by the Defense Department verified just how dangerous a cyber terror attack will be, leading some government officials to label it "the next battlefield for this nation."

Because America's public and private infrastructure is so vulnerable, just one cyber attack has the capacity to collapse our entire country within hours. In a country where business, government, education, and families are both interconnected at the speed of light, our economic well-being is perilously vulnerable. Defending America in cyberspace to this swiftly emerging threat is a national imperative in which we are falling further behind.

ELECTROMAGNETIC PULSE BOMB (EMP)

The threat that scares me the most, even more than a nuclear or dirty bomb, is one few know about but which is frightening real and alarmingly dangerous. A Congressionally-created commission of experts issued a report in 2004 which warns of how one unique nuclear weapon exploded over the United States would be "capable of causing catastrophe for the nation." One lone explosion of an EMP would bring America to its knees yet few mention this weapon when they speak of weapons of mass destruction. Have you ever heard of an electromagnetic pulse (EMP)?

The Commission to Assess the Threat to the Untied States from Electromagnetic Pulse Attack chillingly reported to Congress:

"The electromagnetic fields produced by weapons designed and deployed with the intent to produce EMP have a high likelihood of damaging electrical power systems, electronics, and information systems upon which American society depends. Their effects on dependent systems and infrastructures could be sufficient to qualify as catastrophic to the nation."

In simple language, an EMP is a special nuclear weapon carried by a ballistic missile and detonated at high altitude, and the higher the altitude the larger the affected area, which would send a trillion watts of microwave energy at the speed of light and effect everything in line-of-sight. If the EMP detonated at 300 miles up, all of the 48 states and parts of Mexico and Canada would be impacted. Downrange, everything electrical and electronic would instantly cease to function: power plants, electrical transmission lines, computers, office equipment, car locks, toys and calculators, police radios, stoves and microwaves and refrigeration, ATMs, life-saving hospital equipment, air conditioning, cell phones, air traffic control, cash registers, newspaper presses and television and radio, satellite control, emergency generators, sewer and water pumps, trucks and cars and busses and farm harvesters, movie theaters, manufacturing assembly lines, airplanes and trains and subways and medical helicopters—essentially every component of modern life.

In less time that it takes to blink your eyes, sustaining human life, getting water and food, keeping warm would be impossible for days or weeks or longer. Within minutes or hours cities and towns would burn as fires raged uncontrolled as fire trucks and water systems failed to operate; without electricity cities and towns would become uninhabitable. We would be isolated from every radio and television news source. Without trucks and stores and restaurants, our hunger would quickly grow and it could be weeks before foodstuffs reached us.

The EMP Threat Commission told Congress repairs would take "months to years," outlining the horrific effects of such an attack:

"Depending on the specific characteristics of the attacks, unprecedented cascading failures of our major infrastructures could result. In that event, a regional or national recovery would be long and difficult and would seriously degrade the safety and overall viability of our nation. The primary avenues for catastrophic damage to the nation are through our electric power infrastructure and thence our telecommunications, energy, and other infrastructures. These, in turn, can seriously impact other important aspects of our nation's life, including the financial system; means of getting food, water, and medical care to the citizenry; trade; and production of goods and services."

Can we even comprehend an attack that would endanger the "viability of our nation"? The threat is unfortunately all too real, as the EMP Threat Commission reported to Congress:

'The emerging threat environment, characterized by a side spectrum of actors that include near-peers, established nuclear powers, rogue nations, sub-national groups, and terrorist organizations that either now have access to nuclear weapons and ballistic missiles or may have such access of the next 15 years, have combined to raise the risk of EMP attack and adverse consequences on the U.S. to a level that is not acceptable."

Even more alarming the Commission had more bad news for Congress, telling them that some potential EMP threats may be "unpredictable and difficult to deter." Our acute American vulnerability, amplified by the absence of redundancy and excess capacity, was emphasized by the EMP Threat Commission:

"The U.S. has developed more than most other nations as a modern society heavily dependent on electronics, telecommunications, energy, information networks, and a rich set of financial and transportation systems that leverage modern technology."

127

Not only would our nation come to an abrupt and total halt, so would every domestically-based military unit. Foreign-based units would lose the ability to communicate with home command and control. Our ability to militarily respond to the attack would fail in total. In short, without advance warning we would cease to function as a nation. Al-Qaeda would love such a weapon, and Iran and possibly North Korea now have ballistic missiles needed to deliver such an attack.

Distinguished policy thinker Frank J. Gaffney, Jr., President of the Center for Security Policy, offered this solemn warning: "The price of continued inaction could be a disaster of infinitely greater cost and unimaginable hardship for our generation and generations of Americans to come."

In an instant, a terrorist EMP attack on America would result in a catastrophic disaster of incalculable magnitude, far worse than anything known in world history.

BIOWEAPONS - DISEASE AS TERROR

As horrible as the above weapons' human and economic consequences are, a terrorist attack on the United States using biological warfare agents such as VX, Soman, Sarin, anthrax, Ebola and the other hemorrhagic fever viruses, or smallpox is far more lethal from a human perspective—and has the power to bring this great nation to collapse. Richard L. Garwin, an expert on science and technology at the Council on Foreign Relations, believes that "biological-warfare agents are the biggest menace we currently face."

Smallpox is so deadly it is estimated to have killed between 300 and 500 million people in the twentieth century alone. But the government assures us that the microorganism has been destroyed and that the only remaining live samples are in high-security laboratories in Russia and the U.S. But intelligence confirms that the Soviets secretly relocated samples to a disreputable bio-weapons lab in Siberia and what happened to those specimens is uncertain—maybe they are already in the hands of terrorists.

Given its historic mortality rate of about 30%, introduction of weaponized smallpox into 100,000 people could result in the death of 30 million people within four months.

Smallpox is the perfect weapon of terror—because there are no visible symptoms until nearly two weeks after infection yet for that entire time the carriers are highly infectious. The carriers are happily going about life unknowingly infecting everyone with whom they come in contact, who in turn are spreading the infection even further everywhere they travel. Think about how many people you interact with and how many places in the world you and they travel in any two-week period. Antibiotics are useless against smallpox and there is no effective treatment after its evident you have it.

You do the math, and it is entirely possible that within two weeks the entire nation has smallpox. Granted, this I hope is an unlikely draconian scenario but entirely within the realm of possibility. So reduce the number to say a comparatively measly twenty-five million Americans sick and dying. The consequences are just as horrific and catastrophic, and it is frightening to even contemplate—as my friends in senior government circles must do—the fear and system overloading that would lead to the collapse of utility and transportation and distribution and health care infrastructures, followed by widespread chaos, looting, and a general breakdown of order and civil society.

All in two weeks.

In 2001, before 9-11, the federal government conducted a mock bio-disaster code-named "Dark Winter" where Islamic terrorists discharged smallpox viruses in shopping centers in just three states. The result: one million Americans dead, hundreds of thousands permanently harmed, widespread starvation, and $2 trillion lost as the national economy ceased to function.

Expert Robert Garwin reports there are "many potential biowarfare agents, such as Burkholderia mallet—a contagious bacterium that causes a deadly disease called glanders and for which there is no vaccine. They might be disseminated within large buildings - and distributed by the circulating air in heating, ventilating and air-conditioning systems - or outdoors, to expose whole cities. And in the case of an outside release, even people who were indoors with the windows shut would be at risk of exposure, as air tends to leak through tiny gaps and cracks in most buildings."

The Center for Biosecurity ranks biological and nuclear terrorism as the two most dangerous external threats facing the United States, and that "reliable means" of preventing terrorists from producing biological weaponry and bringing them into our country do not exist and will not soon exist.

CHEMICAL WEAPONS

Chemical weapons are not new; they've been around for four hundred years. And for decades the civilized nations of the world have discussed banning chemical weapons, yet they remain a very dangerous and serious threat to American security. Because chemical weapons may come in liquid, gas, power, or spray form we are seriously prepared to thwart such an attack.

The only known terrorist group to use chemical weapons in an attack is Aum Shinrikyo which used the deadly nerve agent sarin in a Tokyo subway, killing its victims in minutes. Sadam Hussein is known to have used lethal mustard gas on his own citizens, killing tens of thousands. Friends in the intelligence community tell me that Islamic terrorist groups are actively seeking such weapons from several state sponsors of terrorism which have chemical warfare capabilities. Today Russia has the largest hoard of chemical weapons, estimated at 40,000 tons, a poisonous leftover from of the Cold War.

How deadly would such a chemical attack be? Terrorists setting off just one chemical weapon in a crowded area, such as a shopping mall, could wreak havoc with our lives and our economy. The U.S. Army says that "a terrorist attack on a chemical plant which released deadly vapors over a city could result in as many as 2.4 million deaths and injuries."

Speaking at a recent international meeting on chemical weapons, Rogelio Pfirter, Director-General of the U.N.'s Organization for the Prohibition of Chemical Weapons, said "The nature and effect of chemical weapons make unprotected civilians their main target. The materials necessary to produce simple chemical weapons are widely available, and the technology and financial hurdles to be overcome are considerably less problematic than those posed by the illicit manufacturing and use of primitive biological or nuclear weapons. The challenge posed by chemical terrorism is ever greater." Ambassador Pfirter's words are surely not comforting.

ECONOMIC TERRORISM

Nearly forty years ago seventy-seven underdeveloped nation states of the United Nations established the "Group of 77" and a few years later declared economic war on the developed nations. That's us! It's interesting to note that the group's leader was none other than our next door neighbor, Mexican president Luis Echeverria Alvarez.

The Group of 77 joined together in labeling the United States and other developed nations, for economic reasons, as their real enemy.

Today terrorists have the same view, targeting the American economy, its stability and its world financial leadership and striving to disrupt American financial dominance and well-being. If run-of-the-mill daily news can trigger major stock market swings, you can only guess at how extreme would be the impact of the U.S. president and all other senior federal officers being whisked from Washington to an undisclosed secret underground hiding place. This is but one of the way terrorists will try to undermine our economy.

Every banking day roughly two trillion dollars electronically moves in and out of American banks, in roughly four hundred thousand wire transfers. Every day. Extraordinary sums of money, and a lot of it is "dirty money", maybe as much as three hundred billion annually. Even North Korea is accused of flooding the world with billions in counterfeit U.S. $100 bills. With less than 200 employees and housed in a strip mall in the Washington D.C. suburb of Tysons Corner, the Treasury Department's little-known Financial Crimes Enforcement Network is charged with safeguarding the financial system from financial crimes, terrorist financing, money laundering, and other illicit activity—a daunting task by any measure.

Increasingly terrorist groups are engaging in financial crime to fund terror and destabilize the economy. Money laundering and global contraband trading has grown ten times in the last fifteen years to well over $1 trillion annually, about 10% of legitimate global trade. Illicit drug smuggling accounts for about $900 billion annually. According to official sources and trade associations, illegal weapons trade amounts to $10 billion per year; cross-border toxic waste dumping $12 billion; alien smuggling including women and children destined for sexual exploitation, $7 billion; pirated motion pictures, $3 billion; pilfered art, $3 billion. Illegal trade has gone on for centuries, smuggling virtually every form of contraband imaginable including increasingly high-value pharmaceuticals. No taxes or duties are paid, contraband may be hazardous or dangerous, legitimate businesses face unfair competition, other crimes and violence are furthered—all of which has a destabilizing impact.

Federal enforcement efforts are sometimes successful in hindering money crimes, such as one FBI undercover operation in New Jersey interestingly labeled Operation Royal Charm that rounded up nearly 100 suspects at a fake wedding who were arrested for smuggling millions in counterfeit U.S. currency, weapons, counterfeit cigarettes, and illegal ecstasy pills into the United States on container ships using false bills of lading for toys, rattan furniture and other goods. In Southern California, Operation Smoking Dragon nailed 30 suspects for smuggling $40 million worth of counterfeit cigarettes and nearly 10,000 ecstasy pills and Viagra.

Legal global flow of trade and money are being increasingly corrupted, especially by terrorist organizations. As heroic as federal and international law enforcements efforts are, far more must be done is we are not to fall even further behind.

THE ONLY SENSIBLE SOLUTIONS

These are serious times that call for serious measures. If as part of our national security strategy we are to reduce the appeal of extremism and radicalism, our foreign policy apparatus must address the underlying causes by promoting educational opportunities, fostering international understanding, assisting to ensure political rights, advancing the rights and living conditions for women, offer treatment of disease, and expand economic opportunity, especially in the Muslim nations, all while working to minimize or obstruct the insidious spread of weapons of mass destruction.

At the same time, we, as individual citizens and as a nation, need to put in place and maintain sensible security measures. We must understand the world and insist on having leaders who understand it.

And we must insist, even in the face of danger, on maintaining the values and freedoms that make our country worth preserving in the first place. We must not be ruled by fear; we must remain, no matter what confronts us, the home of the brave and the land of the free.

6

FIFTH DANGER – FEDERAL GOVERNMENT STUPIDITY

❦

"There are few examples to be found
in economic history where a government
spent a country into prosperity."
—George Melloan

This chapter and the next deal with a pair of closely linked dangers. One, which we'll talk about here, is the fact that the fate of both the federal government and the economy—and thus the prosperity of our country—are hopelessly entangled with the fate of the American real estate market. Worse, a larger and larger portion of the assets of this jury-rigged system consist of wildly unstable financial instruments that nobody (including, as we shall see, Nobel Prize-winning supposed experts in them) actually understands.

That, all by itself, would be pretty alarming: your fate and mine are tied to the aftermarket in mortgages like the heroine of an old-fashioned melodrama tied to the railroad tracks. What makes it worse—the subject of Chapter 7—is that the train is coming. The subprime-fueled housing bubble is bursting, and it stands to bring large chunks of the American economy down with it.

Now wait a minute, you may be thinking. Markets go up and down all the time, don't they? We saw the collapse of a bubble in Internet stocks less than 10 years ago, and while it was painful, it wasn't the end of the world. What makes this different?

One thing that makes it different is the sheer size of this particular market, and the way it is entwined with the whole economic system. Another is that the federal government was not (for which we bow our heads and thank a merciful God) actively involved in the high-tech industry. It's involved in the housing market, though, up to its elbows.

Have you ever heard of a "GSE"? Well don't feel bad—few people outside of government have either. Simply put, a GSE is a "government-sponsored enterprise", a creation of Congress that almost certainly will drag our nation into further debt, all of which is not reflected in the federal budget.

Take the Federal Home Loan Banks, created by Congress in the depression era of the 1930's as a much-needed source of housing finance. Today the private sector can provide just as well but alas Congress keeps this outdated bank system that pays each of the twelve bank presidents salaries of several hundred thousands of dollars per year, far more than it pays the U.S. Secretary of the Treasury.

The most commonly known GSE's are "Fannie Mae" and "Freddic Mac", which today have become far more than Congress intended them to be when it authorized their creation; they are now an unquestioned and essential component of the credit machine currently propping up the United States. Today our nation depends on credit, and these housing GSE's are the engine driving the credit train and have become the largest and most liquid bond market in the world—

presenting a risk to the national economy Congress never foresaw as our national economic thinkers have connected our future to the fiscal health of the American homeowner!

FANNIE AND FREDDIE—MERCHANTS OF DEBT

Fannie Mae, or Fannie, is an abbreviation for the Federal National Mortgage Association and was created by Congress in 1938 as a government entity to provide a market for mortgages insured by the federal government. In 1970, Freddie Mac (short for Federal Home Loan Mortgage Corporation and mostly known as Freddie) was created by Congress to buy mortgages issued by savings and loan institutions. Their share of the mortgage market has grown steadily, to more than 50% today, far exceeding the intent of Congress.

Their magnitude and power are astounding. They purchase mortgages from lenders, maintain some in their own portfolios, and resell some as mortgage-backed securities. In 2003, the housing GSE's issued more than $1 trillion worth of new debt! And all told, the so-called "housing GSE's" own or guarantee 42% of the $7 trillion U.S. mortgage market. Today the American economy is dependent on homeowners, and over $5 trillion in corporate assets remain safe only as long as the American homeowners pay their monthly mortgages.

The GSE's continue to roll merrily along only so long as there is a constant stream of new homebuyers and refinanced mortgages. Heaven forbid a housing crisis should unfold. Almost $3 trillion in debt and guarantees of the GSE's could become a liability to the American taxpayer of unimaginable proportions if widespread mortgage defaults occur.

Fannie Mae, long representing itself to be an institution of arrogant propriety and stodgy expertise staying above the fray, has in recent years found itself mired in an $11B accounting scandal. (Sounds like Enron all over again!) In his interesting book *The Coming Crash in the*

Housing Market, John Talbott writes:

> "These two monoliths of the residential mortgage business have become the backbone of the entire market. If a contagion reaches into the comfortable offices of Fannie Mae and Freddie Mac, there is no pessimistic scenario I can describe that will adequately depict the ensuing disaster.
>
> "To appreciate the potential calamity involved you are reminded that $1 trillion amounts to one million bags of $1,000,000 each.
>
> "According to their annual reports, in a home mortgage market of $5.7 trillion, one government Agency, Ginny Mae, and two quasi agencies, Fannie Mae and Freddie Mac, hold on their balance sheet or guarantee $3.7 trillion in residential mortgages.
>
> "To put it in perspective, this is getting close to the entire U.S. government debt of $6.3 trillion."

Did you know also that a large portion of the total dollar capital of U.S. banks is held in obligations of Fannie and Freddie? Few people do, but one who does is former Federal Reserve Chairman Alan Greenspan who finds this troubling. As Federal Reserve Chairman, he said: "Mortgage giant Fannie Mae and Freddie Mac could pose a threat to the country's financial system if their ability to take on new debt is not restrained."

SACRED COWS

Unfortunately, there's no one to restrain them. Every time Congress begins to take anything approaching a serious look at Fannie and Freddie, their dependent pals in the homebuilding industry swarm Congress with the persuasive influence of generous campaign contributions and fabricated fears that somehow reform will harm home ownership in their district. Congress hears too from the nation's one million realtors. How about Mary Mancera of the National Association of Hispanic Real Estate Professionals who launched this carefully worded pressure on our elected representatives: "Reform Proposals Will Limit Latinos Access to Homeownership". It's no wonder reform is absent, even though a Federal Reserve study found that the implicit government guarantee for Fannie and Freddie has minimal impact on mortgage rates.

Understandably, few members of Congress grasp the complex technicalities of mortgage finance. But they do grasp, quickly, where their political bread is buttered. One influential observer noted that "the Beltway homebuilders and Realtors have been in bed with Fannie and Freddie so long that they don't even care that their repurchased MBS portfolios do nothing for home ownership." But talk about less threatening campaign contribution reform and public policy is sure to respond.

The larger issue for the American taxpayer and the safety of the American economy is the possibility of a Fannie or Freddie crisis. For years their primary business was buying home mortgages, and then repackaging them into so-called mortgage-backed securities ("MBSs")for sale, thereby creating more liquidity for mortgage funding. OK so far. But Fannie and Freddie have significantly increased their risk in recent years as they have purchased their own MBSs for their own portfolio.

These two financial giant GSE's who have an implicit taxpayer guarantee have endured two accounting scandals and their self-protecting assertions notwithstanding, no one really knows just how safe they are. Absent serious oversight and corrective legislation by Congress, this potential financial danger to the American economy continues to simmer.

DERIVATIVES

Simultaneously, Fannie and Freddie, and the Federal Home Loan Banks, have trillion-dollar derivatives in place to hedge these risks.

For many years I served on a federal banking board on which several of my fellow directors (whose names must be withheld to protect the innocent) were bank presidents. I privately asked several of those bank presidents to explain derivatives to me, and in confidential individual moments, each of them admitted that they couldn't! And yet here we were, approving and authorizing hundreds of millions, even billions, in derivative transactions. What little confidence I then had in derivatives and those who create them was annihilated.

Meanwhile, banks around the world, including the U.S., increasingly look to derivatives for earnings. In fact, eight of America's largest banks derive more than half their total profits from derivatives and currency transactions. A dangerous aspect of the Fannie and Freddie risk is the amount of their assets held in the form of high-risk instruments known as derivatives. Their derivative accounting has been labeled a "black box" mess, and in 2003, Fannie Mae lost an astounding $1.9 billion on its derivatives.

Just so you'll know in case your Member of Congress ever asks you, a derivative is a contract between two parties to exchange value based on an action of a good or service, in which the seller receives money in exchange for an agreement to purchase or sell some good at some specified future date. Got it? They're called derivatives because the value of the transaction is derived from something else, say, the exchange rate between the euro and the Hong Kong dollar a month from next Thursday. You don't actually have to have holdings in euros or Hong Kong dollars to do this; all you have to have is somebody willing to accept the contract and assign a value to it.

This sounds a lot like gambling, and as a matter of fact, that's what it is. Derivatives can involve foreign currencies, commodities, bundled mortgages, interest-rate swaps, and a host of other intriguing but unsettling financial creations, all of which are based on some sort of unregulated and often reckless leverage.

Which is also like more ordinary forms of gambling; just like a guy who gets over-optimistic about his ability to pick winners in college basketball, derivatives investors sometimes find themselves speculating with money that doesn't actually exist.

THE RESCUE

On an autumn day in 1998, William J. McDonough, president of the New York Federal Reserve Bank, urgently convened the heads of several of America's largest banks together with their counterparts from several large foreign banks. This was highly unusual; it was, in fact, the first time in history it had ever happened. Why did McDonough, a reasoned and cautious central banker, do such a thing? He did it because the Federal Reserve feared one company—Long Term Capital Management—was about to expose banks around the globe to a level of "systemic risk" never before experienced.

Talk about money that doesn't exist: can you imagine a company with a balance sheet of about $100 billion being able, through slight-of-hand leverage, to have in excess of $1.25 trillion in derivatives contracts? Seem impossible? Alas, that is what our federal economic system allows. The managers of Long Term Capital Management, a now defunct business operated by two Nobel Prize winners who took huge risks, had an irrationally misplaced confidence in their own ability to compute the odds and borrowed heavily to fund their derivative shenanigans.

Conditions at LTCM had become so dangerously bad that for every $100 in exposure LTCM held only $1 in equity. If market prices shifted one percentage point in the wrong direction, LTCM was finished—and so were the banks. Quietly, the Federal Reserve provided more credit—it's always more credit—and saved the day. All the banks lost money and LTCM's founders lost $4.5 billion, but the financial system survived for another day.

You'd think we would have learned a lesson about derivatives, but such was not the case. The now-infamous Enron earned more in derivative trades in a single year than LTCM did in its entire existence, and while the Federal Reserve saved the world's banks from the LTCM derivative nightmare, Enron was left to fail. The losses there far exceeded those of LTCM, let alone the number of Americans left financially devastated.

While derivatives barely existed a decade ago, this year the global market for credit derivatives passed $8 trillion. The Bank for International Settlements in Switzerland says the face value of all derivative contracts today is almost $370 trillion, an amount that reflects the total value of the actual underlying assets enveloped by the derivatives and is more than seven times the size of the worldwide economy. It's almost unfathomable! There are eighteen funds where the dollar amounts are larger than all but six national economies. The risk is simply catastrophic.

HEDGE FUNDS

A sister danger is the global wave of currency speculation where weaknesses are exploited and accelerated through the use of hedge funds. Of the ten largest U.S. banks, six are heavily involved in hedge funds though they refer to this activity as private equity funds. When a hedge fund fails, the investors are liable for the entire losses of the fund; they have no limit to their total loss exposure. This is insanity! Helping along by accounting rules that classify hedge funds and derivatives as contingent liabilities, banks can keep these immeasurable risks off their official balance sheets and thus banks are not required to set aside any reserves for losses. Double insanity!

A form of legalized bank gambling, hedge funds are now global with hundreds of billions of dollars operating on leverage to greatly multiply their actual assets. They find their profit opportunity in problems in currencies, stocks and bonds, and economic instability, often creating problems just to make a profit. Those dealing in derivatives and hedge funds thrive on instability and chaos, even if they have to create it. The bigger the swing the more the profit—so what's to keep a hedge fund from tipping over the economy of an entire country so they can make a mammoth profit? Absolutely nothing! In the Great Depression banks found creative ways to increase profits, and this time it's with derivatives and currency games.

A HEARTBEAT FROM DISASTER

When LTCM collapsed, the total amount of its outstanding debt was unknown, to anyone. And yet one of the largest consumer banks was their largest investor, with exposure of as much as sixty billion dollars! Just that one hedge fund could have triggered the collapse of one of America's most significant banks—because Congress in its perpetual campaign fund-raising wisdom has amended banking regulations so that derivatives and hedge funds are neither regulated nor supervised. During my years in Washington I have watched the fund managers and the banking industry, including highly paid lobbyists for Fannie and Freddie, prevail on Congress and regulators to chip away at a careful system of watch-care established after the 1929 crash until comparatively very little remains to protect you and me.

Derivatives and hedge funds are enormous time bombs ticking ever more quickly, including for Fannie and Freddie and America's largest banks who get away with things like tiny margins the stock markets would never tolerate. My knowing banker friends tell me its only a question of time before a second depression strikes, likely triggered by derivatives and hedge funds that threaten to demolish our entire economic well-being. America's wealthiest investor Warren Buffet cautions us that the derivatives market is a "mega-catastrophe waiting to happen."

If someone supposedly in the know tells you otherwise, just ask them to explain derivatives.

NATIONAL FLOOD INSURANCE PROGRAM

America has thousands of insurance companies. Why, then, did Congress in its dazzling wisdom feel it necessary to create the National Flood Insurance Program (NFIP), operated by the oft-criticized Federal Emergency Management Agency? Because people who live in flood danger areas can't get private insurance, so Congress generously has the tax payer take the risk. Does this make any sense?

Established in 1969, the program has paid nearly $13 billion in flood insurance claims. As of 2004, NFIP had issued almost 4? million flood insurance policies in 22,000 communities representing $637 billion in coverage. Most years the NFIP collects about the same in premiums as it pays out in damages and has about one billion socked away in reserve. Now along comes Hurricane Katrina and officials estimate claims to NFIP will exceed $10 billion. Will it be your tax dollars to bail out this federal program—to insure homes built in areas that are known to flood? The federal government should get out of this flood insurance business and leave the risk to private insurers.

AMTRAK

And why, in a nation of unmatched business genius and three hundred million people, should our federal government run a railroad? Did you know your federal government is in the railroad passenger business, that it's badly broken, and that you're paying for it?

The concocted political arguments for the government financially underwriting and subsidizing national passenger rail transportation are myriad—but the practical reasons are few. In 1970, Congress funded Amtrak and has every year since, last year to the tune of $1.2 billion. Now in the big federal picture that's not a lot of money, but it all adds up—and for a government that's broke it really counts.

From that inauspicious beginning nearly four decades ago, Congress has declared that their intent was to subsidize passenger rail service only until it became self-sufficient. Every year since Amtrak has operated at a loss and along the route received more than $25 billion in taxpayer subsidy. Yet for all that tax money, according to federal statistics Amtrak represents an infinitesimally small .007% of all daily commuter work trips but the average per rider tax dollar subsidy is around $100. Worse yet, on some cross country passenger rail routes the per passenger taxpayer subsidy exceeds $1,000.

It would be far cheaper just to use tax money to buy commercial airline tickets! But Congress in its political wisdom just keeps spending and spending. Our elected representatives continue to require the government to underwrite this money-loosing enterprise even though we just can no longer afford it.

FUTURE

These are but a representative few of the Government Sponsored Enterprises—GSEs—that our government finds an attractive way to add even more financial risk to the nation and to you. They are also an expedient way for politicians to curry favor, albeit temporarily, with the voters. When will it ever end?

Add to all this the fact that the Federal Financial Management Improvement Act of 1996 required major federal agencies to comply with the same accounting standards as the private sector. In other words, these major departments had to be operated with fiscal competency. What a brilliant notion! Yet, for example, the

Department of Homeland Security with its $35 billion budget has not passed an audit since 2003. The Department of Defense with its annual budget exceeding $450 billion has failed its audit every year. This should give the tax payer great confidence.

7

SIXTH DANGER – THE HOUSING BUBBLE AND BEYOND

✺

"The bursting of this bubble
will be across all countries and all assets."
—Jeremy Grantham

The world-renowned investor and philanthropist Sir John Templeton once described the 1990s tech boom as "the biggest bubble in history" before it crashed. In 2006, The Economist, an equally well respected observer of the financial scene, called the world-wide boom in residential real estate prices "the biggest bubble in history," noting that it was larger than the global stock market bubble in the late 1990s or America's stock market bubble in the late 1920s.

That easy-credit easy-money bubble is now bursting, with an impact that could be catastrophic to our economy. Our national housing boom has exposed the entire American banking system to grave risk: the recent growth in housing units, housing prices, and housing debt is simply unsustainable.

From 2001 to 2004 we lived in sunny golden California, the bellweather state, where we personally witnessed an amazing increase in housing prices. In the four years between 2001 and 2005, California home prices increased by a staggering $1.7 trillion, an amount equal to 35% of personal income. Other states too, like Nevada (mostly because of Las Vegas), sunny Florida, Hawaii, and the greater Washington, D.C. area saw home prices increase more than 20%. Some areas of the U.S. have seen home prices shoot up a whopping 35% in just the past year. Richard Brown, chief economist at the Federal Deposit Insurance Corporation, says "It's a widespread boom and has macro implications."

WHAT GOES UP...

Market downturns do happen, even severe ones. Housing prices skyrocketed in Southern California in the late 1980s; then, suddenly, major cuts in defense spending, coupled with a national recession, caused a housing price collapse all over the state. Many personal friends have told me they could hardly give their homes away. House prices declined and mortgage loan defaults increased, all of which resulted in the failure of some of the largest savings and loan banks.

The process has begun again—nationwide, this time, and most conspicuously in the fastest-growing city in the country, Las Vegas. Foreclosure filings across the United States rose 47 percent in March 2007 from a year previous to 149,150 - one for every 775 households, according to statistics from Realty Trac Inc., a foreclosure listing service. And for the third straight month, Nevada's foreclosure rate led the nation when it rose 220 percent from a year earlier to 4,738 filings, or one in every 183 households. In Clark County, which encompasses Las Vegas, one of every 30 homes began the process toward foreclosure last year, and it has worsened this year.

SPECULATION AND IRRESPONSIBILITY

In 2005, 23% of all houses nationwide, and in Miami 70% of condos, were bought by investors and were not owner-occupied. Nationally, 20% of real-estate transactions came from foreign buyers. To put the speculative nature of the housing boom in even sharper perspective, the annual formation of new households now numbers about only half the number of new housing starts.

Danger signs abound as our American borrow-and-spend mentality has become ever more financially irresponsible, especially as younger consumers turn increasingly to debt for spending. The National Association of Realtors tells us that 25% of all home buyers, and an incomprehensible 42% of first-time buyers, made no down payment on their home purchases last year. Those mortgages are very easy for the borrowers to just walk away from when the market collapses. Other buyers, trying to overcome insane house prices, are resorting to 40-year mortgage loans, which lower monthly mortgage payments but add heavily and unwisely to interest costs.

Banks and mortgage companies only make money if they issue mortgages, so as home prices soared, lenders became ever more creative (and irresponsible) in finding ways to help borrowers qualify for the so-called "sub-prime" loans. In the first half of last year, almost two-thirds of new mortgages were financed with adjustable-interest-rate and interest-only mortgages. In California, often on the forefront of housing growth and decline, interest-only mortgages accounted for over 60% of home-buying mortgages in 2005.

"The boom in interest-only loans—nearly half the state's home buyers used them last year, up from virtually none in 2001—is the engine behind California's surging home prices," said the L.A. Times. But it's even worse: last year, home-equity loans were issued at the same time as the primary mortgage for over 30% of the subprime mortgages issued to homebuyers, up from 7.1% in 2001, so that total mortgage borrowings rose to a mind-boggling average of 91% of the home value! As home prices fall, it's likely the house will be worth less than the mortgage balance owing.

HIGHER INTEREST RATES = HIGHER PAYMENTS = DEFAULT

After several years of record-setting low interest rates we are transitioning to a rising interest rate environment in which some borrowers are unable to meet rising mortgage payments. Furthermore, as interest rates rise, home prices are declining, so borrowers with interest-only sub-prime loans could end up owing more than the value of their homes. Historically, borrowers with less than 20% equity in their homes default in larger numbers when payments go up, because they have less to lose. Business Week magazine reported that "a rise in long-term interest rates, which would push up mortgage rates, could collapse the housing bubble faster than anything else."

Well, those mortgage interest rates are now rising, and American consumers are burdened with debt: high-interest-rate credit cards, car loans, boat loans, home mortgage loans, and home-equity loans, which, if based on adjustable rates, will increase. As those adjustable-rate sub-prime mortgages bump up even a few hundred dollars per month, lots of people run short on spendable cash. Because housing prices have stopped climbing, they will be unable to keep tapping their home equity to pay their monthly bills.

This is a danger to all of us not merely as individuals but as taxpayers, due to the levels of risk created in recent years by the housing GSE's. As the twentieth century came to a close, Fannie and Freddie launched on a mortgage debt marketing path that has added enormous new debt obligations for consumers that many cannot afford while simultaneously multiplying the contingent liabilities of the U.S. government.

WHY THE BUBBLE IS BURSTING

First of all, you have to understand that this really was a bubble— a freak market based on artificially inflated prices. Business Week magazine says "National housing prices going back to 1951… pretty much track the rate of inflation up until 1995. But since then, average prices on new and existing homes have soared more than 35 percentage points beyond the overall rate of inflation. Is that unusual? You bet it is."

And it's more than people can afford. When we purchased our first home, lenders would allow no more than 25 percent of our income to be used on rent or mortgage payments. By mid-2005, a reported one in five new home buyers spent half of their disposable income on housing. Homeowner equity (the part not mortgaged) has dropped in a brief thirty years from nearly 70 percent to now less than 55 percent.

The amount of money American consumers owe today has doubled from what we owed only a decade ago, most of that increase coming from bigger and bigger mortgages and the foolish tendency of homeowners to use home equity loans like a credit card. Home equity loans—once called, and sternly warned against, second mortgages— have become the ATM for maintaining lifestyles we cannot afford. Even former Fed Chairman Greenspan has warned that Americans have become enormously dependent on borrowing against their homes to fuel their spending.

The dot.com bubble burst and home prices surged, at least partly because the Fed kept interests rates artificially low to keep the economy slugging along. Now the time is fast approaching that something will happen to push the current decline into a full-blown market collapse.

WHAT HAPPENS NEXT?

This process has begun, and the largely imaginary nature of current U.S. "prosperity" stands revealed. Debt-fueled consumer spending, together with debt-fueled residential construction, has accounted for 90% of total GNP growth for the past four years. It has also accounted for debt-fueled job growth: more than 40% of all non-government jobs created since 2001 have been jobs relating to housing construction and mortgage financing.

Dean Baker of the Center for Economic and Policy Research points out the severity of the dilemma: "If we do get a spike in mortgage rates, and a modest decline (in the housing market) turns into a rout, there's almost no bottom to that. That's a crash scenario. . . . if housing prices fall at least 10%, it could be even more damaging than the collapse of the high-tech stock bubble in 2000." Many who are close to this liken the impact of a 20% drop in housing prices to a 40% decline in the stock market.

When the dot.com bubble burst, trillions of dollars evaporated from the U.S. economy. The housing bubble burst will likely be far more devastating as mortgage defaults paralyze the economy. The rise in housing prices "created" more than $2.5 trillion in so-called equity between 2001 and 2006, and it may quickly disappear.

As homeowners realize they are paying more each month than their house is worth in the new market, millions are likely to stop making payments. At the same time, as the economy retrenches, consumers will buy fewer new homes. Discretionary consumer spending will evaporate. Corporate earnings will tumble followed by major stock declines. If the bubble burst results in a freeze of new housing construction, as it likely will, unemployment in all construction jobs— once again, more than 40% all non-government jobs created since 2001 have been in jobs relating to housing construction and mortgage financing—will be severe, further constricting consumer spending. It will become a vicious circle.

ONLY THE BEGINNING?

And housing may just be the tip of the iceberg. Legendary investor Jeremy Grantham—the man Dick Cheney and a lot of other wealthy Americans trust with their money—says we are now seeing the first worldwide bubble in history covering all asset classes. "From Indian antiquities to modern Chinese art," he wrote in a letter to clients in late April 2007 following a worldwide tour, "from land in Panama to Mayfair; from forestry, infrastructure, and the junkiest bonds to mundane blue chips, it's bubble time!"

"Everyone, everywhere is reinforcing one another," Grantham writes. "Wherever you travel you will hear it confirmed that 'they don't make any more land,' and that 'with these growth rates and low interest rates, equity markets must keep rising,' and 'private equity will continue to drive the markets.'"

What Grantham is hearing has a grimly familiar ring to anyone who's been following the U.S. real estate market. If he's right, and rampant irresponsible speculation has spread to all global asset markets, we could be in for a very, very bumpy ride. Regardless, the bursting housing bubble may contain the seeds of a catastrophe far worse than the stock market crash of 1929. We are absolutely foolish if we fail to take this threat seriously.

Today in America we live in a financial house of cards—and its teetering. Federal government debt is becoming unmanageable, consumer debt is out of control, mortgage debt is impossible, and the entire U.S. financial system is in peril.

8

SEVENTH DANGER– OUR UNQUENCHABLE THIRST FOR OIL

❦

"America is
addicted to oil."
—George W. Bush

One of the most urgent dangers facing the United States is oil and its declining availability. Every element of our personal and professional lives is affected by oil: the fertilized and harvested foods in our home, the cars, buses, trains, and aircraft we use to get from place to place, the ability to light and heat and cool our homes and offices and schools and hospitals, the factories that manufacture everything from our desk to our bed to the stuff in the medicine cabinet—all of this requires enormous amounts of oil energy.

It's not just about paying more for every gallon at the pump—it threatens our way of existence in America. Every day we delay in securing additional oil threatens our future existence. Highly unusual for a political leader, President George W. Bush was amazingly candid, twice. In his annual State of the Union address before a Joint Session of Congress, he told the nation: "We have a serious problem: America is addicted to oil, which is often imported from unstable parts of the world." And at a meeting of the nation's governors he said, "I spend a lot of time worrying about the disruption of energy because of politics or civil strife in other countries—because tyrants control the spigots."

Like every economy in the world today, America depends on oil and gas to fuel our economic engine. The sources of supply for our rapidly growing energy demands must be reliable and yet we have dangerously allowed ourselves to be dependent for oil and gas on several unstable and increasingly unfriendly countries. We have sold our energy dependent soul to the oil devil, and all the political talk of energy independence at least for the foreseeable future is nothing more than a politician's pipe dream. However, there are three things that are for sure: the days of cheap and readily available oil are over, the days of our economy being driven by oil and gas energy are about over, and energy will be a critical and central issue for years to come.

SOARING WORLD DEMAND

87 million barrels of oil—that's what humankind consumes every day of the year. Every day! That's about 31 billion barrels of oil every year.

All over the world demand for oil is rising like never in history, with the demand increase last year the largest in thirty years. Much of the so-called developing world is marked by high birth rates, growing populations, and modernizing economies and the aggregate impact of these forces is ever more demand for energy. While some energy experts forecast that in just twenty years world oil demand will increase 40%, the U.S. Department of Energy pegs the demand growth at more than 50%. We've failed to pay attention to the rising demand that has sent prices to new high levels—and it's only going to get worse. We've ignored this long enough.

Some experts had predicted that significant price increases would restrain demand; they were wrong. Some predicted that higher pump prices would inspire alternative fuel innovation; they too were mostly wrong. All around the world demand continues to grow.

Right now it appears that our economy is rolling along just fine. Drive to the gas station in your big SUV and you'll have no problem, other than pump prices higher than you don't like, but other than that you feel reasonably comfortable. Since oil's discovery prices have remained comparatively cheap, but alarm bells are ringing as oil prices have more than tripled in less than five years. Tripled—and it's not like we can just decide to do with out it!

Why the tripling in prices and more price increases expected? The primary reason is because worldwide demand for oil is escalating beyond anyone's expectations. As demand rises existing finite supplies become stressed. Every major oil exporting country is already drawing out its oil at capacity, and even if they could expand we have no additional refinery capacity. On top of that there are no extra oil wells, and the additional pipelines and ocean-going oil tankers needed take years to design, permit, and build, and political disruptions are more and more probable. New oil discoveries are occurring in places where it's geographically difficult to get to the oil and get it out, where supportive infrastructures don't exist, and where governments are anything but stable.

Now many energy experts say existing oil field resources are maturing, weakening, and declining and should not be counted as dependable future supply sources. Worldwide annual consumption is now about 31 billion barrels and growing, so based on "known" reserves we've got maybe thirty years left of "known" oil, and prices are sure to soar as we get ever closer to the well running dry. Dr. Colin Campbell testifying before the British House of Commons said, "We now find one barrel of oil for every four we consume. ...The general situation seems obvious."

The International Energy Agency says world demand for oil will further increase this year to 84.3 million barrels each and every day, and that just two nations—the U.S. and China—will account for more than 40% of the 1.8 million barrel-per-day growth in global demand. This year U.S. oil demand is expected to increase to 20.80 million barrels-per-day from 20.52 million barrels-per-day last year, while China's oil demand is seen rising to 6.89 million barrels-per-day this year from 6.43 million barrels-per-day last year.

Those two nations are today driving the world economy and overheating the rising world demand for oil.

CHINA AND INDIA THIRST FOR OIL

Add over one billion Chinese and one billion Indians as oil consumers and the entire world oil equation changes. When I first visited China a quarter-century ago I was taken aback as our chauffeur-driven government limousine raced along the wide expanses of highway encountering surprisingly few vehicles and roadways that were virtually empty of cars. Back then China was East Asia's largest oil exporter. Oh what a change to today when China is now the world's second-largest importer and its demand is skyrocketing. Last year China was responsible for 31% of the total worldwide growth in oil demand, and in the U.S. automobiles consume 40% of total U.S. oil demand, an enormous 12 million barrels-per-day! Consider how much oil China's automobiles will consume and what it will do to oil prices in America as their number of automobiles escalates. According to Fortune magazine, "In the U.S., there are 940 vehicles for every 1,000 drivers. In Japan, the number is 502. In China it is 8." But not for long! In just three years China has doubled its automobile production and in the booming capital city of Beijing, where I saw those vast empty streets, about 30,000 cars are added to its streets every month and Beijing isn't alone. From 1990 to 2004, the number of vehicles on China's roads grew from less than 2 million to over 25 million. Predictions are that by 2010 India will have an almost unbelievable 36 times more cars that it did in 1990 and by then China will have 90 times more! By 2030 China will have more cars than the United States. While China is now only about 40% urbanized, massive population shifts are expected as China becomes 60% urbanized within twenty years as rural residents seek after the improved prosperity of the cities. Per person oil consumption in China is only one-fifteenth of what we consume in America, making Chinese oil demand even more certain to accelerate.

And in India as income levels improve so do car sales, which increased almost 25% in 2004 to help make India the fastest growing car market in the world and expected to have the largest number of cars by 2050. Already importing nearly 2 million barrels-per-day, where will they get oil to fuel all these new cars?

Fueled primarily by Americans' insatiable appetite for cheap consumer goods, business at China's manufacturing plants is mushrooming and so is their need for electricity and natural resources. As China industrializes faster than any nation in history its demand isn't just for oil and gas, but essential base metals are needed in industry and manufacturing—its share of global use of iron ore, nickel, copper, and aluminum has more than doubled over the last ten years and is forecast to double again by the end of this decade. Half of the world's cement, 20% of the world's copper, nearly 1/3 of the world's coal, and 90% of the world's steel were consumed last year by China.

With the 20% of the world's population at 1.3 billion people, every sector of China's energy-dependent economy is thriving and this is resulting in astounding urban and industrial growth and a record-setting pace for adding cars and trucks to already crowded metropolitan area roadways. China today is the world's largest importer of fuel.

China's economic growth, which sees no slowing down anytime soon and is forecast to continue its on-fire 9% annual growth rate, has become the cornerstone of China's foreign policy. As China's political and military might expand, the country is no longer a regional power but is becoming an influence in every corner of the globe. And oil is a constant and challenging factor, especially in the Middle East where China secures almost half of its oil imports.

The Chinese Academy of Social Sciences, a government entity, reported "It is an unarguable fact that China's dependence on Middle East oil is increasing. And this reliance will continue." Last year Saudi Arabia provided 16% of its oil imports, and Oman and Iran together contributed 25%. As import needs increase, China will struggle to find Persian Gulf suppliers.

So China is busy firming relationships with oil producing nations and signing oil and natural gas deals all around the globe, including with outcast renegade governments, unscrupulous regimes, and those openly hostile to the U.S., while systematically positioning themselves to destroy us by using oil as a weapon of economic mass destruction. In Iran, the nation President Bush labeled as part of the "evil Axis" and the world's leading terrorist nation and nuclear threat, China signed contracts for as much as $70 billion in exchange for 150,000 barrels-per-day for 25 years and a deal for natural gas supplies for 20 years. Since then Beijing has constantly thwarted U.S. efforts in the U.N. Security Council to confront Iran's nuclear program. Other China deals are in Latin America with Venezuela, Peru, Ecuador, and Colombia; in Canada; in the Middle East with Egypt, Iraq, Kuwait, Libya, Oman, Saudi Arabia, and Yemen; with African governments in oil-rich Nigeria, Angola, the Central African Republic, Chad, Congo, Libya, Niger, and Sudan (where China is the largest investor in their oil industry); in Asia with Burma, Indonesia, and Thailand; and with former Soviet republics Kazakhstan and others. At the same time, China has continually weakened U.N. resolutions disapproving of Sudan's atrocities in Darfur.

Beyond oil China is busy pursuing other natural resources as it establishes worldwide beachheads that may one day become a point of political or military confrontation with the U.S., developing attractive bilateral trade arrangements, buying foreign oil assets, forgiving national debt, and providing substantial infrastructure aid projects such as highways, harbors, and public facilities. And what does China get? New political relationships and minerals necessary for its robust economy, including gold in Bolivia, coal in the Philippines, oil in Ecuador, and natural gas in Australia.

Last year China's aborted attempt to acquire majority ownership of a Unocal subsidiary was a thinly veiled strategic attempt to acquire vast oil and gas reserves in Indonesia and Thailand. I say strategic attempt because its purpose was broader than merely expanding their energy reserves; it was a military move to diminish U.S. control over Asian oil and gas reserves in hopes of weakening U.S. military strength should a confrontation develop over Taiwan.

Respected national security scholar and former Assistant Secretary of Defense Frank Gaffney who is now President of the Center for Security Policy paints an even more alarming picture, warning that China's oil pursuits are "only part of a larger plan to deny us strategic minerals, strategic choke points, and strategic regions. Their purpose is to deny the U.S. a dominant role in the world and if necessary to defeat us." While they're busy accomplishing that, we have become dependent on too many unstable places for oil, and for such resources as coal and steel in times of national crisis.

Not only is our American political stature undermined by these new, expanding, and competitive relationships but our economy is hindered as well. The unquenchable thirst for oil in America, China, and India will unquestionably have an uninvited impact on world oil prices, driving them higher and higher in a production sector with minimal growth capacity and increasingly vulnerable to disruptions. Unlike the U.S., China and India subsidize oil allowing yet another element of unfair trade competition for goods produced in those two countries.

And Chinese oil demand growth will only continue to climb. The

International Monetary Fund anticipates that in the next five years emerging economies including China will create almost 75% of the increase in world oil demand.

How much oil will China really require? In recent years China's share of world oil demand has more than doubled from under 3 billion barrels-per-day to more than 7 million barrels-per-day today. But that's nothing compared to its expected massive demand of between 14 and 20 million barrels-per-day in the next 10 years. Present resources and capacities simply can't supply that much oil and someone will have to go without. Will it be the U.S.?

The golden age of China is just beginning; some describe China as the America of tomorrow. To get there China must satisfy its desperate need for oil, and as Zheng Hongfei, energy researcher at the Beijing Institute of Technology says, "There is just not enough oil in the world to cover China's and India's growing energy needs."

Unlike most U.S. politicians, China openly considers energy supply as an essential national security concern. Our federal government would just as soon keep this explosive issue out of the public limelight, but we must acknowledge that as China becomes the monster wildcard in world oil markets the Chinese are seriously endangering our national economy, our national security, and our way of life.

Every American needs to ask themselves, "Does China know what they are doing?" Anyone who knows and understands China would have to answer yes.

Two things are for sure: global stress will accompany oil prices that go through the roof, and there isn't enough oil to go around today and its only going to get worse. We must expand our global oil access sources in areas safe for the U.S. and significantly at home.

SHRINKING WORLD SUPPLY

The respected Christian Science Monitor put it this way: "The challenge is huge. For China and India to reach just one-quarter of the level of U.S. oil consumption, world output would have to rise by 44 percent. To get to half the U.S. level, world production would need to nearly double. That's impossible. The world's oil reserves are finite. And the view is spreading that global oil output will soon peak." And Princeton geologist Ken Deffeyes, author of *Beyond Oil: The View from Hubbert's Peak*, warns that global oil production has already peaked and will result in "war, famine, pestilence and death."

China and India aren't alone in their thirst. Worldwide oil and gas demand is suddenly escalating and at a time when instability is increasing in every major oil exporting nation, when many oil fields are aging, when U.S. refining capacity is peaked, and when most new oil discoveries are in places where resources for a host of reasons are difficult and costly to extract. It is an explosive and very real triple-threat to the U.S. economy.

Terrorist threats to oil production facilities are increasingly of deep concern, as is supertanker and pipeline transportation of oil to the United States through some of the most unstable and most dangerous regions in the world, especially the Middle East, the seas around Indonesia, and the predominantly Muslim former Soviet republics. Terrorists are keenly aware that if they disrupt the flow of oil to the United States, or to any industrialized nation, they deal a crippling economic blow.

The area of highest danger, at least right now, is the twenty-two mostly impoverished and corrupt nations of the Middle East. We've enjoyed a half-century of relatively unobstructed oil supply from the abundant Persian Gulf oil fields, but today those resources are in constant risk. Almost half of the world's oil supply is in the world's most dangerous and politically unstable places: Saudi Arabia, Iran, Iraq, Qatar, the United Arab Emirates, and Oman.

Add to that the analysis of some geologists and engineers that the nation with the richest oil reserves, Saudi Arabia, doesn't have what its claims, that its fields are aging and waning, and that worldwide oil production has or will soon peak. In his recent bestseller *Twilight in the Desert*, Houston energy investment advisor Matthew Simmons argues that Saudi fields are so depleted that even current production levels cannot be sustained.

Thomas Friedman, respected New York Times foreign affairs writer, in his intriguing book *The World is Flat* wrote: "If current trends hold, China will go from importing 7 million barrels of oil today to 14 million a day by 2012. For the world to accommodate that increase it would have to find another Saudi Arabia. That is not likely, which doesn't leave many good options."

Simply stated, it appears world supply is declining as world demand is increasing.

BUYING FROM THE ENEMY

The future of America is no longer in our hands; to keep our economic engine humming we've handed our future to dictators, thugs, despots, madmen, religious fanatics, corrupt royals, and even a few countries openly hostile to America. It's in the hands of Saudi Arabia, Iran, Iraq, Nigeria, and Venezuela. Are we nuts? Apparently so, because the terrifying scenarios are numerous and regrettably all too real. Energy intelligence experts with whom I have spoken tell me that in the coming years a major disruption is imminent, maybe even economic strangulation of the western world, and yet we aren't anywhere near ready to cope with it.

SAUDI ARABIA

Over half of all the known oil reserves in the entire world are found in five countries: Saudi Arabia (where reserves by some estimates are worth as much as fifty trillion dollars), Iraq, Kuwait, Iran, and

United Arab Emirates. Following those countries in total known reserves are Russia, Venezuela, China, Libya, Mexico. Nigeria ranks 11th. In spite of our elected officials' efforts to get us to believe otherwise, all in all this is not a list of trustworthy and dependable friends.

Today OPEC (the Organization of Petroleum Exporting Countries) suppliers are pumping at supposed capacity. What would happen to the United States overnight if all of a sudden our imports were reduced several million barrels a day? All it would take is one massive al-Qaeda attack on a Saudi or Kuwaiti refinery or pipeline and our economy would immediately stutter and stumble—this is not an unreasonable possibility.

We all know that at least for the time being world terror centers in the Middle East. Daily the television news programs and the newspapers are filled with reports of improvised explosive devices, suicide bombers, the jihad, and mullahs calls to destroy the Great Satan. Unfortunately, the Middle East is also where the world's largest oil reserves are found and a major disruption of oil supplies would be devastating. It's obvious then that the region is a vital U.S. national security interest.

A conventional attack on any major Middle East refinery would be disruptive but a nuclear bomb attack on oil fields would be economically catastrophic. As radioactivity made oil fields unusable for decades, maybe even one hundred years, a long global depression would be triggered immediately. With the entire Middle East a constant powder keg and with Iran's madman president calling for the nuclear obliteration of Israel, the very real possibility of a pre-emptive nuclear strike by Israel cannot be ignored. The Israelis are armed with a large well-dispersed nuclear arsenal and they won't go down easily. No matter who shoots first, a full-scale nuclear war killing millions in the Middle East would result. Oil production would cease instantly and a worldwide depression would quickly follow.

Even a conventional attack on Saudi Arabia by another sovereign nation, like Iran, could be equally dangerous and devastating. Also keeping the royals awake at night is a potential for an uprising by the Shiite faction which accounts for one-third of the population in the province of Hasa which has over seven hundred wells producing 98% of the entire Saudi output. The days of the House of Saud are numbered, the signs are growing in every quarter, and I believe it increasingly likely they will be overthrown within five years.

Fearing both scenarios the Saudis have established a nationwide self-destruct system for networks of wells, refineries, and oil transportation systems. Were the House of Saud about to be overthrown, or should I say when, some experts believe they would trigger the self-destruct mechanisms to keep the oil supplies, and the oil revenue, from falling into the hands the Shiites. The enormity of world economic impact would be beyond calculation.

Saudi Arabia is a sovereign nation but is operated by the royal family much like a private company. Our supposedly close relationship with the Saudi monarchy would never exist were it not for their massive oil reserves (which they estimate at 262 billion barrels or 22% of the world's total). Until it was discovered their lands sat atop the world's largest oil reserves Saudi Arabia was nothing more than an impoverished barren desert country populated by nomadic wanderers. Now we publicly and falsely proclaim a close and mutual alliance, but in reality the Saudis are anything but a good friend. They talk a convincing line, but the radical faction is driving the future of Saudi Arabia as every young person becomes a potential threat and members of the royal family are funding those who would destroy the United States of America with American dollars—as they haul in the riches from selling us oil. The Gulf Cooperation Council comprised of six Arab monarchies sold some $145 billion worth of gas and oil in 2003; that will double this year. The Saudis took in more oil dollars since 2002 than all of the 1990s.

For a host of reasons including increasing domestic unrest,

declining per capita income, growing world oil demand, and a ravenous royal appetite for more petrodollars, the Saudis' have launched a massive program of 100 new drilling rigs, wells, and infrastructure, at a cost of $50 billion, to expand production to as much as 12.5 million barrels-per-day by 2009, a production increase of 3 millions barrels-per-day that is about the same as total daily production from neighboring Kuwait and less than Iraq.

As the world's voracious oil demand continues to rocket upward, so far our best known source is the Middle East. But there is growing geological question if the Saudis have the oil they say they do. Petroleum investment banker Matthew Simmons presents compelling evidence that Saudi production is peaking and will decline, resulting in a deep and severe oil supply and price shock. They also have a water problem.

The world's largest oilfield is the Ghawar Field and it's considered "the most important near-term resource" for oil, accounting for almost half of the sizeable Saudi output. In the 1970s analysts estimated it contained 60 billion barrels but it has produced 55 billion barrels since then. Would that suggest there is little oil remaining? In his book *Twilight in the Desert*, Simmons says old wells holding 40% water are "almost dead." The Saudis publicly admit their fields are up to nearly 30% water content, but other published reports estimate Ghawar's water content at 30% to 50%. If water content is as high as estimated, Ghawar could rapidly decrease in production. "That will set bells ringing all over the oil world because Ghawar underpins Saudi output and Saudi underpins worldwide production," says expert Jeff Gerth.

Are Saudi oil fields actually full of water? The Saudis say not but Matthew Simmons disagrees. "We are living with an energy illusion of the highest order." The Saudis pump about 10 million barrels of oil every day—but they also pump several million barrels of seawater every day into aging wells. Worst of all, to propel the oil to the surface the Saudis are now pumping nearly 7 million gallons of seawater under Ghawar every day.

Saudi Arabia is not alone. OPEC's present excess production capacity is less than 1 million barrels-per-day. Libya's Energy Minister Fathi Shatwan says "Everybody in OPEC is at full capacity... maybe Saudi Arabia has something left but it is heavy oil, so in physical terms we have nothing." According to Business Week magazine, "Incredible as it may seem, OPEC's production capacity has actually declined over the last quarter century from about 34 million barrels per day in 1979 to about 30 million barrels now."

If experts are correct then Saudi Arabia's splendid oil reserves are nearing old age when things begin to wind down and with it will come severe economic disruption because for years we have depended upon the Saudi source and in times of crises looked to them to ramp up production. Two of Saudi Arabia's largest oil fields, Abqaiq and Ghawar, were discovered over sixty years ago and its third, Safaniya, was discovered over fifty years ago. Someday they will run out of oil. The questions are how soon and how long will we base our national oil security on imports from Saudi Arabia?

IRAQ

As long as Sadam Hussein was in power Iraq was not a dependable supplier of oil for the U.S. Now Sadam is gone and Iraq is still not a dependable supplier. With the world's second largest known oil reserves, Iraq must overcome the problems of terror, insurgencies, civil disorder, centuries-old feuds between Sunni and Shiite Muslims, and the problems and challenges with its neighbors Syria, Turkey, and Iran—all before it can become a dependable supplier of oil.

The United States has far more at stake in Iraq's democratic success than Americans opposing those efforts realize. The people of Iraq are grateful to the United States for their newfound freedom, yet remain either the only hope for a democratic American ally in the Arab Middle East or they are the tipping point for inflamed Middle East instability.

IRAN

My first assignment in the Reagan White House was to coordinate the return of 52 Americans held hostage for 444 very long days by revolutionary fanatics in Iran. From those hostages we have now learned that the man who was recently Tehran's ultra-right mayor and is now Iran's elected president had been one of those youthful hostage-taking insurgents. He hated America then and he still does.

With the election of this madman to oversee Iran's aggressive pursuit of nuclear capability the Middle East and the reasonable availability of Iran's oil have both become ever more uncertain. Already strained U.S.-Iran diplomatic relations overnight became worse. At the same time, Iran, with the third largest oil reserves in the world, is signing multi-billion dollar oil deals with China and Russia.

If Iran appears ready to use its fast-developing nuclear weaponry to attack Israel the probably of an Israeli first-strike is high and Iran instantly ceases to be a source of oil for a very long time. As the United Nations debates sanctions against Iran, western Europe takes the short-sighted view of fearing to lose Iran as a trading partner and supplier of oil.

Iran's leadership—controlling the world's fourth largest known oil reserves—every day grows more fanatical, more overconfident, more vitriolic and venomous, more provocative, and a less certain source of oil. This is the country that also controls one side of the most critical shipping lane in the Middle East, the Strait of Hormuz. Through this vulnerable channel passes the oil from Saudi Arabia, Iraq, Iran, Kuwait, Bahrain, Qatar, and the United Arab Emirates.

NIGERIA

As I have visited Nigeria I have been impressed with two things: the chaos and disorder, and the corruption. Nigeria has vast oil reserves and equally massive political corruption; it is a very unstable and dangerous place vulnerable to civil anarchy and insurgent forces. With a population that's 50% Muslim and its growing challenges with rebellion and uprisings, in the foreseeable future Nigeria cannot be counted as a reliable source of oil for the world.

VENEZUELA

Though Venezuela is the world's fifth largest oil supplier and our third-largest supplier, her new president Hugo Chavez openly detests United States and is more than happy to tell anyone who will listen. With its daily oil income of $100 million of which $60 million comes from the United States, Chavez is anxious to use oil as a weapon against us to destroy our longtime bilateral economic and political relationship and to spread his pro-Castro revolution.

Late last year Chavez told a group of Chinese business executives there to strengthen Chinese ties with Venezuela that "We have been producing and exporting oil for more than 100 years. But these have been 100 years of domination by the United States. Now we are free, and place this oil at the disposal of the great Chinese fatherland."

Last year China signed an agreement with Venezuela to drill for oil—in eastern Venezuela. Chávez is also championing Iran's nuclear ambitions and with his daily hysteria-provoking pronouncements frightening the Venezuelan people of an imminent attack by the American "empire" he mirrors the incendiary Iranian leadership.

To strengthen his power base in South America, where more than half of the 175 million poor now live in cities, Chavez recently started offering Venezuela's neighbors oil at below-market prices, with especially generous terms for his ideological soul-mate Fidel Castro in Cuba. Simultaneously, Chavez has cancelled profit-sharing agreements with several large oil companies, and late last year Venezuela transferred most of its dollar reserves out of the dollar and out of the U.S.

In April, speaking to South American leaders in Paraguay, Chavez said if the United States attacks Venezuela to secure oil, "We won't have any other alternative - blow up our own oil fields - but they aren't going to take that oil."

Chavez' stated goal is to bring down the United States. Speaking to a television audience, Chavez said "Enough of imperialist aggression; we must tell the world: down with the U.S. empire." It would be wise to expect and plan for a disruption of Venezuelan oil supplies to the U.S. in the near future.

RUSSIA

Russia is the world's No. 2 oil producer though not a major source of oil for the U.S. Nonetheless Russia holds a hand of cards deeply hazardous to American interests and is playing them very well. Blessed with vast resources of oil and a third of world natural gas reserves, much of it yet undeveloped, Russia is already using its energy supplies for political leverage, especially with Iran and China and in Europe. Yet all this comes at a time when, according to the International Energy Agency, Russia will fall short of its oil production expectations for the remainder of this decade.

Visiting China in March of this year Russian President Vladimir Putin and 800 "delegates" along to help signed trade agreements affecting everything from agriculture to energy to aviation and terror. Most concerning to the U.S. should be two huge natural gas pipelines from Russia to China, where Russia will supply 60 to 80 billion cubic meters of gas, twice what China consumed in 2004.

The Russian Republic is once again rising, establishing nuclear arrangements with Iran and even flexing its newfound muscles in an attempt to purchase Centrica, Britain's largest energy company. Russia already owns the world's largest natural gas producer, Gazprom, which recently lucratively enticed recently ousted German Chancellor

Gerhard Schroeder to chair its major North European Gas Pipeline project.

When the Soviet Union imploded its several nation states went their independent ways. Now less than ten years later Russia is using energy as the powerful leverage to bring former Soviet states like Armenia, Uzbekistan, and even Georgia back into the Fatherland tent, having already demonstrated by cutting oil supplies that it will use oil as a political tool and a weapon of control.

OUR IMPRISONED UNITED STATES

Until China surpasses us, we are by far the world's largest consumer of oil. With only 6% of the world population we use 25% of all the oil used in the world. Like a junkie we are dangerously addicted, leaving our American economy ever more vulnerable to supply disruption. America's 230 million cars and trucks burn two-thirds of the oil we consume daily. The average American consumes 25 barrels of oil each year, but in China the average is about 1.3 barrels per year and less than one in India.

Only 50 years ago we produced half the world's oil. No more. Since 1970 our oil production has dropped from 10 million barrels-per-day to slightly more than 5 million barrels-per-day. Today to satisfy our unquenchable thirst we import 53% of our oil, much of it from the unstable Middle East.

Do you have any idea how many barrels of oil we import every day? The number is an incredible 12 million barrels—every day of the year—and that already astonishing number will increase to 20 million barrels-per-day in twenty years from sources that are more and more unstable. Side by side with that numerical growth is a soaring export of American dollars to pay for the price-increasing oil, estimated to increase by more than $50 billion this year.

For over one hundred years we have been confident that we'd

always have all the oil we needed. Even in times of war our supplies were never really in grave danger, but today they are and the reasons though many center generally in irresponsible political decision-making, imprudent business choices, and a lackadaisical consuming public.

We must face the reality that as a nation we are at risk. During the Iranian oil crisis in 1979, President Jimmy Carter declared, "Beginning this moment, this nation will never use more foreign oil than we did in 1977—never." Oh how wrong he was! Partisan political arguments aside, if President Clinton had authorized production from Alaska's ANWR field in 1995, today we would have another million barrels a day, about 5% of out total consumption. America's offshore areas and national marine sanctuaries contain an estimated 75 billion barrels of recoverable crude oil and more than 350 billion cubic feet of natural gas, but President Clinton has made them off-limits to exploration or drilling. Government has also prohibited exploration in the eastern Gulf of Mexico and the Outer Continental Shelf. According to the Industrial Energy Consumers of America, such policies contributed to soaring natural gas prices that in the last four years cost consumers an extra $111 billion.

As a nation, spending for the entire energy complex—exploration, drilling, pipelines, storage, refineries—is thirty years behind needs. The last refinery built in the United States was thirty years ago! Mostly because of environmental regulations we have built no refineries since 1976; since then Jimmy Carter, Ronald Reagan, George Bush, Bill Clinton, and George W. Bush have been president! 175 refineries have closed since 1981. The Saudis wanted to build a new refinery here but instead joined forces with ExxonMobil and are building a $3.5 billion refinery in, of all places, southern China.

For a hundred years profit-making oil companies have understandably focused on the easiest oil targets and now we're left to go after the more difficult oil sources. The Rocky Mountain states remain a hope for the United States, and last year energy companies spent almost $11 billion in search of oil and gas in that area and with some success. The largest onshore discovery outside Alaska in a quarter century was in rural Utah where a field containing as much as 1 billion barrels was discovered, but mostly "the lower 48" are drying up as production has decreased by more than 50%.

And we're in trouble with natural gas too. The federal Energy Information Administration says current U.S. demand is around 23 trillion cubic feet per year and in fifteen years expects that demand to shoot up to 34 trillion cubic feet. Yet the U.S. has only 3 percent of the world's known natural gas reserves—Russia, Qatar, and Iran have 58%! —and domestic production has peaked at around 19 trillion cubic feet per year. You do the math.

Hampering domestic energy development is slowly asphyxiating our economy, endangering our national security, and invigorating the economies of our enemies as we growing increasingly dependent on the most turbulent parts of the world. The 2,000 page energy bill passed last year by Congress barely mentions the national security implications of our dependence on imported oil. We must be insane.

American businesses are feeling the financial pain, especially the airline industry which is essential to sustaining our national economy and which last year spent $97 billion for fuel on revenues of about $400 billion. Jet-fuel prices have surpassed $90 barrel in two years.

Of course there are many factors for airlines' financial woes, but fuel is the leading cause. United Airlines, for three years in bankruptcy, has reported twenty-one consecutive quarterly losses. Delta and Northwest were also in bankruptcy protection, expecting to loose billions last year.

Higher oil prices have impacted consumers too, but hey we've found a solution: we won't cut spending because with interest rates low we'll borrow on the equity in our inflated home value. When the housing bubble bursts, then what? Maybe it will be yet higher oil prices that will burst the bubble all the way. Either way, higher oil prices are a certainty and the longer we allow ourselves to remain blind prisoners the closer we stumble to the brink of national financial ruin.

BLOOD MONEY—OIL FOR TERROR

It's time we wise up and get mad. Every day we send billions to countries that use that money against us—to fund those who preach a radical anti-American Islam and those who wage terror against us. Iran and maybe others are using this oil revenue to develop nuclear weapons—to attack us and our allies.

The surprisingly clever Saudis, recognizing we are absolutely dependent on their oil, are spending billions of oil dollars to build thousands of Islamic mosques and schools around the world, where a fundamentalist Whahibbi anti-American doctrine is preached, while at the same time are investing tens of billions in American bonds and stocks and real estate. We are so inextricably interconnected that we are trapped.

But it's worse! The unstable and tumultuous Middle East has caused us to spend hundreds of billions for a U.S. military presence there, politicians' statements to the contrary, to protect our Middle East energy sources. American taxpayers have had to pay for two wars in the Middle East in two decades, yet the outcome is anything but clear. Islamic fundamentalists, extremists, and terrorists endanger the region's unpredictable governments, especially the Saudi monarchy, and could disrupt or destroy production any day. How dumb are we, anyway?

ECONOMIC PARALYSIS

In a best-case scenario we're in big trouble; in a worst-case scenario we face utter economic destruction. Former U.S. Energy Secretary James Schlesinger, known for his highbrow analytical thinking, says "The inability readily to expand the supply of oil, given rising demand, will in the future impose a severe economic shock." If failure to expand production will result in "severe economic shock", think how catastrophic a major disruption in supply or a collapse in production will be.

Those of us old enough remember the painfully long gas lines caused by the surprise 1973 OPEC oil embargo when our friends the Saudis devised a 70% price increase and reduced their production 10%. Our economy took a huge and immediate hit, millions became unemployed, fear was real. A year later we retaliated with a food embargo on OPEC countries, and what resulted was the deep 1974-1975 recession, the deepest slowdown since the Great Depression. We experienced out-of-control inflation and interest rates nearing 20%, and it took ten years to fully recover; some American farmers never have recovered. The three most recent recessions were each the result of oil price jumps, and we're more oil-import dependent than ever before—and so is China, the world's second largest user of imported oil.

There are rising rumblings in the intelligence community that Middle East leaders recognize the Arab street is growing dangerously impatient for a Palestinian state and are keenly mindful of our close supportive relationship with Israel. Pressure on some of those leaders is mounting for shutting off oil exports to the U.S. and there are indications OPEC would join such an embargo—what happens if that becomes the posture of the shaky Saudi royal family? A worldwide recession or worse would be inevitable and instant.

What if Venezuela, whose President is on a public quest to destroy America, and Russia, whose President is on a public quest to return his nation to world supremacy, went along with them? The U.S. strategic oil reserve totaling about 600 million barrels would be quickly depleted, and our very survival as a nation would be threatened as paralyzing economic conditions unseen since the Great Depression reek havoc with our way of life.

OUR DANGEROUS FUTURE

It took the world 125 years to use the first trillion barrels of oil. We'll use the next trillion in 30 years. There are 800 million cars in the world today, a number that is forecast to climb to 3.25 billion cars, or more, by 2050. Vice President Dick Cheney's national energy task force starkly declared: "America in the year 2001 faces the most serious energy shortage since the oil embargoes of the 1970s." That was five years ago, but like so much that is important in the federal city the Cheney report was drowned out in the Washington world of political puffery and the political winds undermined the committee recommendations, and not much of importance has resulted.

It's obvious that to ensure our national security we must reduce our dependence on imported oil, something that cannot be achieved within the window of risk. Lee Raymond, CEO of ExxonMobil, in testifying before Congress said, "Given the scale and long-term nature of the energy industry, there are no quick fixes and no short-term solutions." The International Energy Agency estimates that to meet world demand in the next 25 years will require an investment of $3 trillion in oil production and refining facilities. But Chris Skrebowsky, editor of Petroleum Review and a recently appointed board member of London's Oil Depletion Analysis Center, says "There are not enough large-scale projects in the development pipeline right now to offset declining production in mature areas and meet global demand growth beyond 2007."

The problem is further aggravated because unlike in the past three-fourths of the world's known reserves are now controlled by government-owned companies. University of Houston petroleum engineer Michael Economides puts it this way: "The danger posed by the axis of energy militants—Venezuela, Iran, and, increasingly, Russia under President Vladimir Putin—is that they could not care less. These militants hardly have functioning real economies whose workings would be adversely affected by a recession."

The risk is widely known. For example, the Washington, D.C.-based Heritage Foundation convened a gathering of oil experts for a forum entitled "The Coming Energy Wars: A 21st Century Time Bomb?" The Los Angeles Times reports, "Without a comprehensive strategy designed to prevent China from becoming an oil consumer on par with the U.S., a superpower collision is in the cards." The New York Times says that China's actions threaten "the very stability of the global economy."

In a recent analysis unsettlingly entitled "Imagining the Unthinkable," Defense Department planners foresee that resource wars are soon upon us. "Humanity would revert to its norm of constant battles for diminishing resources. Once again, warfare would define human life."

The evidences of this are growing; China recently dispatched 20,000 People's Liberation Army troops to Africa to protect its oil interests and is aggressively buying oil and gas next door in Canada. The Presidents of Iran and Venezuela have said they will use oil as a weapon.

WHAT WE CAN DO

In face of these growing and immediate threats to our life-giving oil sources, can the United States preserve our national security, our way of life, and our standard of living? The American dream depends on oil and the story just keeps getting worse. The war for the world's remaining oil resources is already underway, and the U.S. position is one of dependency, weakness, vulnerability, and very limited options.

The global oil war has begun.

It is imperative for the United States to develop our own resources and find alternative sources of energy at a much faster pace that at present.

Last fall, the Council on Foreign Relations published a report on

U.S. energy dependency. The work of a blue-ribbon task force headed by former Director of Central Intelligence John Deutsch and former Secretary of Defense and Secretary of Energy James R. Schlesinger, the report makes some very important recommendations:

1. To slow and eventually reverse the growth in consumption of petroleum products, especially gasoline, by any or a combination of:

- A gasoline tax;

- Stricter and more broadly mandated Corporate Average Fuel Economy standards;

- The use of tradable gasoline permits that would cap the total level of gasoline consumed in the economy (in effect, rationing).

2. Urge governments in all countries to reduce subsidies and deregulate the prices of oil and gas. At the same time, remove the protectionist U.S. tariff on ethanol, so U.S. refineries can take advantage of low-cost ethanol producers such as Brazil.

3. Work with both producing and consuming countries to reduce the vulnerability of energy infrastructure, whether to terrorist attacks or natural disasters such as the devastating Gulf Coast hurricanes of 2005.

4. Play a stronger role in promoting better management of hydrocarbon revenues in producing countries. Too often, these revenues accrue to a small minority unaccountable to any representative political authority. This not only undermines governance, it threatens the political stability necessary for reliable production of oil and gas.

5. Improve the ability of the U.S. government to address the threats to national security created by energy dependence. The Task Force recommends the creation of a small energy security directorate within the National Security Staff to coordinate interagency policy-making on energy security issues. It also recommends that the secretary of energy be involved in any foreign policy deliberations that involve energy issues.

The Task Force also recommended increased development of U.S.

energy resources, offshore, in Alaska, and elsewhere, both to make a (modest) addition to available resources and, more importantly, as a way of showing the rest of the world we're serious about this.

As is often the case with sensible advice, the CFR report has been greeted by a crashing silence in Washington. Doing what it recommends would involve some pain to everyone:

• You and I would pay more for gasoline, use less of it, and drive smaller cars.

• The Chinese, the Russians, and others who subsidize below-market gasoline in their own countries would face stiff domestic resistance to realistic pricing.

• All governments and oil companies (including our own) would have to spend money and allow international inspection to make oil fields and refineries safer and less vulnerable.

• Oil tyrants" in Africa, the Middle East, Russia, and elsewhere would dislike being asked—and prodded—to share the wealth with their own people.

• And to make energy issues a real—and publicly acknowledged—part of U.S. strategy and foreign policy, the White House, the State Department, and the Pentagon would have to operate somewhat more openly and cede some turf. (Making this happen is going to be a lot harder than getting Americans to pay more for gas and use less of it. The people who live in America, by and large, seem to have far better sense than the people who run it.)

On the other hand, no pain is not an option. We can have some pain now or a lot of pain soon. Think about the issues we've covered in this chapter. Call your elected representatives and ask them what they're going to do about it. If you don't get an answer that makes sense, hang up and vote for his or her opponent in the next election. This is important; our future hangs on it. Only when you and I take it seriously will they take it seriously. Throughout our national history our creativity and innovation have risen to the occasion, and we must do so now—before we find ourselves stranded and thirsty in a post-oil world.

9

EIGHTH DANGER –
IMMIGRATION
INSANITY

※

"If the immigrant is illegal, this means that the
first act of this person coming to America
is to break the law."
– Brian Tracy in *Something for Nothing*

Immigration is a nation-threatening danger, growing worse by the
day. The numbers are colossal, and illegal immigrants now out-
number legal immigrants. If our borders aren't sovereign then how
long can America remain sovereign?

Last year over 400 million people entered the U.S. by land and
another 85 million came by air and 10 million came by sea. They
arrived on 600,000 commercial aircraft, 130 million automobiles, 11
million trucks and 214,000 ships. On top of that over 2.4 million railroad freight cars and 9 million oceangoing containers entered our
country. We have over 300 ports of entry and 3,700 shipping terminals. Is it any wonder we are in trouble?

But what can we do about it, if anything? Our solutions are limited. We can either enforce the existing laws, at a financial cost we can't afford, or we can repeal those laws, or we can ignore them—which is pretty much what we are doing now.

Speaking to a Joint Session of Congress in his 1986 State of the Union speech, President Ronald Reagan, said, "You can move to Paris and live their all your life and never be accepted as French. You can move to London and live there all your life and never be accepted as British. You can move to Berlin and live all your life and never be accepted as German. But you can move to America and be accepted as an American from the first day." Our national welcome mat is out, maybe too far out.

The United States is the only country in the world, ever, that codified its purpose as "life, liberty, and the pursuit of happiness." An extraordinary notion then and now, and thus it remains the dream of most every nation worldwide: the American dream. Have you ever heard the expression "German dream" or "Mexican dream"? An estimated 1 billion people in the world live on less than $2 per day, and until that changes they will continue to come in ever greater numbers, unless something drastic is done to stem this crisis.

OUR POROUS BORDERS

Our national borders are lengthy—nearly 7,000 miles of land borders with Mexico and Canada and nearly 2,000 miles of coastal border. We are the only developed nation to share such a lengthy and insecure border with a developing nation. Our country deploys over 11,000 U.S. Border Patrol agents to protect those elongated borders, a task laughingly beyond existing resources and capacities. For most of the nearly 2,000-mile-long border with Mexico there are no agents, no border fences; it's a wide open desolate frontier. And all this poses a considerable threat to the security of our country.

The 9/11 Commission wrote in its report: "More than 500 million people annually cross U.S. borders at legal entry points, about 330 million of them noncitizens. Another 500,000 or more enter illegally without inspection across America's thousands of miles of land borders or remain in the country past the expiration of their permitted stay. The challenge for national security in an age of terrorism is to prevent the very few people who may pose overwhelming risks from entering or remaining in the United States undetected." Illegal immigrants aren't the only thing crossing our porous borders. For example, in a 2005 test of border security in Washington and Texas federal undercover agents using counterfeit documents brought in enough radioactive material to make two "dirty bombs". And more than 75% of the illegal drugs in the U.S. cross our porous borders.

Some federal officials say there are officially seven million illegal immigrants in America today, other feds say eleven million, and the Pew Hispanic Center says nearly 12 million. Nobody really knows, but whatever the number is it's larger than a multiple of Denmark or Norway or Ireland. Unofficially, reasonable estimates are as high as thirty million people spread out all over the country, and almost 40% of illegal immigration has occurred since 9/11.

We lived in greater San Diego where so typical of any metropolitan area we would watch the illegal immigrants openly clustered on street corners every morning waiting for work. We would often drive out along our border with Mexico and watch illegals, ever alert for green and white Border Patrol SUVs, scamper from the border across barren stretches of the desert or even into the bright lights of San Diego to vanish into America in pursuit of the American dream—in western states for farm and ranch jobs, in the Midwest for meatpacking jobs, in the south for chicken processing and Christmas tree jobs, or in the east for restaurant and service jobs.

OTMs—OTHER THAN MEXICANS

It's not only Mexicans seeking jobs—illegals are pouring in from all over the world largely undetected. Border Patrol agents report discovery of discarded packages and clothing with Arabic writing on them. Human smuggling networks use a complex network for illegals from the Middle East and Asia, through the Balkans and into countries of the European Union, then through Central or South America across our broken border with Mexico and undetected into our southern deserts and long weedy beaches and on to Los Angeles or Phoenix or Las Vegas, and beyond. And along with smuggling people they smuggle dangerous weapons and illegal contraband. Border patrol agents have arrested dozens from such countries as Iran and Yemen.

In Border Patrol jargon these illegals are the so-called "OTMs" or "other-than Mexican nationals". Because the immigration jails are full about 70% of OTMs are issued a notice to appear in court—what experienced Border Patrol agents call a "notice to disappear"—and are simply turned loose in the U.S. to await eventual deportation hearings. Is it any surprise that most of them don't show up for those hearings? For those few who are jailed, even those from terrorist watch countries are released into the U.S. after a 180-day detention. The number of OTMs penetrating our borders is exploding and the Border Patrol expects the number to reach 150,000 this year alone. So far, ICE— Immigration and Customs Enforcement, the largest investigative branch of Homeland Security—has released about one million illegals into the United States.

Immigration activists argue they are harmless, but in testimony before the U.S. Senate, Homeland Security Deputy Secretary James Loy disclosed "Recent information from ongoing investigations, detentions, and emerging threat streams strongly suggests that al Qaeda has considered using the southwest border to infiltrate the United States. Several al Qaeda leaders believe operatives can pay their way into the country through Mexico and also believe illegal entry is more advantageous than legal entry for operational security reasons." How are we sure these OTMs aren't planning to destroy our country? The answer is that we have absolutely no idea who they are or what they're up to!

THE SPECIAL CHALLENGE OF MEXICO

Mexico has successfully invaded the United States, without firing a single shot. Somewhere between 10% and 20% of Mexico's population has slipped over our border—unlike anything seen before in history.

Our relationship with Mexico, the most populous Spanish-speaking nation in the world with a population of 105 million, is unlike that of any two nations in the world, and it is all about money, not barriers. Mexico is dependent on the U.S. for buying nearly 90% of its exports, accounting for close to 25% of Mexico's gross domestic product. We are Mexico's largest foreign investor, accounting for over half of total foreign direct investment. And illegals send home billions of American dollars each year to family members who remain behind.

It's no wonder Mexicans are streaming into the U.S. in unprecedented numbers: Mexicans need American money and jobs. In 2004, the median hourly wage for a Mexican working in the U.S. was nearly five times greater than in Mexico—$9 vs. $1.86 in Mexico. Recently a Pew Hispanic Center survey found almost half of Mexico's population wish to leave immediately for the U.S.—that's about 50 million people!

No country has a greater diplomatic presence all across the U.S. In addition to its embassy in Washington DC and at the U.N. in New York, Mexico operates almost 50 diplomatic offices in the U.S. There were less than 10 million Hispanics in the U.S. in 1970; today there are more than 40 million, not all from Mexico of course but the vast majority are. Some experts predict Hispanics will account for one in three U.S. residents by 2050.

Mexican corruption is another acute problem. While U.S. officials publicly profess we're close friends and essential trading partners, U.S. federal law enforcement officials privately acknowledge the widespread corruption by border region Mexican military and police who are often on drug cartel payrolls to facilitate drug smuggling, and their corruption is becoming increasingly blatant. Federal border officials report over two hundred border crossing incidents by Mexican military and police, in which several American Border Patrol agents have been wounded.

WORKFORCE SHORTAGE

Standing on the porch of my father's home in tiny tony Tubac, Arizona, a short twenty mile walk north of the U.S.-Mexico border, under the moonlight sky I watched as the desolate and cruel desert seemed to move. The nighttime sagebrush floor was crawling with illegals, running perilously north to where the jobs are, to Denver and Chicago and New York and Atlanta and beyond, melting silently into our vast nation. As long as a worker can make more in one hour in the U.S. than in a whole day in Mexico, especially in the rural areas, the flood of immigrants will continue to grow. Jobs here abound in construction, service, and especially in agriculture, where most U.S. farmers struggle to survive and depend on illegals to harvest crops for market; more than half of all farm workers are illegals; in California estimates are as high as 90%. Over 10 million illegals are essential to the American workforce, without which the work would not get done.

But the workforce problem is much deeper than low wage workers. As baby boomers reach retirement age beginning in 2007, labor officials estimate a potential workforce shortage of between 4 and 10 million by 2010. The "baby boomers" number 78 million but the succeeding "gen x" numbers just 46 million, leaving an enormous and obvious workforce shortage. Worse still, half of all federal government employees become eligible to retire in 2007.

COSTS OF ILLEGALS

If something else doesn't bankrupt our nation first, the burdensome and growing costs of illegals may just do it.

Take health care for example. Some studies estimate that we are spending over $70 billion for health care, education, and related costs each year for illegals, including upwards of $2.5 billion annually just for Medicaid. The federal Centers for Disease Control reported nearly 40,000 cases of tuberculosis in California, many of which are Multiple Drug Resistant Tuberculosis which is 60% fatal and for which treatment costs $200,000 to $1,200,000 per patient. Immigrants account for more than half of the tuberculosis cases in the U.S., and have ten times greater chance of contracting tuberculosis than native born Americans. Illegals also bring with them sexually transmitted diseases such as gonorrhea and syphilis. Over 7,000 cases of leprosy in just three years have illegally entered from Mexico, Brazil, and India. Unlike those who enter the country legally, illegals receive no health examinations.

Mexicans who live near the border constantly cross illegally to seek medical care in the U.S. and you are paying for it. If they die, you pay for it; border states must shell out burial costs of illegals who cross the border and then die. In American border cities and towns, hospitals are filled with illegal Mexicans needing treatment. Pregnant Mexican women often sneak across the border soon after going into labor—so that their children will be born in the U.S.A., thus as "anchor babies" making them U.S. citizens, and the medical care will be superior and free.

Our granddaughter was born in a sparkling new hospital in

greater San Diego, about three miles from the Mexico border. It was a first class facility, and just four years later it is closed—because like dozens of others hospitals the illegals have caused it to go bankrupt. Between 1994 and 2003, 84 California hospitals closed because emergency rooms are required by law to treat every patient, including illegals. One study in Arizona found that in 2002 illegals cost Arizona medical centers losses of over $150 million. The American Hospital Association says that nationally uncompensated care for patients, many of them illegals, costs in excess of $20 billion each year.

Beyond health care costs, the financial impact of illegals on your tax dollars is ferocious. Billions are spent on food stamps for illegals. Over 25% of the prisoners in federal prisons are illegals, costing you nearly $1 billion each year to house and care for them; some estimates say the numbers are even higher in state and local jails. The Center for Immigration Studies in Washington estimates that illegal aliens have cost U.S. workers $133 billion in job losses. We spend probably $8 billion annually for educating illegals' children. And the list goes on and on.

For several years the State of California has suffered staggering state budget deficits. It is estimated that about a quarter of its nearly $40 billion annual deficit is directly tied to immigration.

Federal, state, and local jails are overflowing with illegal immigrants. Federal estimates for the "costs associated with the incarceration of undocumented criminal aliens" cost state and local governments more than $15 billion last year.

GOVERNMENT GONE MAD

Living in enchanting San Diego County we witnessed firsthand the ever-expanding daily cost of absurd legislation intended to benefit illegal immigration. As California fast becomes an Hispanic state, observant politicians are rushing to curry favor with the rapidly changing electorate and public policy reflects it.

In the 1970 census, California's total population was about 20 million. Today it is upward of 36 million, including at least 2.7 million illegals mostly from Mexico, and by 2030 California's population will likely exceed 50 million. Today one third of California's population is Hispanic, but the makeup is forecast to change so dramatically that by 2040 only one third will be white. Thirty years ago there were less then 10 million Hispanics in the U.S.; now the number exceeds 40 million. Some population forecasts estimate by 2050 one out of every three Americans will be of Hispanic heritage.

California is one of nine states that allows illegal immigrants who grow up in the state to pay in-state tuition at public colleges—but a U.S. citizen growing up legally in an adjoining state must pay higher out-of-state tuition to attend that same college. Three states offer tax-payer-funded scholarships to illegal immigrant students. Lawmakers in several states now require tax-payer funded health care to children regardless of their illegal immigration status, and in generous New Jersey and Nebraska lawmakers arranged for complete pre-natal care for expectant illegal mothers.

It is frighteningly appalling how frivolously generous self-serving politicians at all levels of government can be with our tax money when it may just help them get re-elected.

THE ONLY RATIONAL CHOICE

Immigration is a crisis, and extraordinary complex. Our northern and southern land borders are a several thousand mile long sieve leaking undocumented illegals by the millions including would-be terrorists and smugglers of all kinds, drugs and other contraband, and potentially dangerous weaponry. We have nearly 11,000 Border Patrol agents and the government says that number is being doubled. How, I don't know, because currently available resources can only train about 1,500 agents each year.

President George Bush, speaking in Arizona, a state increasingly desperate for border fortification, correctly said that "Securing our border is essential to securing the homeland." More than at any time in our national history, as a nation we are under threat—by terrorists—and knowing who is entering our country is more important than ever before. Border security is widely acknowledged to be inadequate in every measure, and when we apply one fix it creates a problem in another place, much like the famous Little Dutch Boy who when he stuck a finger in the hole to stop a leak the dike quickly sprung a leak somewhere else.

But solving the problem is not as simple as building a 7,000 mile long border fence with Mexico and Canada. On our borders freight trucks and railroad boxcars join millions of pedestrians lining up on the other side 24-hours every day waiting to cross, part of nearly $2.5 trillion in annual international trade which must cross our borders. Immobilize the borders and you immobilize our economy. Customs officials and border inspectors are mindful, maybe overly, that to slow up the line to open and inspect those semitrucks or railcars and business and the economy will suffer. At one port, according to Congress' General Accountability Office, worried that false radiation alarms would back up trains and block an adjacent military base, a U.S. border official solved the problem with immediate creativity: he shut off the radiation detector.

American business has a "next quarter" perspective, about as visionary as most American politicians. Until we take the long-term view of protecting our nation, its people and its economy, we remain in grave danger. Smugglers of humans, known on our Mexican border as "coyotes", who are willing to endure hardship and risk arrest and even death just to earn a few hundred dollars smuggling in a farm worker are surely willing to earn far higher dollars to bring in OTMs carrying bioweapons. Our border security is an absurdity, and something must be done soon or it will be too late—if it isn't already.

The on-going political debate is all about which finger to stick in the proverbial dike, and ignores the compelling reason millions of Mexicans come to America. They come because things are economically tough "at home" and are better here. If we put ourselves in their position—with a family to support and no way to make a decent living—we would each likely do the same thing. Most of us, in fact, have ancestors who did do exactly the same thing. Only when conditions "there" become livable enough that immigrants would rather remain "at home" can we begin to stem the immigration tsunami crashing over our national borders. For our own national security we must work with Mexico and other nations, not in conflict with them, in creating a meaningful and lasting solution to immigration insanity.

10

Ninth Danger–
Pandemic Plagues,
an Invisible Enemy

❦

"The world is now in the gravest
possible danger of a pandemic."
—Shigeru Omi (World Health Organization)

Bangalore, India is a thriving metropolis of nearly seven million people blending the rich traditions of heritage and culture with the energy and vibrancy of modernity, a pleasant year-round climate and every modern convenience. Its crowded streets are tree-lined and there is an abundance of fragrant flowers and lush greenery, leading to its long-standing designation as the "Garden City" of India. In recent years it has become the center of India's exploding technology boom, now home to thousands of high-tech companies, and today Bangalore is known worldwide as the "Silicon Valley of India" with reportedly more engineers than in the entire state of California.

Bangalore is a city of wealth, or so it seems. Like so much in today's world, what we see is not really the whole truth. Over one million of its people live in its seven hundred slums, where life is hard and a daily wage is just a few rupees. Thomas Friedman, writing in the New York Times, described Bangalore this way:

"Sure Bangalore has a lot of engineering schools, but the local government is rife with corruption; half the city has no sidewalks; there are constant electricity blackouts; the rivers are choked with pollution; the public school system is dysfunctional; beggars dart in and out of traffic."

Racing along with seemingly reckless enthusiasm, our police escort motorcycles sirens blaring, our Indian government motorcade of a dozen new armored Mercedes Benz limos arrived at Bangalore's largest public hospital, a government-run facility reflecting the faded glory of the colonial era once obviously proud but now decaying from lack of maintenance and attention. At the entrance to the unkempt hospital grounds was a very large pile of unprotected and diseased hospital surgical waste, dogs and children running freely to and fro.

A gentlemanly but obviously overworked physician kindly gave us a tour of hospital facilities, and the evidences of poverty were everywhere as an understaffed yet dedicated cadre of doctors and nurses worked against seemingly overwhelming odds. The orthopedic surgery recovery ward, typical of every unit, consisted of one nurse working a 12-hour shift and 34 surgery patients stacked bed-to-bed. Meals were being cooked by relatives under patients' beds. A mother slept on the cold slab floor beneath her newborn infant's crib. Human excrement lay in hospital corners. Mounds of surgical and medical waste littered the once-lush tropical grounds.

Corruption is rampant, even in public hospitals. Before mothers are allowed to see their new baby, a nurse will whisk the infant away and a bribe is demanded. If the mother wants to see her baby, the price is often several dollars per baby—an enormous amount for slum dwellers. And all this in one of India's most wealthy cities.

I asked the young physician what he felt was his biggest single concern? His answer was much different from what I expected. "We need more money, more nurses, more doctors, more facilities, but most of all we need something to protect us from infectious diseases. We simply have no way to stop them here."

As we consider dangers facing America and the world, little-discussed but racing in deadliness are infectious diseases which are emerging as one of the world's most urgent problems. 75% of new human diseases in the last quarter century have been animal-borne, and we have seen comparatively little yet. Today we live in a high risk world that is as if it were designed just to spread infectious diseases: gigantic growth in sprawling global cities as the impoverished relocate from poor rural areas in search of elusive jobs, ever increasing human interaction with wildlife as cities expand into previously undeveloped lands, agriculture production that is no longer local and round-the-world food distribution that ships not only food but harmful microorganisms, and planes crisscrossing the globe carrying every infection imaginable in a matter of hours—all conditions fraught with danger.

Synonyms listed for "pandemic" are plague, epidemic, virulent disease, Bubonic plague, deadly disease. The dictionary definition of "pandemic" is "a widespread epidemic that affects people in many different countries; a disease found in a large part of a population;" no pandemic—a worldwide epidemic—has even been controlled.

For years health experts have been warning a pandemic influenza outbreak is overdue, warnings we have largely ignored, and now they are warning the deadly pandemic is fast upon us. Michael T. Osterholm, Director of the Center for Infectious Disease Research and Policy, says, "A pandemic is coming. It could happen tonight, next year, or even ten years from now. This is a critical point in history. Time is running out to prepare for the next pandemic." He is joined by Dick Thompson, spokesman for the World Health Organization in Geneva: "We don't know the timing of the next pandemic, how severe it will be. We don't know what drugs will work. We don't have a vaccine."

NO ORDINARY FLU

The last major worldwide pandemic, the infamous 1918-1919 flu pandemic, killed between 50 and 100 million people. What's fast approaching may well be far worse! Today health practioners around the world are urgently but belatedly bracing for a lethal universal pandemic of Asian bird flu, medically known as avian influenza strain H5N1, which they expect could be more contagious than any respiratory disease since 1918, kill many millions of people, and destabilize the global economy. Even at 1918 rates, medical experts project 90 million infected, 45 million hospitalized and about 2 million dead in just the United States.

Health and Human Services Secretary Michael O. Leavitt and I have a thirty year friendship. I know him to be a sincere and open public official who speaks with clarity and homespun candor. When he said "Pandemics happen. We're overdue and underprepared," we should listen carefully. And Leavitt is not alone in sounding the alarm.

Asia has become the recurring incubator for dangerous viral outbreaks, and it now appears we are entering a period of horrifying new health danger. H5N1 was first detected in 1997 in hundreds of thousands of dying chickens in Hong Kong and reappeared in Southeast Asia in 2003, killing 80 to 100% of the birds infected. It then appeared in China where the government initially concealed and denied its existence. Since then it has pursued a relentlessly aggressive and unstoppable expansion, spreading like an uncontrollable Texas prairie fire. In only a matter of months it swept across whole continents, carried unknowingly by migratory birds which are no respecters of national boundary lines. "We expected it to move, but not any of us thought it would move quite like this," said Dr. David Nabarro, the United Nations' bird flu coordinator. "Something generally disturbing is going on at the moment. It's certainly in the bird world, and it's pushing up against the human world in a serious way."

At first it killed only domestic birds, killing or forcing the slaughter of more than 140 million birds in Asia alone and more than 200 million birds globally, according to the World Health Organization. But as this deadly virus spread geographically it also mutated and spread from chickens to migratory birds, and bird deaths have now spread along migratory bird pathways across Siberia, through Russia and Turkey, to the Mediterranean and into countries in Europe and Africa, leaving health officials stunned in its wake. It is known to already have infected domestic cats and mammals like martens in Germany, tigers and leopards in Thailand, and a dog in Azerbaijan.

As of this writing it has spread to more than sixty countries— many of which are poorly equipped, financially unable, and marginally competent to deal with the contagion. One dangerous example is Nigeria, with a human population of about 130 million people and a poultry population of about 140 million birds. Officials there have chosen to ignore international recommendations and thus far the rapidly-spreading virus has killed at least 100,000 birds.

As the Washington Post explains: "In the worst possible case scenario the H5N1 virus was detected this month in Nigeria, Africa's most populous country and one of its poorest. If there was a country least equipped to deal with avian flu, Nigeria is at the top of the World Health Organization list. It has weak veterinary and public health infrastructures and a very large and poor population that depends on poultry for food."

For Cambodia's 13 million people their government has budgeted a miserly reprehensible $2,500 for education about bird flu dangers. And the list of ill-equipped and careless countries goes on and on.

What we are witnessing in Asia is but a brief glimpse into the deepening economic impact. China has 14 billion farm poultry and is now attempting the daunting task of vaccinating all of them. Thailand, Laos, and Vietnam are far smaller nations, and the bird virus there has so far resulted in $10 billion in damages as millions of domestic poultry birds were destroyed. And yet there are eyewitness accounts of how poor farmers are hiding their poultry while government officials attempt to kill millions of infected birds. In Africa, it will likely be even worse.

The economic consequences of the preventive slaughter or the flu killing billions of poultry birds are immeasurable, staggering, and potentially too severe to contemplate. Yet the greater fear of health officials is the Asian H5N1 strain will mutate and trigger a human flu pandemic. The 1918 flu's deadly reputation notwithstanding, only one out of every 100 people infected died. As the dangerous H5N1 has now begun to mutate further and jump to humans throughout Asia, in Indonesia, Turkey, Egypt, and elsewhere it has consistently killed a terrifying 56% of those infected. Some health officials have said H5N1 poses "a greater threat than North Korea's nuclear arms." We are a world without protection from a killer on the loose that respects neither governments nor borders.

Now the United Nations has a pandemic flu authority who warns that up to 150 million people could die and nation's leaders are suddenly paying attention. All it would take to detonate the flu's ticking time bomb of worldwide spread would be for just one infected human who was unaware of that infection to board an overseas flight. And the consequences could be unspeakable in the magnitude of suffering, beyond description in the measurement of cost. Federal officials say more than 200,000 Americans could die in a moderate bird flu pandemic and two million in a severe outbreak, and the U.N. bird flu coordinator says he expects bird flu to reach the Americas in a migratory bird in the next six to 12 months. H5N1 is a superflu that may kill tens of millions of people within two years. With millions of travelers jetting all over the world every day, world health officials are frightened that the flu could reach hundreds of cities in a matter of days. No nation, no city would be safe.

THERE IS NO VACCINE

Since its spread appears unstoppable, logically our primary remaining recourse and protection is vaccinating billions of people against the virus. But that is completely impractical for four alarming reasons. First, no vaccine exists, and experts estimate an effective vaccine is at least six months away. Most of the world's flu vaccine is produced in nine countries, 70% of it in Europe. Second, we must expect that in an outbreak Europe will understandably first take care of Europe, not the U.S.A. Third, vaccine may take years to produce and neither time nor worldwide capacity exists to produce sufficient volume. In a very-best-case scenario, for the first six months only highly limited supplies of vaccine would be available. Some authorities believe a pandemic flu vaccine will not be widely available before 2010. And fourth, this dodgy virus is constantly mutating and as it does prediction of its mutation path is impossible, potentially allowing it to infect billions of people—far more than any terrorist attack.

Dr. Robert Webster of St. Jude Children's Research Hospital in Memphis, who has studied avian flu for decades, says "I've worked with flu all my life, and this is the worst influenza virus that I have ever seen. If that happens in humans, God help us." This vicious killer is no ordinary flu.

ECONOMIC DISASTER

During the 1918 flue pandemic, the streets filled with dead bodies, factories and schools closed to prevent infection, and in some places anarchy and civil disorder resulted. The flu killed more people in 24 weeks than AIDS has killed in 24 years, and H5N1 is considerably more lethal. Add to that our population today is older, with many more elderly people who have naturally weakened immune systems.

In his final speech as Secretary of Health and Human Services, Tommy Thompson called a flu pandemic his "gravest concern." His successor Mike Leavitt has been no less publicly worried: "If a pandemic hits our shores, it will affect almost every sector of our society, not just healthcare but transportation systems, workplaces, schools, public safety, and more. We are inadequately prepared."

The poultry death toll would be financially catastrophic to the American poultry industry, and hence to the American consumer. Human deaths, numbering in the tens of thousands each day, and all the costs that entails, would likely be staggeringly high. But those costs pale in comparison to the potentially devastating hit to our national economy, likely greater than any prior event. Imagine hospitals so overwhelmed they turned away the sick and morgues filled to overflowing and no one available to care for the bodies. Life as we know it would come to a screeching halt.

Michael T. Osterholm, Director of the Center for Infectious Disease Research and Policy and Associate director of the Department of Homeland Security's National Center for Food Protection and Defense, outlines just how potentially ruinously disastrous a pandemic is:

"The pandemic-related collapse of worldwide trade and its ripple throughout industrialized and developing countries would represent the first real test of the resiliency of the modern global delivery system. Given the extent to which modern commerce relies on the precise and readily available international trade of goods and services, a shutdown of the global economic system would dramatically harm the world's ability to meet the surging demand for essential commodities such as food and medicine during a crisis.

"There is no model for how to revive the current global economy were it to be devastated.

"Even in unaffected countries, fear, panic, and chaos would

spread as international media reported the daily advance of the disease around the world.

"In short order, the global economy would shut down.

"The labor force would be severely affected when it was most needed. Over the course of the year, up to 50% of affected populations could become ill… There would be major shortages in all countries of a wide range of commodities, including food, soap, paper, light bulbs, gasoline, parts for repairing military equipment and municipal water pumps, and medicines, including vaccines unrelated to the pandemic. Many industries not critical to survival—electronics, automobile, and clothing, for example—would suffer or even close. Activities that require close human contact—school, seeing movies in theaters, or eating at restaurants—would be avoided, maybe even banned."

IMPACT ON THE UNITED STATES

A key financial management tool of American business today, including hospitals, has been to maximize efficiencies and minimize inventories. Failure of "just in time" inventories, including medical supplies, will result from worker absenteeism and precipitate massive disruptions of distribution and services. The federal "bird flu plan" anticipates that "widespread breakdown in municipal services and social order" could occur, including the "loss of public transportation and electricity, and food shortages." Federal predictions are downright frightening: Over 30% of the population would be infected, with 40% of children being infected. 20% of working adults would become sick. The entire health care system would be overwhelmed. Most every piece of our lives would be cancelled, including schools, churches, funerals, airports, factories, train stations, subways, and where we work. All malls and stores would be closed. Consumer sales would plummet and the housing bubble would burst all the way, if it hasn't already by then. As millions of Americans missed work, they would then miss mortgage payments and banks could be forced to curtail or suspend any new lending.

In 1918 coal was the major source of energy. When the Spanish flu struck, the price of coal jumped nearly 180%. What if gasoline would suddenly shoot up 180%? What if international borders are closed, even for a short time, and oil tankers cannot deliver our daily fix of oil? What happens if oil workers are too ill to work the rigs or the refineries or the delivery trucks?

AIDS: GROWING GLOBAL EPIDEMIC

Twenty-five years ago, a federal health official briefed several of us in a White House conference room about a new disease call AIDS, first recognized then among five homosexual men in Los Angeles. Since then this killer disease has spread with such astonishing pace that worldwide it is today the leading cause of death among men and women between the ages of 15-59, and half of all new infections are now in young people. If you can, set aside the considerations of relentless human suffering for those infected with the AIDS virus and consider only the economic dimensions of this escalating global health threat.

According to the United Nations, more than 46 million people worldwide, including a record one million in the U.S., are now infected with AIDS, over half of whom are women and children. An astounding 7.5% of the people in Africa are infected with AIDS. Last year alone AIDS infected nearly five million people, three million of whom are in sub-Saharan Africa. Since it first appeared in the early 1980, AIDS has killed about 25 million people; last year 3.1 million died. In Africa, 14 million children are orphans because of AIDS.

As its spread accelerates the UN has labeled AIDS "an epidemic that is continuing to spiral out of control." In Russia it is spreading at a shocking rate: the Woodrow Wilson International Center for Scholars estimates one million people are infected there—three times the number officially reported by Moscow.

Millions of new cases are causing Southeast Asia to lead the world in the pace of AIDS spread. Though public health efforts have reduced the rate of increase in Cambodia and Thailand, in Indonesia, Myanmar, Vietnam, and Papua New Guinea infection rates are soaring. Last year in East Asia the number of AIDS-infected cases shot up 24%, according to the UN, but it may be even worse than measured. Few Muslim countries collect AIDS data, so in those nations nobody really knows.

In India, brothels staffed by illiterate young women prostitutes are common and widespread. In Mumbai, formerly known as Bombay, officials estimate that 40% of the 25,000 "commercial sex workers" there have HIV/AIDS, though most of the infected do not know it. While the government of India says the country has 5.1 million AIDS victims, the real numbers are far higher, and according to the U.S. National Intelligence Council as many as 25 million Indians will be infected with AIDS by 2010.

In China, where the government has a long history of fudging health statistics downward and where the leading cause of AIDS is selling blood using unsterilized equipment, it is known that 80,000 suffer from AIDS (though 85% don't know it) yet the entire nation has only 50 AIDS doctors.

The epidemic crisis remains rampant in sub-Saharan Africa, where anti-retroviral treatment coverage remains abysmally limited. In Zambia, for example, one of every four people is HIV-positive, two-thirds of them are women, most of these are mothers, and many of them are themselves widowed by AIDS. In Nigeria, an estimated 8 million who will soon die of AIDS are farmers; who will take their place to produce food crops? And in Zimbabwe orphanages for AIDS orphans cannot be build fast enough to house all its orphans. And the numbers are worse in South Africa. "Today," says a U.N. report, "if you use a stereotype, the face of AIDS is a young woman from Africa."

The staggering economic cost worldwide is growing daily, a quiet yet real danger of immeasurable human and monetary cost. The death toll is now 8,500 every day. Dr. Peter Piot, UNAIDS Director, says "Nothing less than an exceptional response will do because AIDS is an unprecedented crisis and poses exceptional challenges. It is indeed one of the make-or-break global threats of this century, in the same league as mass poverty and climate change, not one of many infectious diseases. AIDS is truly an unprecedented crisis that demands nothing less of us than an exceptional response. And there are no shortcuts or quick fixes." This one disease is killing the human spirit, vitality, energy, productivity, and life on an entire continent. It may do so worldwide unless stopped.

WHAT DO WE DO?

President George Bush has already raised the question of military quarantine and cordoning off states or regions, though flu is no respecter of national or state borders. If you want to know what things could be like in a pandemic plague, look at Hurricane Katrina—where federal aid was slow and lacking, where communities were on their own, where public transportation systems collapsed and emergency medical facilities were overwhelmed. In a national pandemic every region of the nation could be similarly paralyzed.

Dr. Grattan Woodson, author of *The Bird Flu Preparedness Planner,* points out that typically help comes from outside the region in a disaster such as an earthquake or hurricane, but "when we have a pandemic, there is no outside. There won't be a cavalry coming over the hill to rescue us. We'll all be on our own, each town, each village, each neighborhood, and the neighbors are going to need to pull together to take care of each other." And conditions could "spill into civil effects, resulting in a period of anarchy and civil disorder." He points out that the last pandemics in 1957 and 1968 were mild. "It was a big deal for hospitals. There were not enough ventilators. Some schools closed down for a couple of weeks. The only thing you have to do to get ready, if that's what's coming, is hope the feds know what they're doing."

The estimated direct economic consequences to the U.S. economy vary, but all are in the hundreds of billions; former Senate Majority Leader Bill Frist pegs it at $675 billion. But none of these costs include the immeasurable cost of disruptions to critical supplies and services, to factories, stores, restaurants and all of Main Street, or the lost federal dollars your local school depends on. A more likely economic cost is in the trillions. The Administration has warned this flu could kill up to 2 million Americans and infect one in three. One in three Americans is 100 million people!—one hundred million Americans too sick to work, too sick for school, too sick to haul freight, too sick to tend the farms!

The man in charge, Secretary Leavitt, acknowledges "we have limited tools" and are "inadequately prepared." Despite unprecedented cooperative prevention efforts by health officials around the globe, the Avian bird flu cannot be stopped. If it migrates to humans in any significant degree, as it could, and a worldwide pandemic occurs, as it could, we will experience massive global economic disruption. Panic is then likely in every city in the world, and the results will be financially devastating. The possible effects from this threatening crisis are as deep, as terrifying, and as damaging as we can even imagine.

The encouraging thing is that Americans have an astonishing tendency to pull together in times of crisis. When, for example, we look back on the 9/11/01 attack on the World Trade Center in New York, we tend to think of the heroic labors of the Police Department and the Fire Department. They did a magnificent job, but it is no disrespect to them and their sacrifices to point out that they were not, in fact, the first responders to the crisis. The authorities are almost never the first responders to a crisis, because they normally aren't there when it happens.

The first responders were ordinary citizens who kept their heads and did what they saw in front of them to do. In the buildings, a considerable number of lives were saved by people who ignored the contradictory instructions they were getting from officialdom, groped through the smoke to an exit, and led their fellow workers downstairs to safety.

Meanwhile, tens of thousands of office workers attempting to flee the scene found themselves trapped at the end of the island south of the towers. Boat pilots in the harbor and the mouth of the Hudson, seeing this, swung over to Battery Park, picked people up, and ferried them across the river to New Jersey. This went on all day; it was the largest peacetime waterborne evacuation in the history of the United States, and no one at any level of government played a role in organizing it. People just saw what needed to be done, and did it.

They don't always, of course; there may in fact be civil unrest and chaos if the terrible things we've been talking about in this chapter come to pass. But you don't have to be part of the chaos, and you don't have to stand around with your hands in your pockets waiting for somebody with a uniform and a bullhorn to come and tell you what to do.

If this happens, it will be bad, but we've been through bad things before, and we can get through this as well. If you're sick, find somebody to help you. If you're healthy, take care of your family. If your family is squared away, take care of your neighbor. If you're in public, take care of the person next to you.

You don't need to be a scientist or a policeman to know what to do: you already know. Respect others and their property. Tend the sick. Bury the dead. Feed the hungry. Shelter the homeless. Comfort the desperate. And fear not. You do that, and help others do it, and wherever you are, the government of the United States will still be functioning. You are the government of the United States; you're an American citizen, which means all those people in blue suits are your employees. You own this country, and it's your responsibility. Remember that and do the right thing, and one way or another we'll get through this. We'll get through anything.

11

TENTH DANGER – AMERICA'S FAILING INFRASTRUCTURE

❧

"There's no limit to how complicated
things can get, on account of
one thing always leading to another."
—E. B. White, in *Charlotte's Web*

There's nothing very exciting about transportation systems or electric power or water or essential services. The whole subject is really downright boring—but it is nonetheless a rapidly-developing danger for our national well-being. The infrastructure of our country is so badly broken because for years both we and our politicians have spent our time tending to supposedly more important matters, and now we are going to have to come up with a whole lot of money in a hurry to fix it.

I have chosen to mention here only a few of the more serious infrastructure failings that, unless resolved, will have harsh consequences for our economy and our way of life. Because of costly government entitlement programs, excessive debt, and a host of other factors, it's also going to require some harsh choices to make the needed fixes in time.

AMERICA'S WATER SUPPLY

I live in the Great American West and know from daily experience the abundance of challenges related to the rapid population growth its facing, everything from inadequate road systems to overcrowded schools to electricity shortages. But those challenges pale in comparison to one overarching problem: a growing shortage of water. Drive through the vast deserts of the southwest and the Rocky Mountain states and the dry desert heat and the miles and miles of scorched earth tells the story. There are considerable areas of this nation where water is obviously lacking; note the gravel gardens of Phoenix. But the water problems of America today are much deeper and far more widespread.

The western states of Montana, Wyoming, Idaho, Colorado, New Mexico, Utah, Nevada, California, and parts of Washington and Oregon, - the nation's fastest growing states—all lack sufficient water to maintain current lifestyles and industrial and agricultural consumption. Much of western water comes from the Colorado River, controlled by agreements made by seven states over eighty years ago as to how the water would be divided. Back then Arizona and Nevada were tiny states, their soaring population growth not even dreamed of, and now their geometric growth depends on that same amount of 1922 water. Only because the upper Colorado River states of Utah, Colorado, and Wyoming have not yet used their full allocation have Las Vegas and Phoenix had water to drink and to waste. Those days are about over.

Water too is short in the Great Plains states, where the vast underground water supplies of the Ogallala aquifer, the world's largest underground water supply system, are running dangerously low. Some experts say it once contained enough water to cover the entire United States to a depth of one and a half feet. But its drying up and towns small and large and countless farmers are desperately seeking for other sources of water.

The Ogallala aquifer provides irrigation water to one-third of the nation's corn crops and providing drinking water to eight rapidly growing states: Texas, New Mexico, Oklahoma, Kansas, Colorado, Nebraska, South Dakota, and Wyoming. For decades the Ogallala has been a seemingly inexhaustible watering hole for America's bread basket, ensuring our unending supply of comparatively cheap and abundant food for us and for the world.

In some places the aquifer has dropped a whopping twenty-five feet in the last ten years. Once plentiful streams have stopping running altogether and rivers are but a trickle. An economy based on farming and ranching lacks water to irrigate crops, and small towns are enduring extreme costs of importing water for human consumption. State and federal governments finally acknowledge this life-giving water aquifer may well dry up within twenty years. Then what do we do? Agriculture is a vital, fundamental, bedrock ingredient of our national economy, and without water we have no agriculture.

But this danger isn't limited just to the U.S.: over 70% of the water consumed in the world is consumed by agriculture, with 525 million small farms in the world and two and a half billion people living off the land. The United Nations also reports that 20% of the world population lives without safe drinking water. Former Soviet leader Mikhail Gorbachev recognizes that "we stand today on the brink of a global water crisis." The two major legacies of the 20th Century— the population and technological explosions —have taken their toll on our water supply.

AMERICA'S ELECTRICITY

In so many countries I've visited electricity is inadequate and treasured, generally available intermittently and usually for only a few hours each day. It is undependable, unreliable, and unappreciated. In so-called developing nations electricity is a luxury, unlike in the United States where it is something taken for granted and used with careless abandon without a thought given to its source or supply. Our comfort levels are misguided, because the American electricity grid can fail, as it did in 2003, and we could run short on electricity.

Today the U.S. Department of Energy predicts that by 2020, the United States will almost double its electrical power consumption—to more than 800,000 megawatts. To supply that American power need will require 1,300 to 1,900 new power plants—well over one hundred new power plants each and every year. As a nation we are no where even close to meeting this need.

At most we are annually building a handful of new power plants. Next time you hear a politician say we have what we need, run for cover! States like California are digging their grave by passing preposterous laws that will in the end result in crippling power shortages and widespread economic disruption.

THE MIGHTY MISSISSIPPI

The great Mississippi River is a grand liquid thread that binds this nation together, giving life and work to tens of millions of Americans. It is a watery ribbon of commerce carrying agricultural crops and manufactured products for export and bringing debt-financed consumer goods from oceans away. It's economic importance cannot be overvalued.

Way back in 1879 Congress created the Mississippi River Commission to oversee the mighty river by preventing flooding and improving navigation. The building of flood control levees was a local responsibility paid for by tax-paying citizens who lived along the river. But just like every other government program, four decades later the feds took control—and failed. Hurricane Katrina, one lone hurricane, brought about the failure of those levees protecting New Orleans and nearby southern Louisiana where the damage is estimated by some experts to exceed $200 billion.

The Mississippi River is a natural power beyond the capacity of man to control or contain. Mark Twain wrote that "The Mississippi River will always have its own way; no engineering skill can persuade it to do otherwise..." But hey, what did Mark Twain know? Two hundred years ago the French encouraged the building of the city of New Orleans below sea level, though it was beyond logic and fiscal sanity. Now we are faced with that same fiscal insanity to shore up and rebuild the failed levees and rechannel the watercourse.

Some Americans, stunned by the damage to New Orleans and the seeming inability of government at any level to deal with it, have advocated simply abandoning the place and settling what remains of the population elsewhere. This is not possible. Some 60% of the grain exported from the U.S. comes down the Mississippi to the sea, as does a staggering amount of petroleum products, iron & steel, rubber, paper, wood, coffee, coal, and chemicals. In terms of tonnage, La Place, Louisiana, which lies in the New Orleans basin, is the largest port in the world. For there to be a port, there have to be people to operate the port, which means there has to be a city for them to live in.

New Orleans has a richly deserved reputation as one of the most corrupt and ill-run cities in the country. However, spending the money to fix and protect it is not a boondoggle. It's essential to the American economy.

Maybe we should have listened to Mark Twain.

AIR TRAFFIC CONTROL

Airplanes of every size and model have taken me several million miles to hundreds of places around the world, and to far too many crowded airports. The West African country of Guinea has nearly ten million people, and it seemed like nearly all of them were swarming in the sweltering Conakry Airport as I tried to board a flight already four hours late in departing. It was the same in Cairo, Egypt except I think the multitudes were larger and the heat was hotter.

Over-flowing airport terminals used to be the exception but no longer. In less than ten years the number of people boarding planes in the U.S. will nearly double—to more than one billion people flying America's friendly skies each year, according to the Federal Aviation Administration.

The structure to support this growth, unfortunately, is non-existent. Air traffic control systems in the U.S. are widely recognized as not merely antiquated but obsolete. The FAA is years behind in its "eight-year upgrade," and the nation's air traffic control system's improvements are facing obsolescence before they will be completed—at least that's the admission of the U.S. Department of Transportation. A program to update its aging air traffic control system begun in 1996 will not be completed for another five years or longer, and is costing nearly double what was originally projected. Even worse, says the DOT, "components being purchased today are now facing obsolescence, even though they were modern in 1996." As more and more aircraft compete for the same airspace, the CEO of Delta Airlines has predicted that "rationing" of access to the air is fast upon us.

Speaking at a symposium on the future of our national airspace system, John S. Carr, President of the National Air Traffic Controllers Association, gave a dire warning:

"Technology and people are the two pillars of air safety. Are we going to fall short on both? I can tell you that the prospect of not enough experienced controllers working on too much old technology doesn't appeal to me. The General Accounting Office estimates that 5,000 controllers may leave in the next five years, twice the attrition rate of the previous five years. FAA estimates that 7,000 controllers will leave by 2010. GAO thinks the number is higher because almost 70 percent of controllers will become eligible for retirement by 2011. Twice as many leaving in the next five years and it takes five years to train a first-rate controller. From where I sit, things look more like, 'One step forward and two steps back.'"

Once again the executive branch and Congress in their near-sighted spending priorities have given short shrift to an impending retirement and system danger as the needed automation platforms continue to deteriorate.

AMERICA'S HIGHWAYS

Every time Reagan's presidential campaign plane took off, the sound system came alive with Willie Nelson singing "On the Road Again"—"just can't wait to get on the road again." And I can still hear Woody Guthrie singing "This Land is Your Land" while driving to our Montana ranch.

"This land is your land, this land is my land
From California, to the New York Island
From the redwood forest, to the gulf stream waters
This land was made for you and me
As I was walking a ribbon of highway
I saw above me an endless skyway
I saw below me a golden valley
This land was made for you and me."

Great songs of the road. Having traveled the roads of all fifty states and nearly one hundred countries I feel somewhat qualified to draw comparisons of roadways, of that ribbon of highway, that endless skyway. We have more miles of paved roads than any country, an intricate asphalt network connecting the distant towns and cities of a great nation, an interconnecting system to move the economy of America.

And it's in big trouble. Highway travel is increasing faster than highway capacity. In the past thirty years passenger travel nearly doubled in the U. S. and road use is expected to increase even more by nearly two-thirds in just the next twenty years. Within fifteen years we face a major crisis in our ability to move goods to market. As a nation, in recent years we have seriously under-invested in needed road repairs while passenger and commercial use of our highways has sky-rocketed.

Transportation experts say highway transportation infrastructure annually requires $94 billion in improvements, yet we are spending less than two-thirds that amount and falling further behind each year. Federal highway surveys report one-third of America's urban and rural roads are not in good condition, and driving on roads in need of repair costs U.S. motorists $54 billion per year in repairs and operating costs—$275 per motorist. Congestion costs add another wasted $67.5 billion annually in lost productivity and wasted fuel.

The American Association of State Highway and Transportation Officials estimates that capital outlay by all levels of government must increase a whopping 42% to $92 billion just to remain at present conditions and nearly double to reach the $125.6 billion for needed improvements. And our country simply doesn't have the money.

AMERICA'S BRIDGES

According to the American Society of Civil Engineers, between 2000 and 2003 "27% of the nation's 590,750 bridges rated structurally deficient or functionally obsolete. However, it will cost $9.4 billion a year for twenty years to eliminate all bridge deficiencies." That's $188 billion, in today's dollars. Those are extraordinary numbers.

Yet total bridge expenditures by all levels of government, for everything from bridge repairs to new bridges, was only $8.8 billion in 2003. But the risk is really more critical than it appears at first glance, because in the cities where large concentrations of jobs and the population are located, one in three urban bridges—nearly 44,000 bridges—is classified as "structurally deficient or functionally obsolete." One in three!

Our national highway and transit systems have long been recognized as among the world's finest, but that system is slipping badly as political leaders continue to shortchange funding for much-needed road and bridge repairs. We simply are falling farther and farther behind.

AMERICA'S NURSES

Go to a hospital emergency room and if you're not about to die see how long you have to wait. One night not long after midnight I accompanied a young man delivered by ambulance to the emergency room where he was checked and then left on a gurney to moan in pain in the waiting room for six hours! When I asked what was taking so long to treat his injury, the nurse was abrupt in telling me "we don't have enough nurses."

Health care providers in every region of the country are sounding the alarm about what they term "an acute worldwide nursing shortage" that will only worsen in the immediate future years, a potentially catastrophic crisis in health care. According to Edward O'Neil, director of the Center for Health Professions at the University of California, San Francisco, solutions won't be easy. "This is not just another cyclical shortage of nurses that can be rapidly cured by paying nurses higher wages and enrolling more students in nursing schools. The aging of the nursing workforce, the upheaval in the health care system and more attractive career opportunities for women [who make up 94% of the nursing workforce in California] are combining to produce a chronic shortage of nurses." Sigma Theta Tau International Honor Society of Nursing describes the growing scarcity "a major threat to the future of the world's health care system."

Some American hospitals are already canceling surgeries deemed less than urgent and are closing beds and emergency rooms, leaving them able to admit only a reduced number of patients. In California, for example, studies estimate the state will be short an astounding 25,000 registered nurses within the next five short years. But it's not just a U.S. crisis. Canada, Australia, much of Asia, and western Europe also report problems. So our traditional American ability to hire nurses from foreign lands is also at danger stage.

There have been nursing shortages before, but this time it is different. Fewer and fewer individuals, especially women, are choosing the nursing profession because of declining job satisfaction in the new environment of managed care. According to the American Nurses Association, a recent survey found that 54% of nurses surveyed said they would not recommend their profession to their children or their friends. That is not very encouraging.

And all this is happening at the same time as the baby boomers are growing older and requiring increasing health care. But that aging bubble is also affecting nurses; today the average registered nurse is age 47 and Sigma Theta Tau estimates within ten years 40% of working nurses will be over age fifty and reaching retirement. As they do retire, it's forecast that there will be a 20% danger level shortage of nurses by 2020.

SO WHAT DO WE DO?

When was the last time you heard a political "leader" talking about this growing infrastructure crisis? Never? Because it's dull and unexciting, not the stuff that will get politicians on the evening news or on cable talk shows. In a private conversation with a national network news anchor I criticized him for his failure, and the general failure of media, to talk about important issues facing our nation, and I will never forget his ready answer. "Viewer ratings mean everything in our business, and we don't get ratings with light—we get ratings with heat." It's obvious these dangers will just continue to fester below the radar until they reach chaotic conditions of widespread collapse and system failure and outpace our national financial capacity.

And then what? None of these problems have cheap or quick solutions, but it's sort of like fixing your car: if you depend on it, and it breaks down, you're going to find the money to get rolling again. It may hurt, and you may have to do without other things for a while, but mobility isn't optional. Neither is this.

In terms of specifics, any one of these problems probably doesn't have a good answer. It's entirely possible that there will never be enough water to support the people and agriculture we've taken on in the American West, which means population growth may have to turn into mass population relocation. There's plenty of livable and arable land available in the United States; that's not the problem. The problem is that a lot of that land isn't near a mountain or a seacoast, which is where a lot of people want to live.

They may not all get to. The brute fact is, we can't have a town everywhere it's pretty, and we can't have farming everywhere there's land. There isn't enough water, and there's no place to get any more (except through wise conservation).

As to electricity, there needs to be a meeting of the minds among utilities developers, politicians, and the public. Everybody's going to have to give something, and nobody's going to want to.

Ditto for highways and bridges. This is, by the way, a bipartisan mess. In the West, it's been mostly Republicans pretending the problem would go away all by itself. In the cities of the East (conspicuously New York; the engineers who built the Brooklyn Bridge said, in 1882, it would need to be replaced in 50 years), it's been mostly Democrats.

The Canadians privatized air traffic control, which seems to be working pretty well for them. (It's hard to imagine that a consortium of, say, Dell, Microsoft, and Cisco couldn't upgrade the technology better than DOT is doing.)

Whoever does it—this applies to utilities as well—will need to be watched like a hawk. The U.S. isn't a particularly corrupt country, but there are pockets of corruption here, and any large-scale public works project is in danger of being one of those pockets. The ancient and dishonorable tradition of Somebody Important's Brother-in-Law needs to be replaced by transparent, closely monitored bidding practices, bolstered by laws with real teeth.

On the people side, we're treating air traffic controllers and nurses like overpriced industrial parts that need to be utilized to the max. The nurses need to be given more money and a lot more respect and autonomy, period, or they aren't going to be there, and we can't afford for them not to be there. The air traffic controllers make a lot more money, but they too feel resented, shoved around, and bargained down. Money to deal with this will probably have to come from elsewhere in the system; "managed care" may have to get a little less managed, and airline tickets are almost certainly going to cost more. Food will, without question, become more pricey.

Which is all too bad, but if the alternative is pushing the switch and not having the lights come on, or turning on the tap and not having water come out, or dying in a bridge collapse or a plane crash or on an operating table, or not having food to eat, a little infrastructural investment is suddenly going to seem pretty attractive.

———

Part Three

SOLUTIONS AND
THE FUTURE

12

POLITICAL
COWARDICE

❧

"I don't mind what Congress does,
as long as they don't do it
in the streets and frighten the horses."
—Victor Hugo

"Suppose you were an idiot.
And suppose you were a member of Congress.
But then I repeat myself."
—Mark Twain

I've listed ten dangers; there are countless others. Congressional inaction in most of these dangers is the eleventh danger and maybe it's
the central cause of the other ten. Or maybe we, the citizens, are the
real cause. The whole bizarre mess of our government is truly unfathomable to me, and yes the problem lies with the politicians and with
us the voters! The Founders began this nation with a belief and a
vision and ideals that guided the decisions of sincere men and women
who were dedicated to a government that provided for the national
defense while ensuring life, liberty, and the pursuit of happiness. Those

were bold and visionary objectives framed in a sense of prudence, practicality, fiscal responsibility, and desperation with their status quo, yet from that welcome beginning we have deteriorated into a virtual insane asylum of federal disarray, discord, distrust, runaway spending, and no accountability.

Ronald Reagan once said that "government is like a baby—an alimentary canal with a big appetite at one end and no sense of responsibility on the other." It is that very government, with its inexorable growth of spending at all levels that is leading this nation over the cliff into an abyss of financial disaster. On another occasion Reagan said, "Government's view of the economy could be summed up in a few short phrases: If it moves, tax it. If it keeps moving, regulate it. And if it stops moving, subsidize it."

Truly, the insane asylum is out of control and the inmates are running the circus.

AN EPIDEMIC OF GOVERNMENT
INCOMPENTENCY, STUPIDITY, & WASTE

Revered American political satirist and funny man Will Rogers made us laugh about government. Said he, "I don't make jokes. I just watch the government and report the facts." If things today weren't so deeply concerning maybe government would still be funny.

Former U.S. Senator Zell Miller, a fireball of passion and angered and appalled at the government's inept practices and wasteful spending, said this: "The federal government spent nearly $25 billion in 2003 that we can't account for." (That's billion, with a "b". Twenty five billion is one thousand dollars twenty five million times—that's a whole lot of money to lose track of. They know they spent it, they just don't know where.) "We overpaid $20 billion in 2001 and didn't reclaim a dime. We wasted $100 million on unused flight tickets because we never collected refunds on reimbursable tickets. We are owed $7 billion from contractors that we have never collected." Is this how you manage your home or business finances?

The magnitude of such unacceptable stupidity might be laughable were its consequences not almost beyond comprehension. That $100 million of unused airlines tickets was our Defense Department, not claiming a refund for 270,000 unused commercial airline tickets. That same department also paid twice for the same airline tickets 27,000 times. Our federal Education Department has an astounding $22 billion of student loans in default. The list of astonishing incompetencies goes on and on. Add to that the enormity of federal spending waste—even the Rock and Roll Hall of Fame received federal funds—and it makes one almost cry.

Then there is government stupidity. One glaring example involves our nation's soldiers heading to war. As reported in Reason magazine, members of the 48th Brigade Combat Team of the Georgia National Guard were heading to Kuwait, armed as they should be with their weapons. As they boarded a charter flight at Georgia's Savannah Airport our brilliant government inspectors confiscated their pocket knives, nose-hair clippers, and cigarette lighters. Will such stupidity never end?

Thomas Jefferson warned, "Were we directed from Washington when to sow and when to reap, we should soon want bread." We should have listened to Tom. Our nation is run by politicians, men and women who lack real understanding of money and finance and who always manage to craft a publicly acceptable solution no matter the long-term reality. Even the federal Office of Management and Budget recognizes how bad things are: they rate just 17% of federal programs as "effective".

PUBLIC SERVICE: DECENCY LOST

Serving in government throughout modern American history has

227

been a noble duty. Issues of great moment were considered and debated in a respectful and deferential manner. There were men and women from all walks of life, fallible humans trying with sincerity to do their best and give their best for our nation and its communities. Such is still the order of the day in our Supreme Court, but contrast this with the pitiable and pathetic dissonance, disharmony, and madness across South Capitol Street in the Capitol Building. Walking along that reasonably narrow tree-lined roadway one gets a sense of how enormous the divide.

Theodore Roosevelt once remarked that the most practical kind of politics is the politics of decency. Sadly, the word decency and all that it entails is glaringly absent in today's political environment. Civility has become a value of the past, replaced with an inflexible partisan division that threatens meaningful public policy debate with an atmosphere of poison by regularly impugning the integrity of our nation's leaders and keeps our elected leaders from truly addressing the serious problems we face as a nation.

It was fun to sit on the sidelines and watch President Ronald Reagan and Speaker of the House Thomas "Tip" O'Neill, two old Irish-American pols who never agreed on any substantive issue of American public policy. Awed by a sense of place, history, and purpose, their long relationship was marked not by partisan vitriolic and personal attack but by friendship, civility, mutual respect, and an understanding that they were about the people's business and had a duty-bound obligation to work together for the public good.

When I first went to Washington as a high school senior I was privileged to meet Senator Wallace F. Bennett, the distinguished four-term senior senator from my home state (and father of current Senator Robert F. Bennett, a public servant of equal integrity). I was in awe of the United States Senate, a body known for the first two centuries of our country's history as the most deliberative body in the world. Personal competing ambitions, a maze of soaring egos, and considerable differences in philosophy notwithstanding, debate and deliberation by trusted friends were marked by shared respect, personal dignity, and the interests of the nation generally before the interests of political party. In its early days the members of the Senate were foremost concerned with national interests and watched out for the nation, but in the intervening years they have come to represent first the parochial interests of their home states.

When I returned to that same Senate in later years as a senior White House advisor, I found a Senate resembling its lower house sibling, filled with politicians beholden to special interests who seemed to view each other not as trusted colleagues dedicated to the common good of the nation but as combat targets on the political battlefield. Yes, some devoted public servants today remain there, but far too many of them now spend their days playing to the cameras, more interested in appearance than reality.

STATESMEN NO MORE

The historic decency and integrity of public office and the noblesse oblige of civic service, which I love, have to a great extent surrendered to the modern money-driven American political world of electronic media, mass advertising, focus groups, and daily opinion tracking polls. We have created a polarized political process that is now too often too distasteful and hampers men and women of exemplary character and strong leadership from entering what President Theodore Roosevelt called "the arena" and heaps unrealistic expectations on the person occupying the presidency. Many Americans naively maintain an optimistic yet unrealistic view that Members of Congress are busy serving the public and anxiously watching over the interests of the country. To be sure, some are, and I thank them and salute them. But far too many are not. Other Americans, including me, have grown ever more cynical, seeing far too many office holders continually confuse the public interest with their personal obsession of re-election. Politics has always been a human process and often a ruthless one; today it has also become spectacularly self-centered.

Ronald Reagan gave an apt description of what modern politics has unfortunately become. "Politics is supposed to be the second oldest profession. I have come to realize that it bears a very close resemblance to the first." A lobbyist friend once pointed out a Member of Congress to me and said, "He can't be bought but he sure can be rented."

The mother's milk of modern politics—money—ever setting newer and higher records, perpetuates the cowardice of politics. As the country races on its runaway path toward economic Armageddon, the intensity of Washington's partisanship permeates and then suffocates intelligent decision making as those we have elected to "lead" are engrossed with making sure the "donor base" remains strong. Everything in Washington is measured in money (and by its twin sister, power)—as the saying goes, "in order to win the battle of ideas, you first have to win the battle of money." Little would they dare vote against the interests of a key donor group. Have you ever wondered why Congress can't agree on some form of life-saving Social Security repair?

Many who come to Washington to serve are absolutely well intentioned. They swear a Constitutional oath of office to serve the nation, but soon seem to forget and think more of pleasing the voters in their home town. Something happens when they taste the power, the influence, the daily praise and adulation they receive, and they often begin to believe their own press releases and for far too many the politics of service is overtaken by the politics of greed and elective survival. All the while vigilantly attuned to the instincts of political survival at the next election, elected representatives navigate through Washington's treacherous political waters feeling incessantly indebted to major campaign contributors and vocal special interest groups, receiving their instructions from highly-paid consultants and lawyers and advisors, and searching for any hint of possible scandal they can use to attack and blemish the opposition. Their days are consumed by endless meetings of little meaningful action, endless fund-raisers to fuel the perpetual campaign engine, and endless genuflection and acquiescence to essential voter support groups.

The noise level in turf-conscious Washington has reached unprecedented levels of premeditated harshness and partisan rancor, where style trumps substance in the incessant pursuit of television air time. Whereas I once loved the Washington political theater, which in former years was filled with serious purpose, drama, and occasional comedy that was mostly in good sport, today I am sickened and saddened by the whole madhouse of calculating self-interest in what one knowing pundit has characterized as an "adversarial soap opera." And there is sufficient blame on both sides of the aisle, where bipartisanship is almost a memory of history. The political win-at-all-costs mentality has overwhelmed the national policy process and debased and degraded what was once noble representation in the federal city.

The worst is found in the House of Representatives, the so-called "lower" house (which has a double meaning), where all 435 members face re-election every two years. My friends on both sides of the House aisle tell me the intensely crass partisanship has made the House all but dysfunctional and brought about a feeling of exhaustion. It has become one continual round of campaigning and fundraising and advertising and self-promoting, all at the cost of public advocacy and good public policy.

There are 435 computer-drawn Congressional Districts mapped out by partisan state legislatures with the unstated but widely acknowledged purpose of political advantage, each consisting of more or less 700,000 people, and with such statistical accuracy that most experts agree that in only about 10% of all 435 districts is there an equal chance for either party to carry the district. In California in the 2004 elections there were 153 congressional and state legislative districts up for election, and not one changed parties.

Increasingly it is a challenge to differentiate on domestic issues between the two major parties, at least in the federal Congress. While the ideology-based platforms of the two parties are surely different in principle, something has become seriously lost in practice. In an apparent disconnect with their professed values, the Administration's 2007 budget reveals federal spending of almost 50% more than Bill's Clinton's final budget. Our American Congress, populated by seasoned self-promoters devoted to political self-preservation, is ignoring the warning signs yet you can rest assured they will take none of the blame when things come crashing down all around them. Like one irresponsible Congressman disdainfully said in speaking of fixing Social Security, "I'll be dead in 2042." Now that is statesmanship!

John Danforth, a former Senator from Missouri, was quoted as saying: "I've never seen more senators express discontent with their jobs. I think the major cause is that, deep down in our hearts, we have been accomplices to doing something terrible and unforgivable to this wonderful country. Deep down in our hearts, we know that we have bankrupted America and that we have given our children a legacy of bankruptcy. We have defrauded our country to get ourselves elected."

FISCAL COURAGE

The word "politics" originated in ancient Greece and meant the art of governing, the science of the state, and the art of organizing and administering the destiny of a nation. Take a quick look at our bankrupt federal government and it's evident that definition is lost and our government has become an inept and ineffective institution propelled by self-interested politicians where wasteful spending is par for the course.

The word "courage" means daring, brave, gutsy—words that have little application to Congress. Those two words simply cannot be linked in today's political world of round-the-clock television news cycles, sound bites, and political correctness in an environment of rampant destructive partisanship.

This very day, our representatives on Capitol Hill are already running for re-election, even though for some it's still four years away. And to earn political favor with the voters, rather than exercising political courage and reducing deficit spending and instead incurring ever-greater debt, they pass more and more costly programs to satisfy special interest voting blocks—knowing that when the real problem of their selfish votes comes home to roost, they are already retired on a more-than-generous congressional retirement. With reckless disregard for fiscal wisdom, they are buying votes with your money and with trillions of dollars of debt being amassed on your grandchildren. In the short time since 2001, discretionary spending has grown by 36% in real terms. The number of pork projects in appropriations bills grew from 2,100 in 1998 to 12,999 in 2005.

Short-sighted politicians who lack courage, who are gutless and seek only the perpetuation of their positions of power and who sacrifice strategic thinking for quick-gain political gimmicks, are bankrupting America. Nikita Krushchev, long-time leader of the Soviet Union, once said that "Politicians are the same all over. They promise to build a bridge even where there is no river." Such is regrettably an apt description of today's Congress.

Jay Ambrose boldly described Congress in the Washington Times: "There is no discipline, no sense of responsibility, apparently not even a love of country or sense of patriotic duty amongst most members of Congress, for if there were you would never get the 3,000-page, omnibus-bill abomination that is economically threatening and virtually an act of mass thievery."

Runaway federal spending, especially the so-called entitlement programs which are now so entrenched that few politicians have the political courage to propose their end, ensures politicians continued employment but ignores a growing apocalyptic economic threat.

Maybe they are just economically ignorant; surely they can't be that lacking in conviction and responsibility, trading principle for political advantage.

DROWSY BUREAUCRACY

For just a moment set aside the politicians and focus on the bureaucrats, that vast lethargic throng of complacent career employees whose entire career is often devoted to seeing how slowly things can move, how much delay they can inflict. That is not to say that there are not tens of thousands of dedicated hard-working professionals amongst the ranks of career government workers; there are and they are a credit to the nation, but they are a noticeable minority.

Recently I went to a Department of Agriculture office where after standing alone at the reception counter for ten minutes a woman approached and just looked at me. I told her what I needed, and politely she told me she had no idea where to find that but she would look. While she was looking, or maybe pretending to look, she told me that she only had to "do two more years" and she would retire and "escape to retirement". I felt like telling her she had already retired, at least in spirit. If you haven't had a similar experience you haven't had anything to do with government.

Never before has there been known a more change-resistant group than federal bureaucrats. With a few noble exceptions they are devoted to hand wringing, propagating endlessly intrusive and costly regulations, perpetuating their careers, and ensuring their generous pensions—rather than striving for cost-efficiency, fiscal prudence, and serving the American public.

UNITED NATIONS

In theory I am a supporter of the United Nations, purportedly a house of peace and a place of world dialogue where civilized nations reason together. In theory. I have attended many meetings and sessions there, and participated in relief and democracy-building activities in many countries. All of that tentative respect notwithstanding, I have come to seriously question the value of this costly expense for the United States.

The United Nations today seems to have embraced the primary principles of strategy expressed fifteen hundred years ago by Chinese military philosopher Sun Tzu: deception and surprise. In a tranquil environment of decorum and inhabited by pompous, arrogant, and insincere diplomats most of whom in their home countries never lived so lavishly, a system of anti-American deception, delay, stupidity, procrastination, and avoidance has developed, all of it enveloped by a bloated officialdom of unaccountable U.N. bureaucrats. In a mockery of common sense and logic, recognized terrorist state Libya has been designated chair of the Human Rights Commission, and the U.N. continues mollycoddling murderous dictators around the world. And all the while costing the United States about $10 billion each year, and the United States is now billed nearly one-third of all peacekeeping costs. Of nearly one hundred and ninety member nations, thirty countries pay 98% of that budget while 158 nations pay only 2%. Of the total U.N. budget, the U.S. assessment is a lopsided 27%. Are we getting our money's worth? Now along comes the United Nations with its headquarters building in New York is falling apart and asks the U.S. to pay for renovations, in the form of an interest-free $1 billion loan. Repairs are expected to cost U.S. taxpayers about $600 million over 30 years. Why should we fix their building? Let China or France or Iran pay for it!

When do we say enough is enough? Last year, the United States tried when our then Ambassador John Bolton, chairing the U.N. Security Council, attempted to clean up the systemic misbehavior, shameful corruption, and abusive humanitarian activities. Once again demonstrating the failed thinking and absurd fiasco that the United Nations has become, seventy-seven member nations (known as the G-77) joined together—not to join the U.S. in our call for reform of the fraud and abuse—but to protest the U.S. bringing them before the Security Council.

There is a fundamental need for an assembly of all nations to join together to promote peace between nations, to advance civilization, to cultivate human rights, to nurture the economies of nations, to combat global spread of disease, to supply relief in exceptional natural disasters, and to most importantly facilitate global discourse and exchange. Those admirable goals were the original intent of the United Nations, but without substantial and persistent reform the United Nations will continue to be just one more bottomless sinkhole for American dollars.

OUR CIVIC DUTY

Democracy works. Since the revolutionaries and patriots first convened in the 1770's, our country has been a confirming example, a showcase of citizens uniting to achieve thoughtful solutions to complex problems. For two hundred years we've mostly elected leaders who truly served the country, and who inspired us to a higher good.

But in recent years we've lost this, and now we must play catch-up. Far too many—in both political parties—who we've elected and sent to Washington and to our state capitols have forgotten why they were elected and have wandered off course. Their undisciplined behavior, like a compulsive shopper run amok, is a national disgrace and has lead the most powerful and prosperous country in the history of the world into technical bankruptcy. In our elected representatives nonstop upward spiral of borrow and spend they evermore enslave you and me with debt that will never be repaid but instead shoved forward and repeatedly refinanced until there's nothing left.

Laurance J. Kotlikoff, who has conducted extensive research on "intergenerational accounting", estimates that when a child born today reaches adulthood he or she will be paying between 76% and 84% of his or her income in taxes—just to fund the entitlements Congress has already authorized today. And this presumes that Congress authorizes no further entitlement programs in the next half century! Sadly, there is no sign that Congress will ever get serious about reducing (let alone eliminating) the deficit, or even reducing exorbitant spending, unless we face a desperate crisis. I have so lost confidence in Congress to do the right thing that my feelings are much like those of Ronald Reagan, who said "I have wondered at times about what the Ten Commandment's would have looked like if Moses had run them through the U.S. Congress."

As citizens we must awake from our national stupor and acknowledge how truly serious is the dilemma before us. Less than half of registered voters actually vote in Congressional elections, and "We the people" are severely lacking in this process. Today we must demand elected officials who will actually lead, who will replace party line allegiances and personal ambition with serious regard for the best interests of the country—but that's probably too much to hope for. We must demand that politicians at every level are held accountable for what they say, that they become more informed, that we tolerate human shortcomings but do not tolerate political meanness, and that opportunistic politicians motivated by money and votes are sent packing.

Over two hundred years ago Alexander Hamilton said "The natural cure...is a change of men." It's time we had a "change of men" in Congress. Simultaneously, it's time we as citizens changed our personal behavior, and stepped forward and did our duty with a renewed civic interest and seriousness of involvement and purpose.

But until that happens, our best hope is that China, Japan, and other nations keep loaning us money.

13

HOW TO
PROTECT YOURSELF

❧

"If you would be wealthy, think of saving
as well as getting."
—Benjamin Franklin

"Just because you do not take an interest in politics
doesn't mean that politics won't take an interest in you."
— Pericles

By nature I'm an optimistic guy who doesn't worry, but right now I'm worried, as you can tell. I am not alone in my concerns. David Walker, our country's Comptroller General, is unusually blunt about the fiscal danger I've been describing: "The United States can be likened to Rome before the fall of the empire. Its financial condition is worse than advertised."

Now, then: why am I telling you all this? Ronald Reagan, who taught me many priceless lessons, once told me something I will never forget. I had come into the Oval Office, a humbling room filled with history and majesty and the heavy air of duty and power, and presented him with the dimensions of a rather complex problem. Period; I just told him what was wrong. The President looked at me with his hall-mark twinkle, and in his soothing gentlemanly voice said, "I pay you to bring me solutions, not problems."

I never made that mistake again, and believe it or not, I'm not making it now. The solutions to what confronts us must come from the genius that has always preserved America, which resides in the American people. But until we understand the problems, we can't employ that genius. That's why I've been telling you all this: you're the solution. There are times when Americans have heard the clarion call of national need and responded with great energy and brilliance. We must do it again, while there is still time.

Throughout our history, we Americans have always been bigger that ourselves in adapting and finding solutions. Today, as my wise friend Neal Maxwell used to say, we are "bogged down in the thick of thin things," spending our time and energies on selfish gratification. The time has come again for us to be selflessly bigger, to focus on what matters most, to help each other, and to help our country right itself.

The world we've known our entire lifetime has changed. Worldwide terror targeted at the U.S. is with us for the long term and at some point a major attack on our homeland will occur, we all know that. In September it was six years since 9/11 and that's a long time for Islamic planning. In this changed world personal complacency is now not only irresponsible but suicidally dangerous, and there are no panaceas, no quick and easy solutions.

To help you be prepared for the avalanche that may come I offer ten common sense recommendations:

1. RAISE YOUR AWARENESS LEVEL

It has been said that "knowledge is power." Empower yourself by becoming knowledgeable about the issues facing elected decision leaders. We must shake ourselves awake and become more attentive than you have ever been before to money matters and especially to national and international trends of concern. Read the daily newspaper and news magazines, and watch television news programs. And don't just read and listen to the people you agree with; get as many points of view as you can. Argue the issues, not in anger but thoughtfully. Understand the world you live in. Involve yourself in civic democracy—at the local, state, and national levels.

2. JOIN WITH OTHERS

Think of our nation's founders. They didn't succeed as individuals in securing our nation, but together they brought about extraordinary things. Those same organizing principles are valid today; groups can leave an important impact. The old saying that "there is strength in numbers" is as true today as ever, maybe even more so. Join with groups of other interested citizens, in church or civic or community groups, because your voice is then more likely to be heard.

3. GET OUT OF DEBT

As a nation and a people we have become compulsive debtors, and it must stop. Last year Americans spent $2 trillion on credit! The single most important action you, your family, and our government can take is to get out of debt. Not only is our government enslaving us and our children and grandchildren to federal debt obligations, but we are enslaving ourselves to mountains of personal debt. Protect your core assets.

No matter the status of your income, your debt keeps accruing interest every hour of every day. Seek counsel and advice from financial experts. Get out of debt as fast as you can. Then should difficult times come, you are in a position to not only withstand the hardship period but to preserve your core assets as well.

4. SAVE SOME MONEY

Many Americans have no savings—the U.S. savings rate is at its lowest level since the Great Depression—but they do have lots of debt. The U.S. Commerce Department reported that the average American household saved zero last year, and many families dipped into their savings for living expenses and to maintain lifestyle.

You may be one of them. If a personal or national crisis occurred, you would instantly be financially overwhelmed. Last year when Hurricane Katrina destroyed tens of thousands of homes and businesses in Mississippi and Louisiana, we witnessed first-hand the quickness with which total financial ruin can occur.

Without personal savings, you are in a very weak and precarious position to survive any disaster—be it natural, disease, or financial. Saving "for a rainy day" is sound advice.

5. OPT OUT

At your earliest opportunity opt out of your employer's pension plan and instead put your money into an individual retirement account, known as an IRA. While no financial instrument is 100% safe, an IRA in a carefully selected financial institution may offer the most security. Employer-administered pension plans and retirement accounts are increasingly insecure places to save for retirement.

6. CONSERVE ENERGY

All it would take is for Saudi Arabia or Iran to reduce their oil exports to the U.S. by 50% and oil would shoot past $100 a barrel or more. All it would take is for terrorists (or another huge natural disaster) to destroy a major pipeline or a major refinery or a major port, and prices would soar.

You cannot avoid the rising costs of an energy crisis. It will happen; it's just a question of when. A common sense measure to protect yourself is to drive vehicles that get more miles per gallon and live near public transport systems. Follow conservation measures in every other element of your life as well.

7. STOCKPILE SOME CASH

No one knows if or when a terrorist or avian flu will strike, but when it happens the impact will strike humans with ruthless cruelty—and you may need a little cash for groceries or to fill up your car at a gas station. Remember, automatic teller machines require electricity to dispense cash and in certain emergencies there will be no electricity. While governments mobilize to protect you, to protect yourself keep some cash for emergency use, even $100, in a waterproof, fireproof locked box hidden in a safe place and take the recommended home storage precautions. Stash a roll of quarters in the trunk of your car for when your cell phone quits working.

8. WORK FOR CHANGE

On my office wall are the words of a simple yet profound statement made by Boyd K. Packer, a former teacher and today a deeply respected religious leader: "Things that don't change, remain the same." The more I've pondered that simple thought the more meaning it has come to have for me—that there must be real change and soon because things can't remain as they are. It's time you and I got really angry about unnecessary, excessive, needless, and costly government programs and voiced our annoyance to our elected representatives. We must stop the ballooning spending at all levels of government, demand spending cuts, followed by true tax reform and tax cuts. "Business as usual", especially in Washington, must cease.

A serious disruption in America—a terror attack, an economic crash, a flu pandemic—might be good for us in that it would wake us up, and as a people and a nation we seem to always do better when we pull together in times of crisis. It will be far less painful to avoid a crisis. A very long time ago Plato said, "The price good men pay for indifference to public affairs is to be ruled by evil men." We must rid ourselves and our nation of indifference and complacency, and remember these words from Ronald Reagan: "No arsenal, or no weapon in the arsenals of the world, is so formidable as the will and moral courage of free men and women."

9. SPEAK UP AND WRITE

Years ago a senator shared with me a story about how Congress works that I have never forgotten. A prominent senator was headed to the Senate floor for a vote. He stopped and asked a staffer what his office had heard from the constituents back home. "We've received five letters—four against and one for." Whereupon the senator went to the well of the Senate and made an impassioned speech about his constituents being against this dreadful legislation by an overwhelming margin of 4 to 1. And the legislation was defeated.

Nothing changes in Washington until politicians feel a sense of urgency, and today they are hearing our apathetic silence. Your letters do matter, they do get read. Don't be afraid or hesitant to write to your Senator or Representative, or your state and local officials, and tell them how you feel. After all, remember that they do work for you— and we need to remind them from time to time!

10. DEMAND ACCOUNTABILITY

Whether in the workplace or the classroom or even in heaven, accountability is required. So why not in the government? It's time you and I held our elected representatives accountable for the deals they cut, the actions they take, and the votes they cast. It's time we held elected leaders to the same standards they legislate for you and me, whether it be retirement benefits or Social Security or OSHA or a host of other federal regulatory burdens they place upon us. If they are good enough for you and me, isn't it time they were good enough to be placed on Congress too? A democracy is a place where everyone plays by the rules, and no one is above the law.

As we exercise our individual right and responsibility of citizenship to vote, we must elect political officials at every level of government who will unhesitatingly exercise moral and political courage and valor, and who will place the national interest ahead of personal political interest. And we must hold them accountable to us the citizens of this nation. To do otherwise is totally unacceptable.

No matter how difficult the days ahead, if we are prepared we shall not fear.

14

THE END OF AMERICA AS WE KNOW IT

⊛

"The means by which we live have
outdistanced the ends for which we live.
Our scientific power has outrun our spiritual power.
We have guided missiles and misguided men."
—Martin Luther King, Jr.

Nationally known and highly respected political journalist Jack Germond has covered American politics and public life for over forty years. I have been a reader of this man for years and have known him during several presidential campaigns. A political reporter of the first magnitude, a grumpy curmudgeon in the old-fashioned model, his reporting, no matter how unpleasant or direct, is always honest. In his recent book *Fat Man Fed Up*, he puts forth a passionate, contemptuous, and often disparaging judgment of the state of American politics today, and then offers his view of the ability of the American political apparatus to solve the enormity of problems which confront our nation. His words echo my feelings.

"Books like this are supposed to end with an optimistic chapter describing 'solutions' to the problems the author has been whining about in all the previous chapters. But I doubt there is any easy way—or, for that matter, any way at all—to fix the things that are wrong with American politics today. They are too deeply rooted. They are too much a part of a pattern of mindless behavior in our culture. We worship all the wrong gods—money, celebrity, and television, most notably. We listen to the loudest voices. We pay obeisance to false standards imposed on us by those with an ax to grind. We are too lazy intellectually to go beyond the glib language of politics. After fifty years as a newspaper reporter, most of them covering national politics, I am both fed up and dismayed. American politics has gone sour."

Yes, American politics "has gone sour." General Douglas MacArthur in speaking to Congress said the solution "must be of the spirit if we are to save the flesh." The sour spirit can and must be replaced if we are to save this nation.

I love this country, it is my country. I love the proven process of democracy, the acknowledged divine right to pursue happiness, the equalizing power of the personal ballot, and the supposed will of the people. And yet too many of those we have elected and entrusted and empowered to manage our national economy, preserve our American way of life, and ensure our freedom are instead focused on their personal first priority of political self-perpetuation because what they really care about is winning their next election and consolidating their power base, not about the sustainable safety, security, and health of this nation. Their rhetoric is sometimes noble, their speeches filled with lofty platitudes, their promises appealing yet pretentious—and we believe them time and time again and all the while they exploit us as they deepen our culture of spending and debt, entitlement and dependency.

At another time of national peril, President Franklin D. Roosevelt said "we have nothing to fear but fear itself." To that I would today add inaction. We must fear inaction—by ourselves and by those we elect to represent us. President Roosevelt also said, "When you get to the end of your rope, tie a knot and hang on." It's time to tie a knot, hang on, and demand action.

I was disheartened by a recent letter to the editor in TIME magazine where a reader wrote these sad words about our country: "Loathed around the world, deeper in debt than at any other time in history, engaged in a war we started without good reason and in defense of nothing, rife with scandal in the highest offices of the government, the United States has nothing to cheer about." I disagree strongly! We have so much to cheer about—or why else would we be flooded by illegal immigrants pursuing the American dream?—and we should be cheering. This letter writer should be cheering—that our nation allows the freedom to write such critical letters. We should each stand up and cheer about what's good in this country and demand that our leaders do the same. To his everlasting credit President Bush does this constantly, often to the displeasure of others. We should cheer that we do enjoy freedom, and peace, and liberty, and the right to pursue happiness. But while we're cheering we should simultaneously demand responsibility and accountability at every level of government, and in our own lives and homes, because our future depends on it.

Addressing a Joint Session of Congress six decades ago, President Roosevelt urged America to look to the future, to meet the challenge of change and the need for leadership that looks forward, not backward. "Throughout the world," he said, "change is the order of the day. In every nation economic problems long in the making have brought dangers to many kinds for which the masters of old practice and theory were unprepared." He also reminded America that "the future lies with those wise political leaders who realize that the great public is interested more in Government than in politics."

William Bonner, writing in *Financial Reckoning Day*, wrote:

"Leading a wild cavalry charge, the last thing you would want would be a group of intellectual kibitzers by your side. Instead, you would want real men... whose thoughts are as uncomplicated and blunt as mace.

"With such men behind you, you might have a chance of success—of crashing into the enemy line and breaking it up. But any hesitation or doubts, and you would be finished.

"Neither the god of war, nor the god of love, favors half measures. 'Audacity,' said Danton to France's generals in 1792. 'We need audacity, more audacity and always audacity.'"

One such man of audacity was President Theodore Roosevelt, who considered the White House a bully pulpit and who had no hesitancy using it. I served another man of audacity who also loved to use the White House bully pulpit, Ronald Reagan. As he entered the House of Representatives for his first address to Congress since the assassination attempt that nearly took his life, the chamber was electrified. Standing, shouting, tumultuous were the members of both parties; it was an evening of American spirit I shall never forget.

As the nation's representative leaders stilled and listened with rapt attention, Reagan evoked the words of the great American poet Carl Sandburg's poem "Washington Monument by Night". Said Reagan:

"'The republic is a dream. Nothing happens unless first a dream.' And that's what makes us, as Americans, different. We've always reached for a new spirit and aimed at a higher goal. We've been courageous and determined, unafraid and bold. Who among us wants to be first to say we no longer have those qualities, that we must limp along, doing the same things that have brought us our present misery? I believe that the people you and I represent are ready to chart a new course. They look to us to meet the great challenge, to reach beyond the commonplace and not fall short for lack of creativity or courage. Someone, you know, has said that he who would have nothing to do with thorns must never attempt to gather flowers. Well, we have much greatness before us. We can restore our economic strength and build opportunities like none we've ever had before. As Carl Sandburg said, 'all we need to begin with is a dream that we can do better than before. All we need to have is faith, and that dream will come true. All we need to do is act, and the time for action is now.' "

Our nation requires elected leaders, regardless of partisan affiliation, who will dare to take these steps in these difficult times to address the pending dangers regardless of their daunting complexities or political consequences. Our nation and way of life are in danger and we desperately need a courageous and comprehensive national strategy to protect our economy, before it's too late. Will it be enough, we don't know. But we do know that today an avalanche builds and will continue to do so until something lurking but unseen triggers it, and then as it comes crashing down the time to prepare will be no more. As a nation and a people that is a risk we cannot afford.

Through the history of this nation, in times of great national challenge we have drawn deeply on our national character and turned to God. Upon resigning his military commission in 1793, George Washington spoke these words to Congress:

"Glorious indeed has been our Contest: glorious, if we consider the Prize for which we have contended, and glorious in its Issue; but in the midst of our Joys, I hope we shall not forget that, to divine Providence is to be ascribed the Glory and the Praise."

"I consider it an indispensable duty to close this last solemn act of my Official life, by commending the Interests of our dearest Country to the protection of Almighty God, and those who have the superintendence to them, to his holy keeping."

251

As a nation we today face national challenges as serious as we have ever known. We must invite a national civic discourse on the survival of America, we must invigorate civic democracy, we must stand fast by our Constitution and its foundational principles, and as George Washington counseled we must "commend the Interests of our dearest Country to the protection of Almighty God."

I am neither confident nor hopeful that our elected federal government will make the urgently needed spending reductions, refocus public policy toward a safer and more stable economic base, place national interests above partisan rancor, or even come close to resolving the lurking terror threats. In 1775, Patrick Henry said "the battle, sir, is not to the strong alone; it is to the vigilant, the active, the brave"— and we must demand such vigilance, activity, and bravery from our elected leaders. We have the opportunity now, but if we fail this time we do so at our national peril.

The events that are likely to unfold across these United States in the next coming years won't be pretty. The suffering and hardship we last experienced in this country in the Great Depression may grab us again, but this time it will be worse because we've carelessly exhausted our remedies. Arnold Toynbee once observed, "The fall of a great nation is always a suicide." Whatever happens, we did to ourselves.

"The United States can be likened to Rome before the fall of the empire. Its financial condition is worse than advertised. It has a broken business model. It faces deficits in its budgets, its balance of payments, its savings - and its leadership." These are not the words of a novelist, but David Walker, Comptroller General of the United States, and they starkly convey the ominous magnitude of our growing American crises.

In my lifetime no American leader so consistently expressed his unwavering confidence in the American citizen as did President Ronald Reagan, who believed that "No crisis is beyond the capacity of our people to solve; no challenge too great."

Before the hour grows too late, each of us as Americans must rise to the challenge facing this nation. In my White House office hung a simple yet powerful slogan which meant much to me then and to our country now: "Failure is not an option." For you and for me, failure to act, to demand action of our elected officials, to cease our tolerance of those (including ourselves) who would spend us into bankruptcy and hardship, and to fail to build vital bridges of understanding around the world—that failure is not an option, or it will sadly be the end of America as we know it.

Abraham Lincoln once characterized America, a nation different from all other nations of the world because its very existence centers in its Constitution, as "the last best hope of earth." It was then and it remains so today. It's all up to you and me.

Sources and References

Der Spiegel, February 22, 2006

Economist, September 3, 2005, p. 25.

Brad Macdonald, "The Asia Effect," The Philadelphia Trumpet, April 2006.

Washington Times, November 20, 2005.

Steven R. Weismann, "Just when It's Needed, Russia's Not There," The New York Times, April 9, 2006

Bill Gertz, "China stocks nukes as anti-U.S. tactic", The Washington Times, July 29, 2005

John Wiley & Sons, Hoboken, NJ, 2006

USA Today, November 16, 2005.

Random House, New York, NY, 2004

J. Reuben Clark, Conference Report, April. 1938, p. 103.

Justin Fox, "Now please fix the $50 trillion mess we're in," FORTUNE, November 29, 2004.

Lois M. Collins, "Panel Fears Collapse of U.S. Health System," Deseret Morning News, July 23, 2005.

"Home Alone", Economist, June 11, 2005., p,. 8.

James Hoagland, The Washington Post, "Nations Ignore Major Census Trends", May 3, 2004.

Robert J. Samuelson, "Economic Death Spiral," Washington Post, April 6, 2005; Page A19.

Human Events, July 4, 2004, p.5.

"Three Out of Four U.S.'s Biggest Airlines in Bankruptcy Court," Associated Press, Daily Herald, Sept 15, 2005, p C6.

Kim Clark, "Pension Tension", U.S. News & World Report, Jan 24, 2005, p. 44.

Katherine Shrader, "Bush Administration Warns of Future Terrorist Acts," Daily Herald, Feb 17, 05. pA14.

John Negroponte, HYPERLINK "http://www.nti.org" www.nti.org, February 28, 2005

Congressional Research Service Report, September 22, 2004.

Richard L. Garwin, "The Technology of Megaterror,", Technology Review, Sept 1, 2002.

Council on Foreign Relations, "Responding to Chemical Attacks", January 2006.

Mortimer B. Zuckerman, "In No Uncertain Terms," US News & World Report, March 20, 2006, p. 72.

George Melloan, "Global View: Washington's Spending Spree and the Dangers It Poses", The Wall Street Journal, July 12, 2005, pA17.

John R. Talbott, "The Coming Crash in the Housing Market", p. 127-128. Associated Press, February 24, 2004

Carrick Mollenkamp and Charles Fleming, "Why Students of Prof. El Karoui are in Demand", Wall Street Journal, March 9, 2006, p. A1.

Associated Press, April 29, 2007, reported by Ryan Nakashima.

"Concerns Mount About Mortgage Risks", Wall Street Journal, May 17, 2005, p.1.

David Streitfeld, "They're In—But Not Home Free," Los Angeles Times, April 2, 2005.

Business Week, April 12, 2004

Noelle Know, "43% of First-Time Home Buyers Put No Money Down", USA Today, January 18, 2006, p. 1A.

Brett Arends, TheStreet.com, April 27, 2007.

Ronald Bailey, "Presidential Energy," The Wall Street Journal, February 2, 2006.

The Christian Science Monitor, January 20, 2005.

Ronald Bailey, "Peak Oil Panic", Reason, May 2006, p. 22,

Business Week, August 2004

Peter Enav, "Uncertain Saudi Supplies Hold Key to China's Growth", The Durango Herald, August 24, 2005, p. B1.

James Schlesinger, The National Interest, winter 2005-2006.

National Security Consequences of U.S. Oil Dependency, Independent Task Force Report No. 58, Council on Foreign Relations, October 2006.

9/11 Commission Report

Shaun Waterman, "Analysis: Porous borders a back door for terrorists?" Washington Times, March 14, 2005.

Wall Street Journal, March 4, 2005, p.1.

Peter Piot, "Facing the Challenge", USAID Speech, May 15, 2006.

UNAIDS/WHO (2006), "UNAIDS Report on the Global Aids Epidemic, Annex 2: HIV/AIDS estimates and data, 2005.

Trevor Neilson, 'Money Needed for AIDS", Washington Times, Nov 29, 2004,

USA Today, December 7, 2005, p.1.

Jia-Rui Chong, "Bird Flu Defies Control Efforts", Los Angeles Times, March 27, 2006

Epidemic and Pandemic Alert and Response, Cumulative Number of Human Cases of Avial Influenza A/(H5N1) Reported to WHO, 2 April 2007.

World Health Organization, "Epidemic and Pandemic Alert and Response."

"Bird Flu Expert: H5N1 is the worst he's seen", Daily Herald, May 5, 2006, p. A4.
Nancy Shute, "The Fear Factor", TIME, Nov 21, 2005, p. 71.

Michael T. Osterholm, "Preparing for the Next Pandemic," Foreign Affairs, July/August 2005, p. 31-32.

"A Man with an Antiflu Plan", U.S. News & World Report, November 154, 2005, p 32

Garance Burke, Associated Press, "Plains Towns Hunt to Buy Water as Aquifer Shrinks," Deseret Morning News, Feb 12, 2006.

"World's Water Problems, Solutions can be Found on the Farm," Daily Herald, March 19, 2006, p. A4.

USA Today, "FAA Predicts Billion Passengers by 2015", March 18, 2005, p3A. Sara Kehaulani Goo, Washington Post, "DOT Says Air Traffic Overhaul is Flawed", November 30, 2004; Page E5

John Carr, Air Traffic Control Reform Newsletter, Dec. 2003.

The Road Information Project, Key Facts: America's Road and Bridge Conditions and Federal Funding, 2004, www.tripnet.org.

American Society of Civil Engineers, The Road Information Project, Key Facts America's Road and Bridge Conditions and Federal Funding, 2004

Peter Piot, "Facing the Challenge", UNAIDS speech.

Zell Miller, A Deficit of Decency, p. 130.

Brian Tracy, "Something for Nothing", Nashville: Nelson Current, p. 174.

USA Today, November 15, 2005.

Jack W. Germond, "Fat Man Fed Up," New York: Random House, 2004, p. 199.

William Bonner, "Financial Reckoning Day," Hoboken, New Jersey: John Wiley & Sons, p. 178.

Acknowledgements

My grateful thanks to George Bush, Ronald Reagan, and Gerald Ford—for inviting me into the arena.

To respected friends Conrad Gottfredson, Robert Robb, Brent Beesley, Maura Carabello, Hugh O'Neill, Phil Harris, Jim Davies, Rick and Denise Nydegger, Sterling Brennan, Dale Greenwood, Richard Hill, Jamey and Catherine Johnston, Wayne Hilbig, Sherm Robinson, Douglas Thayne, Frank Thorwald, and Bob Warnick—for taking time beyond the call of friendship to offer invaluable advise about this book and its content.

To Hugh Hewitt, America's best national radio talk show host and political commentator, for his words of wisdom over lunch and for his friendship.

To three distinguished colleagues and treasured friends, statesmen all in their respective vocations and each with a rich love of America's Constitution. The late Neal A. Maxwell, a brilliant thinker and extraordinary human being, whose insight and understanding of America and our quiet conversations I miss dearly. M. Russell Ballard, a courageous man of principled action, for his enduring friendship, for his uncommon vision about common problems, and for his patience with me. Senator Orrin Hatch, always sincere through countless political battles and to whom I am grateful for lessons taught.

To Peter Johnston, a superb editor, and Kelly Sobotka, a master at publication details.

To Mark, Chris, David, Wes, and Michael for their insightful and on-going critiques, and ever helpful Jessica for mastering the computer.

And to Bonnie, for being ever patient and loving.

Bibliography

The Man Who Changed China: The Lift and Legacy of Jiang Zemin, by Robert Lawrence Kuhn. Crown, 2005.

Blood and Soil: Land, Politics, and Conflict Prevention in Zimbabwe and South Africa. by International Crisis Group. International Danger Group, 2004.

Rogue Regime: Kim Jonh Il and the Looming Threat of North Korea. By Jasper Becker. Oxford University Press, 2005.

The World is Flat: A Brief History of the Twenty-first Century. By Thomas L. Friedman. Farr, Straus & Giroux, 2005.

The United States and the World Economy: Foreign Economic Policy for the Next Decade. By C. Fred Bergsten and The Institute for International Economics. Institute for International Economics, 2005.

The Idea of Pakistan. By Stephen Philip Cohen, Washington: Brookings Institution Press., 2004.

The European Dream: How Europe's Vision of the Future is Quietly Eclipsing the American Dream. By Jeremy Rifkin. New York: Tarcher, 2004.

China, Inc.: How the Rise of the Next Superpower Challenges America and the World. By Ted C. Fishman. Scribner, 2005.

China: The Gathering Threat. By Constantine C. Menges. Nelson Current, 2005.

Plagues and Peoples. William H. McNeill. History Book Club, 1976.

Germs: Biological Weapons and America's Secret War. Judith Miller, Stephen Engelberg, William Broad. Simon and Schuster, 2001.

The Coming Crash in the Housing Market. John R. Talbott. McGraw-Hill, 2000.

Inside the Asylum: Why the United Nations and Old Europe are Worse Than You Think. Jed Babbin. Regnery Publishing, 2004.

The West's Last Chance: Will We Win the Clash of Civilizations. Tony Blankley. Regnery Publishing, 2005.

While Europe Slept: How Radical Islam is Destroying the West from Within. Bruce Bawer. Doubleday, 2006.

Imperial Hubris: Why the West is Losing the War on Terror. Anonymous. Brassey's Inc., 2004.

Comments and questions for Stephen M. Studdert, as well as inquiries regarding his availability for speaking engagements, may be sent to:

studdert@criticalissuespress.com

For subscriptions to Mr. Studdert's newsletter visit:

www.criticalissuespress.com